CYBER INFRASTRUCTURE PROTECTION

Tarek Saadawi
Louis Jordan
Editors

May 2011

The views expressed in this report are those of the authors and do not necessarily reflect the official policy or position of the Department of the Army, the Department of Defense, or the U.S. Government. Authors of Strategic Studies Institute (SSI) publications enjoy full academic freedom, provided they do not disclose classified information, jeopardize operations security, or misrepresent official U.S. policy. Such academic freedom empowers them to offer new and sometimes controversial perspectives in the interest of furthering debate on key issues. This report is cleared for public release; distribution is unlimited.

*****

CONTENTS

PREFACE

The Internet, as well as other telecommunication networks and information systems, have become an integrated part of our daily lives, and our dependency upon their underlying infrastructure is ever-increasing. Unfortunately, as our dependency has grown, so have hostile attacks on the cyber infrastructure by network predators. The lack of security as a core element in the initial design of these information systems has made common desktop software, infrastructure services, and information networks increasingly vulnerable to continuous and innovative breakers of security. Worms, viruses, and spam are examples of attacks that cost the global economy billions of dollars in lost productivity. Sophisticated distributed denial of service (DDoS) attacks that use thousands of web robots (bots) on the Internet and telecommunications networks are on the rise. The ramifications of these attacks are clear: the potential for a devastating large-scale network failure, service interruption, or the total unavailability of service.

Yet many security programs are based solely on reactive measures, such as the patching of software or the detection of attacks that have already occurred, instead of proactive measures that prevent attacks in the first place. Most of the network security configurations are performed manually and require experts to monitor, tune security devices, and recover from attacks. On the other hand, attacks are getting more sophisticated and highly automated, which gives the attackers an advantage in this technology race.

A key contribution of this book is that it provides an integrated view and a comprehensive framework of the various issues relating to cyber infrastructure protection. It covers not only strategy and policy issues, but it also covers social, legal, and technical aspects of cyber security as well.

We strongly recommend this book for policymakers and researchers so that they may stay abreast of the latest research and develop a greater understanding of cyber security issues.

CHAPTER 1

INTRODUCTION

Tarek Saadawi
Louis Jordan

This book is intended to address important issues in the security and protection of information systems and network infrastructure. This includes the strategic implications of the potential failure of our critical network and information systems infrastructure; identifying critical infrastructure networks and services; analysis and risk assessment of current network and information systems infrastructure; classification of network infrastructure attacks; automating the management of infrastructure security; and building defense systems to proactively detect network attacks as soon as possible once they have been initiated.

The chapters in this book are the result of invited presentations in a 2-day conference on cyber infrastructure protection held at the City University of New York, City College, on June 4-5, 2009.[1]

The book is divided into three main parts. Part I deals with strategy and policy issues related to cyber security and provides discussions covering the theory of cyberpower, Internet survivability, large scale data breaches, and the role of cyberpower in humanitarian assistance. Part 2 covers social and legal aspects of cyber infrastructure protection and discusses the attack dynamics of political and religiously motivated hackers. Part 3 discusses the technical aspects of cyber infrastructure protection including the resilience of data centers, intrusion detection, and a strong emphasis on Internet protocol (IP) networks.

STRATEGY AND POLICY ASPECTS

The four chapters in Part I provide a good framework for the various issues dealing with strategy and policy of cyber security. In Chapter 2, Stuart H. Starr presents a preliminary theory of cyberpower. The chapter, attempts to achieve five objectives. First, it will establish a framework that will categorize the various elements of the cyber domain. Second, it will define the key terms of interest. Third, it will begin to make clear the various benchmarks and principles that explain the various cyber categories. Fourth, it will characterize the degree to which the various categories of the cyber domain are connected. Finally, it will anticipate key changes in the cyber domain and provide a basis for analyzing them.

However, it must be emphasized that this evolving theory is in its preliminary stages. Thus, it is to be anticipated that it will not be complete. In addition, given the long gestation period for theories of "hard science" (e.g., physics, chemistry, and biology), it is likely that some of the elements are likely to be wrong.

In Chapter 3, Mike Chumer addresses the survivability of the Internet. The use of the "commodity" Internet, referred to simply as the Internet, is the cornerstone of private and public sector communication, application use, information sharing, and a host of taken-for-granted usages. During a recent planning symposium in 2007, hosted by SunGard and the New Jersey Business Force, the key discussion question was, "Will the Internet Be There When You Really Need It?" The planning symposium focused on how the internet will be effected if a pandemic based upon H5N1 (the bird flu) was to break out in the United

States. In this chapter, Mr. Chumer addresses the following issues that resulted from this symposium:

- Foreseeable short- and long-term impacts if the Internet either "crashes," "goes down," or "stops working";
- Whether existing protocols for providing collaboration and coordination between U.S. service providers (cable, telephone, and "last mile" providers) are sufficient enough to preserve Internet access and limit overload;
- Points of Internet failure that planners must consider when modifying or developing business practices;
- The effects on computer applications and/or protocols if the Internet slows down rather than halting during a pandemic, as well as mitigation strategies;
- In the face of heavy demand on the Internet, which features or services should contingency planners expect to shut down or redirect to conserve or preserve bandwidth;
- Whether contingency planners should expect attacks from hackers during a state when the Internet is weakened;
- Whether we as a nation are becoming too dependent on the Internet and underestimating its risks for the sake of cost, convenience, and efficiency;
- Will the Internet be resilient enough to hold up under the onslaught of school, business, home enterprise, emergency management, and recreational users during a pandemic?

Mr. Chumer concludes the chapter with a set of recommendations drawing upon those presented during the symposium.

Chapter 4 by, Douglas Salane, posits that despite heightened awareness, large scale data breaches continue to occur and pose significant risks to both individuals and organizations. The recent Heartland Payment Systems data breach compromised financial information in over 100 million transactions and involved financial records held by over 200 institutions. An examination of recent data breaches shows that fraudsters are increasingly targeting institutions that hold large collections of credit card and social security numbers. Particularly at risk are bank and credit card payment processors, as well as large retailers who do not properly secure their systems. Frequently, breached data winds up in the hands of overseas organized crime rings that make financial data available to the underground Internet economy, which provides a ready market for the purchase and sale of large volumes of personal financial data. Credit industry studies based on link analysis techniques confirm that breached identities often are used to perpetrate credit fraud soon after a breach occurs. These studies also show that breached identities may be used intermittently for several years. We conclude that strong data breach notification legislation is essential for consumer protection, and that the direct and indirect costs of breach notification provide significant economic incentives to protect data. Our analysis also concludes that deployment of privacy enhancing technologies, enterprise level methods for quickly patching and updating information systems, and enhanced privacy standards are needed to mitigate the risks of data breaches.

Chapter 5, "The Role of Cyberpower in Humanitarian Assistance/Disaster Relief (HA/DR) and Stability and Reconstruction Operations," by Larry Wentz, explores the role and challenges of cyberpower (information and communication technologies [ICT]) in humanitarian assistance/disaster relief (HA/DR) and stability and reconstruction operations. It examines whether a strategic use of cyber assets in U.S. Government (USG) engagement and intervention activities such as HA/DR and stability and reconstruction operations could lead to more successful results. Certainly, the information revolution has been a dynamic and positive factor in business, government, and social arenas in the Western world. The combination of technology, information content, and people schooled in the use of each has reshaped enterprises and activities of all types.

Complicating the challenges of HA/DR and stability and reconstruction operations related to failed-state interventions are the exacerbating difficulties that typically consist of: spoilers interfering with the intervening forces; refugees and internally displaced persons requiring humanitarian assistance; buildings requiring reconstruction; roads, power, water, telecommunications, healthcare, and education systems that are disrupted or dysfunctional; absence of a functioning government and laws, lack of regulations, and enforcement mechanisms; widespread unemployment and poverty; and a shortage of leaders, managers, administrators, and technical personnel with 21st century technical and management skills. Additionally, the operations lack a U.S. whole of government approach; a lack of trust among stakeholders; a lack of policy, procedures, business practices, and people; and organizational culture differences. It is not a technology challenge per se, generally, technology is an enabler if properly employed.

The chapter concludes that civil-military collaboration and information sharing activities and the smart use of information and ICT can have decisive impacts if they are treated as a core part of the nation's overall strategy and not just as "nice to have" adjuncts to HA/DR initiatives, or to the kinetic phases of warfare and stability and reconstruction operations. It is further suggested that utilizing the elements of the information revolution and the whole of government in a strategic approach to HA/DR and stability and reconstruction operations can have positive results and sets forth the strategic and operational parameters of such an effort. Finally, enhancing the influence of USG responses to HA/DR and interventions in stability and reconstruction operations will require a multifaceted strategy that differentiates the circumstances of the messages, key places of delivery, and sophistication with which messages are created and delivered, with particular focus on channels and messengers.

LEGAL AND SOCIAL ASPECTS

Cybercrime and attack dynamics are explored in Part II of this book. The first chapter is presented by Michael M. Losavio, J. Eagle Shutt, and Deborah Wilson Keeling. The chapter examines how public policy may evolve to adequately address cybercrime. Historically, legal protections against criminal activity have been developed in a world wherein any criminal violation was coupled with physical proximity. Global information networks have created criminal opportunities in which criminal violation and physical proximity are decoupled.

In Chapter 6, the authors argue that cyberspace public policy has not adequately incentivized and supported protective behaviors in the cyber community. They examine the roles that user-level/consumer-level conduct, social engagement, and administrative policy play in protecting information infrastructure. They suggest proactive work with laws and administrative/citizen-level engagement to reform the cyberspace community. To that end, they examine applicable legal and transnational regimes that impact such a strategy and the options for expanding administrative and citizen engagement in the cyber security enterprise.

Chapter 7, by Thomas J. Holt, is titled, "The Attack Dynamics of Political and Religiously Motivated Hackers." There is a significant body of research focused on mitigating attacks through technical solutions. Though these studies are critical for decreasing the impact of various vulnerabilities and hacks, researchers still pay generally little attention to the affect that motivations play in the frequency, type, and severity of hacker activity. Economic gain and social status have been identified as critical drivers of computer hacker behavior in the past, but few have considered how nationalism and religious beliefs influence the activities of some hacker communities. Such attacks are, however, gaining prominence and pose a risk to critical infrastructure and web-based resources. For example, a number of Turkish hackers engaged in high profile web defacements against Danish websites that featured a cartoon of the prophet Muhammad in 2007. To expand our understanding of religious and nationalist cyber attack, this chapter explores the active and emerging hacker community in the Muslim-majority nation of Turkey. Using multiple qualitative data sets, including interviews with active hackers and posts from multiple web forums, the findings explore the nature of attacks, target selection, the role of peers in facilitating attacks, and justifications through the lens of religious and national pride. The results can benefit information security professionals, law enforcement, and the intelligence community by providing unique insights on the social dynamics driving hacker activity.

TECHNICAL ASPECTS

The five chapters in Part III characterize the technical and architectural issues of cyber security.

Chapter 8, by Yehia Khalil and Adel Elmaghraby, deals with the topic of the resilience of data centers. Data centers are the core of all legacy information in a cyber society. With the incredible growth of critical data volumes in financial institutions, government organizations, and global companies, data centers are becoming larger and more distributed, posing more challenges for operational continuity in the presence of experienced cyber attackers and the occasional natural disasters. The need for resilience assessment emerged due to the gap in existing reliability, availability, and serviceability (RAS) measures. Resilience as an evaluation metric leads to better system design and management; this chapter illustrates why resilience evaluation is needed and it surveys the continuing research.

Chapter 9, by Edward Wagner and Anup K. Ghosh, covers the development of high fidelity sensors for intrusion activity on enterprise networks. Future success in cyber will require flexible security, which can respond to the dynamic nature of current and future threats. Much of our current defenses are based upon fixed defenses that attempt to protect internal assets against external threats. Appliances like firewalls and proxies positioned at network segment perimeters similar to the Maginot Line attempt to shield us from outsiders attempting to break in. There are other mechanisms such as public key infrastructure and antivirus software within the network perimeter. This added layer is referred to as "Defense in Depth" methodology. However, in each component of security architecture, vulnerabilities are revealed over time. These defenses lack any agility; their defenses must become agile and responsive. They propose high fidelity sensors in the form of virtualized applications on each user's machine to complement network-based sensors. In addition, they equip each user such that even as they are reporting intrusions, their machine and data are protected from the intrusions they are reporting. Their approach is able to protect users from broad classes of malicious code attacks, while being able to detect and report both known and unknown attack code.

IP networks are no longer optional throughout the business and government sectors. This fact, along with the emergence of international regulations on security, reliability, and quality of service (QoS), means that IP network assessment is also no longer an option. With IP networks representing the core of our cyber infrastructure, the lack of deep understanding of such networking infrastructure may lead to drastic strategic implications and may limit our ability to provide a solid cyber infrastructure. The remaining chapters in Part III focus exclusively on IP networks.

In Chapter 10, Angelos Keromytis, indicates that voice over IP (VoIP) and similar technologies are increasingly accepted and used by enterprises, consumers, and governments. They are attractive to all these entities due to their increased flexibility, lower costs, and new capabilities. However, these benefits come at the cost of increased complexity, reliance on untested software, and a heightened risk of fraud. In this chapter, the author provides an overview of VoIP technologies, outlines the risks and threats against them, and highlights some vulnerabilities that have been discovered to date. The chapter closes with a discussion of possible directions for addressing some of these issues, including the work in the ANR VAMPIRE project, which seeks to understand the parameters of the problem space and the extent of VoIP-related malicious activity.

Chapter 11, by Rajesh Talpade, discusses foolproof IP network configuration assessment. IP networks have come of age. They are increasingly replacing leased-line data infrastructure and traditional phone service, and are expected to offer Public Switched Telephone Network (PSTN)-quality service at a much lower cost. As a result, there is an urgent need for assuring IP network security, reliability, and QoS. In fact, regulators are now requiring compliance with IP-related mandates. This chapter discusses the complex nature of IP networks, and how that complexity makes them particularly vulnerable to faults and intrusions. It describes regulatory efforts to mandate IP network assessment, explains why many current approaches to assessment fall short, and describes the requirements for an effective solution to satisfy business, government, and regulatory requirements.

In Chapter 12, Nirwan Ansari and Amey Shevtekar provide an overview on the new breed of denial of service (DoS) attacks on the Internet. Denial of service attacks impose serious threats to the Internet. Many attackers are professionals who are motivated by financial gain. They bring a higher level of sophistication along with inventive attack techniques that can evade detection. For example a shrew attack is a new type of threat to the Internet; it was first reported in 2003, and several of these types of attacks have emerged since. These attacks are lethal because of the inability of traditional detection systems to detect them. They possess several traits, such as low average rate and the use of transmission control protocol (TCP) as attack traffic, that empower them to evade detection. Little progress has been made in mitigating these attacks. This chapter presents an overview of this new breed of DoS attacks along with proposed detection systems for mitigating them. The chapter will lead to a better understanding of these attacks, and will stimulate further development of effective algorithms to detect these attacks and to identify new vulnerabilities which have yet to be discovered.

ENDNOTES – CHAPTER 1

1 . Available from *www.ccny.cuny.edu/cip09*.

PART I

STRATEGY AND POLICY ASPECTS

CHAPTER 2

DEVELOPING A THEORY OF CYBERPOWER*

Stuart H. Starr

INTRODUCTION

The goal of this chapter is to develop a preliminary theory of cyberpower. A theory of cyberpower will try to achieve five objectives.[1] First, it will establish a framework that will categorize the various elements of the cyber domain. Second, it will define the key terms of interest. Third, it will begin to make clear the various benchmarks and principles that explain the various cyber categories. Fourth, it will characterize the degree to which the various categories of the cyber domain are connected. Finally, it will anticipate key changes in the cyber domain and provide a basis for analyzing them.

However, it must be emphasized that this evolving theory is in its preliminary stages. Thus, it is to be anticipated that it will not be complete. In addition, given the long gestation period for theories of "hard science" (e.g., physics, chemistry, and biology), it is likely that some of the elements are likely to be wrong.

---

* The views expressed in this article are those of the author and do not reflect the official policy or position of the National Defense University, the Department of Defense or the U.S. Government. All information and sources for this chapter were drawn from unclassified materials.

ELEMENTS OF A THEORY

Categorize.

In analyzing the cyber domain, four key areas emerge (see Figure 2.1). These include the cyber-infrastructure ("cyberspace"), the levers of national power (i.e., diplomacy, information, military, economic [DIME], or "cyberpower"), the degree to which key entities are empowered by changes in cyberspace ("cyberstrategy"), and the institutional factors that affect the cyber domain (e.g., legal, governance, and organization). For the purposes of this chapter, this framework will be employed to decompose the problem.

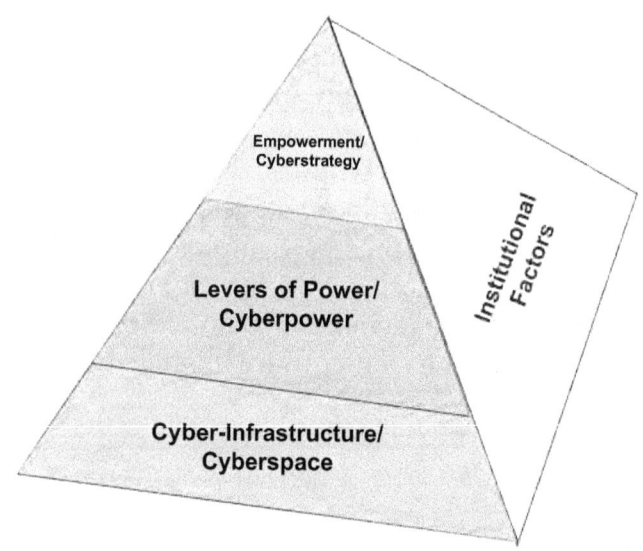

Figure 2.1. A Framework for Categorizing the Cyber Problem.

Define.

Although the definitions of many of these terms are still contentious, this chapter will use the following definitions of key terms. First is the formal definition of cyberspace that the Deputy Secretary of Defense formulated: ". . . the interdependent network of information technology infrastructures, and includes the Internet, telecommunications networks, computer systems, and embedded processors and controllers in critical industries."[2] This definition does not explicitly deal with the information and cognitive dimensions of the problem. To deal with those aspects explicitly, we have introduced two complementary terms, "cyberpower" and "cyberstrategy," which were defined by Professor Dan Kuehl, National Defense University (NDU).

The term cyberpower means "the ability to use cyberspace to create advantages and influence events in the other operational environments and across the instruments of power."[3] In this context, the instruments of power include the elements of the DIME paradigm. For the purposes of this evolving theory, primary emphasis will be placed on the military and informational levers of power.

Similarly, the term cyberstrategy is defined as "the development and employment of capabilities to operate in cyberspace, integrated and coordinated with the other operational domains, to achieve or support the achievement of objectives across the elements of national power."[4] Thus, one of the key issues associated with cyberstrategy deals with the challenge of devising "tailored deterrence" to affect the behavior of the key entities empowered by developments in cyberspace.

Explain.

Cyberspace. Over the last 15 years, a set of rules of thumb have emerged to characterize cyberspace. Some of the more notable of these rules of thumb include the following:

- Moore's Law (i.e., the number of transistors on a chip approximately doubles every 18 months);[5]
- Gilder's Law ("total bandwidth of communication systems triples every 12 months");[6]
- Proliferation of IP addresses in transitioning from IPv4 to IPv6 (e.g., IPv6 will provide 2^{128} addresses; this would provide 5×10^{28} addresses for each of the 6.5 billion people alive today).

In addition, recent analyses have suggested the following straw man principles for cyberspace. First, the offensive has the advantage. This is due to the challenges of attribution of an attack and the fact that an adversary faces a "target rich" environment. Consequently, if cyberspace is to be more resistant to attack, it may require a new architecture that has "designed in" security.

Cyberpower. Robert Metcalfe formulated one of the oft-quoted laws of cyberpower.[7] He characterized the value of a network as "N^2," where N describes the number of people who are part of the network. However, more recently, it has been demonstrated that the value of a network tends to vary as N*log (N). Note that this equation suggests that the "value" of a network is substantially less than "Metcalfe's Law."[8]

In addition, there have been many studies about the contribution that net-centricity can have to mission effectiveness. For example, studies of air-to-air combat suggest that the value of a digital link (e.g., Link 16) can enhance air-to-air loss exchange ratios by approximately 2.5.[9] This is due to the enhanced situation awareness, improved engagement geometry and the efficiency of the engagement. However, the complexity of modern conflict is such that it is difficult to assess the affect of net-centricity on complex missions. Thus, for example, studies of air-land operations are much more complex and very scenario-dependent. In addition, preliminary studies of humanitarian assistance/disaster relief and stability operations are currently underway. Chapter 5 in this book will provide preliminary results for those operations.

Cyberstrategy. Recent studies have suggested that the "low end" users (e.g., individuals, "hacktivists," terrorists, and transnational criminals) have considerably enhanced their power through recent cyberspace trends.[10] This is due, in part, to the low cost of entry into cyberspace (e.g., the low cost for a sophisticated computer or cell phone; the extensive investment that the commercial world has made in cyberspace (e.g., applications such as Google Earth); and the major investments in cyberspace that have been made by governments (e.g., the Global Positioning System).

Similarly, potential near-peer adversaries are aggressively exploring options to exploit attributes of cyberspace (e.g., exfiltration of data; distributed denial of service attacks, and implementation of innovative cyber stratagems). These activities have been well-documented in recent news accounts.[11]

From a U.S. perspective, new concepts and initiatives are emerging from the Comprehensive National Cyber Initiative (CNCI). At a minimum, it has been recommended that the United States must incorporate a creative and aggressive cyber "opposing force" to stress the system in future experiments and exercises.

Institutional Factors. Over the last several years, a number of studies have been conducted to address the issues of cyberspace governance, the legal dimension of cyberspace and cyberpower, the tension between civil liberties and national security, and the sharing of information between the public and private sectors. In the area of cyberspace governance, there is a growing appreciation that one should seek *influence* over cyberspace vice *governance.* In the near term, there are a number of policy governance issues that remain to be addressed (e.g., the extension of the contract of the Internet Corporation for Assigned Names and Numbers [ICANN]; and the role of the International Telecommunications Union [ITU] in cyber governance).

The legal dimension of cyberspace has barely addressed the key issues that must be resolved during the next decade. For example, the issues of concern include: what is an act of cyber war; what is a proportionate reaction to an act of cyber war; how should one treat intellectual property in cyberspace; how should one resolve differences in sovereign laws and international treaties.

It is broadly recognized that there is a need for a framework and enhanced dialogue to harmonize the efforts of civil liberties and proponents of enhanced national security. This issue is being pursed as a component of the CNCI initiative.

Finally, many studies have cited the need to address the issue of sharing of cyber information between the U.S. Government and industry. However, there is still a need to provide guidance and procedures to clarify this issue.

Connect.

It is well understood that the various categories of the cyber domain are strongly interconnected. To address this problem, there is a need for a family of Measures of Merit (MoM) to provide that linkage (see Figure 2.2).

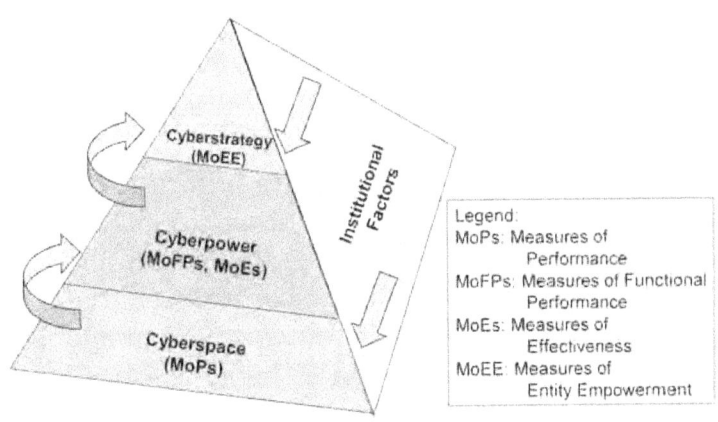

Figure 2.2. Representative Measures of Merit.

For example, cyberspace can be characterized by a set of Measures of Performance (MoPs). These might include performance in cyberspace (e.g., connectivity, bandwidth, and latency) and resistance to adversary countermeasures (e.g., resistance to distributed denial of service attacks, resistance to exfiltration attempts, and resistance to corruption of data).

In the areas of cyberpower, it is useful to think about Measures of Functional Performance (MoFP) and Measures of Effectiveness (MoE). For example, in the case of air-to-air combat, appropriate MoFP might be the range at which air combatants are able to detect, identify, and characterize unknown aircraft. Similarly, loss exchange ratios may be suitable MoE.

In the area of cyberstrategy, one might use political, military, economic, social, information, and infrastructure (PMESII) measures to characterize Measures of Entity Empowerment (MoEE). Thus, for example, one could characterize the extent to which changes in cyberspace might effect changes in politics (e.g., the number of people who vote in an election), military status (e.g., the enhancement in the security of the population), economic factors (e.g., the change in unemployment statistics), social (e.g., ability of diverse social groups to live in harmony), information (e.g., the extent to which social networks support political activity), and infrastructure (e.g., the extent to which improvements in supervisory control and data acquisition [SCADA] systems enhance the availability of electricity and clean water). The actual MoEE will have to be tailored to the entity that is being empowered by changes in cyberspace. Thus, a terrorist, who seeks to, *inter alia,* proselytize, raise money, educate, and train, would have a different set of MoEE.

Finally, one needs to formulate MoMs that are appropriate for issues of governance; legal issues, civil liberties, critical infrastructure protection, and cyber reorganization. Work is currently ongoing in those fields.

Anticipate.

From the perspective of a senior decisionmaker, the key challenge is anticipating the key issues of interest and performing the analyses needed to make knowledgeable decisions.

In the area of cyberspace, it is important to perform technology projections to identify potential key breakthroughs (e.g., cloud computing); explore options to enhance attribution in cyberspace; develop techniques to protect essential data from exfiltration or corruption; and formulate an objective network architecture that is more secure and identify options to transition to it.

In the area of cyberpower, it is important to extend existing analyses to assess the impact of changes in cyberspace on the other elements of power (e.g., diplomatic and economic) and to perform risk assessments to guide future policy decisions.

In the area of cyberstrategy, additional research is needed to guide the development of "tailored deterrence" (particularly against nonstate actors) and to explore options to thwart the efforts of key entities to perform cyber espionage.

In the area of institutional factors, the major challenges are to address the legal issues associated with the cyber domain and to harmonize civil liberties and national security.

Overall, there is a need to develop assessment methods, tools, data, services (e.g., verification, validation, and accreditation [VV&A]), and intellectual capital to assess cyber issues. Figure 2.3 suggests the relative maturity of key tools in the areas of cyberspace, cyberpower, cyberstrategy, and institutional factors.

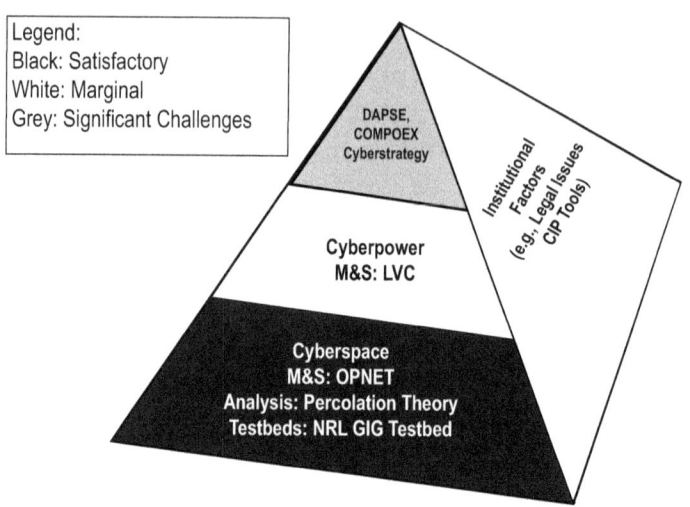

Legend:
Black: Satisfactory
White: Marginal
Grey: Significant Challenges

DAPSE, COMPOEX Cyberstrategy

Cyberpower M&S: LVC

Institutional Factors (e.g., Legal Issues CIP Tools)

Cyberspace
M&S: OPNET
Analysis: Percolation Theory
Testbeds: NRL GIG Testbed

Figure 2.3. State-of-the-Practice in Assessing Cyber Issues.

In the area of cyberspace, there are several tools that the community is employing to address computer science and communications issues. Perhaps the best known is the operations network (OPNET) simulation that is widely employed to address network architectural issues.[12] From an analytic perspective, techniques such as percolation theory enable one to evaluate the robustness of a network.[13] Looking to the future, the National Research Laboratory (NRL) has developed a Global Information Grid (GIG) Testbed to explore the myriad issues associated with linking new systems and networks.

In the area of cyberpower, the community has had some success in employing live, virtual, and constructive simulations. For example, in assessments of air-to-air combat, insights have been derived from the live Air Intercept Missile Evaluation/Air Combat Evaluation (AIMVAL-ACEVAL) experiments, virtual experiments in the former McDonnell Air Combat Simulator (MACS), and constructive experiments using tools such as TAC BRAWLER. However, the community still requires better tools to assess the impact of advances in cyberspace on broader military and informational effectiveness (e.g., land combat in complex terrain).

In the area of cyberstrategy, a number of promising initiatives are underway. In response to a recent tasking by Strategic Command (STRATCOM), a new methodology and associated tools are emerging (i.e., Deterrence Analysis & Planning Support Environment [DAPSE]).[14] However, these results have not yet been applied to major cyberstrategy issues. In addition, promising tools are emerging from academia (e.g., Senturion; GMU's Pythia) and Defense Advanced Research Projects Agency (DARPA) (e.g., Conflict Modeling, Planning & Outcomes Experimentation [COMPOEX]). However, these are still in early stages of development and application.

Finally, as noted above, there are only primitive tools available to address issues of governance, legal issues, and civil liberties. Some tools are being developed to explore the cascading effects among critical infrastructures (e.g., National Infrastructure Simulation and Analysis Center [NISAC] system dynamics models); however, they have not yet undergone rigorous validation.[15]

KEY CHALLENGES

Theories for the "hard" sciences have taken hundreds of years to evolve. However, this preliminary "theory of cyberpower" is approximately only 1-year old! As a consequence, there is a great deal of work that remains to be done in each of the areas of interest.

In the area of Categorize, it is understood that the preliminary framework is just one way of decomposing the problem. It is necessary to formulate alternative frameworks to support further decomposition of the cyber domain.

In the area of Define, there has been a great deal of contention over the most basic terms (e.g., cyberspace and domain). Steps must be taken in the near term to develop a taxonomy that will formulate and define the key terms of interest.

In the area of Explain, it is understood that we are just beginning to deal with a very complex and time-variable problem set. It is vital to conduct studies to create benchmarks and to gain a deeper understanding of key cyber issues.

In the area of Connect, the selection of MoMs is in its infancy. We must consider all of the entities that are being empowered by changes in cyberspace and develop appropriate MoMs for them.

Finally, in the area of Anticipate, we understand the challenge in trying to predict the evolution of cyberspace. At a minimum, we need to generate a research agenda to address unresolved cyber issues. This should include the development of methods, tools, data, services (e.g., VV&A), and intellectual capital to attack many of these problems.

ENDNOTES - CHAPTER 2

1. Dr. Harold R. Winton, "An Imperfect Jewel," presented at INSS workshop on the Theory of Warfare at the National Defense University, Washington, DC, September 2006.

2. Deputy Secretary of Defense Memorandum, "The Definition of Cyberspace," Washington, DC: Department of Defense May 12, 2008.

3. Daniel T. Kuehl, "From Cyberspace to Cyberpower: Defining the Problem." in Franklin D. Kramer, Stuart H. Starr, and Larry K. Wentz, Eds., *Cyberpower and National Security,* Washington, DC: Center for Technology and National Security Policy, National Defense University, Potomac Books, Inc., 2009, p .48.

4. *Ibid.,* p. 40.

5. Sally Adee, "37 Years of Moore's Law," *IEEE Spectrum,* May 2008.

6. Rich Kalgaard, "Ten Laws of the Modern World," April 19, 2005, available from *Forbes.com.*

7. George Gilder, "Metcalfe's Law and Legacy," *Forbes ASAP,* September 13, 1993.

8. Bob Briscoe, Andrew Odlyzko, and Benjamin Tilly, "Metcalfe's Law is Wrong," *IEEE Spectrum,* July 2006.

9. Dan Gonzales *et al.,* "Network-Centric Operations Case Study: Air-to-Air Combat With and Without Link 16," Santa Monica, CA: RAND Corporation, National Defense Research Institute, 2005.

10. Irving Lachow, "Cyber Terrorism: Menace or Myth?" Chap. 19, *Cyberpower and National Security,* Bethesda, MD: Potomac Press, 2009.

11. John Markoff, "Vast Spy System Loots Computers in 103 Countries," *New York Times,* March 29, 2009.

12. Emad Aboelela, "Network Simulation Experiments Manual," Amsterdam: Morgan Kaufmann Publishers, 3rd Ed., June 2003.

13. Ira Kohlberg, "Percolation Theory of Coupled Infrastructures," 2007 Homeland Security Symposium entitled "Cascading

Infrastructure Failures: Avoidance and Response," Washington, DC: National Academies of Sciences, May 2007.

14. "Deterrence in the 21st Century: An Effects-Based Approach in An Interconnected World, Vol. I," Nancy Chesser, ed., *Strategic Multi-Layer Analysis Team*, USSTRATCOM Global Innovation and Strategy Center, October 1, 2007.

15. Colonel William Wimbish and Major Jeffrey Sterling, "A National Infrastructure Simulation and Analysis Center (NISAC): Strategic Leader Education and Formulation of Critical Infrastructure Policies," Carlisle, PA: Center for Strategic Leadership, U.S. Army War College, August 2003.

CHAPTER 3

SURVIVABILITY OF THE INTERNET

Michael J. Chumer

INTRODUCTION

In 2007, a symposium was sponsored by the New Jersey Business Force (NJBF) and SunGard. During the symposium, a panel of experts posed a series of questions that were then addressed in detail by workgroups drawn from the symposium participants. This chapter presents the key issues identified by those issues that affect the resilience and survivability of the Internet during a pandemic declaration.

The use of the "commodity" Internet, referred to simply as the Internet, is the cornerstone of private and public sector communication, application access and use, information sharing, and a host of taken-for-granted usages. During the SunGard[1] and NJBF[2] symposium in 2007, the key question posed and addressed was, "Will the Internet Be There When You Really Need It?"[3] The planning symposium focused on the effects on the Internet if a pandemic based upon H5N1 (the bird flu) was to break out in the United States. In addition, the symposium addressed reciprocal effects on businesses given a marginally functioning Internet.

From the middle of April 2009 to the present, the United States has been in a pre-pandemic event suggested by the World Health Organization (WHO) as stage 5.[4] This in turn has caused many private sector organizations to review their pandemic plans and take the necessary steps to revise and adjust them in anticipation of a pandemic declaration. The virus strain is called H1N1 (swine flu) instead of the H5N1, but that does not alter the business planning process or the steps that make sense for organizations to take in preparation of such a declaration.

As the symposium suggested, a pandemic plan should consider the availability of the Internet for business continuity, given that social distancing will be required. Social distancing will affect all employees, to include "key" personnel. As personnel work from home, the traffic on the Internet will change in a way where certain Internet Service Providers (ISP) may encounter Internet traffic loads that were not anticipated.

SYMPOSIUM DATA COLLECTION

The symposium was conducted as a modified table top exercise (TTX). In the morning, presentations were given that addressed the H5N1 virus along with predictions on how it might spread in the United States; who would be at risk; the role of the public sector, personal protection and the responsibility of the individual; and some initial thoughts about the role and concerns of business and business continuity planning in general. Initial presentations by 10 experts were followed by a facilitated panel discussion designed to surface issues that would later be discussed in detail by the symposium participants.

Subsequent to the panel discussion, the 110 participants were divided into workgroups which engaged in a TTX that addressed in more detail the major questions that surfaced during the panel discussion.

Data that resulted from the panel discussion and from the individual workgroup TTXs were captured and analyzed by a team of researchers. The key items in the panel and TTX data were identified, resulting in a white paper jointly authored by the NJBF and SunGard.[5] Most of the material contained in the white paper has been incorporated and reassessed in this chapter.[6]

In the white paper, a series of topical area issues posed as questions were developed:

- **Business continuity effects due to Internet reduced availability**. What are the foreseeable short-term and long-term impacts if the Internet either "crashes," "goes down," or "stops working"?
- **Service provider collaboration for the collective good**. Explain whether existing protocols for providing collaboration and coordination between U.S. service providers (cable, telephone, and "last mile" providers) are sufficient enough to preserve Internet access and limit overload.
- **Points of Internet failure**. What must planners consider when modifying or developing business practices?
- **The effects on computer applications and/or protocols**. What are the effects on applications and/or protocols if the Internet slows down rather than halting during a pandemic, as well as mitigation strategies for such an event?
- **Increased Internet demand**. In the face of heavy demand on the Internet, which features or services should contingency planners expect to shut down or redirect to conserve or preserve bandwidth?
- **Hacker Attacks**. Should contingency planners expect attacks from hackers during a state when the Internet is weakened?

- **Growing Internet Reliability**. Whether we as a nation are depending too much on the Internet and underestimating its risks for the sake of cost, convenience, and efficiency?
- **Internet Resilience**. Will the Internet be resilient enough to hold up under the onslaught of school, business, home enterprise, emergency management, and recreational users during a pandemic?

CURRENT ESCALATING SITUATION

On June 11, 2009, the WHO raised the pandemic alert level from phase 5 to phase 6, which indicates the start of a full-fledged worldwide pandemic. This declaration, in turn, suggests that certain actions or behaviors should be "triggered" within organizations (the public and/or private sector). The general discussion that follows in the next section reveals answers to questions about the effects of a pandemic declaration on the Internet. Many business organizations, in turn, are reviewing their current continuity of operations plans (COOPS), and public sector organizations also are reviewing their continuity of government plans (COOGS). The next section also provides guidance to organizations about what issues they need to address to ensure that business can continue to function and continue to survive during a pandemic.

That section also indicates that the "commodity" Internet plays a significant and vital role in the ability of business to do business. The Internet is a critical component within the supply-and-value chain of each organization, linking businesses as the producers of products and/or the providers of services to the customers that benefit from those products and services.

The reliance on the Internet has grown over the past 16 years (the backbone of the Internet was contracted in 1993 or outsourced by the National Science Foundation to the private sector). This growth has been exponential and, along with it, a growing dependency and interdependency has occurred, with the tacit belief that the Internet will always be there. Businesses have developed processes and procedures where the Internet is a critical component. If the Internet slows down significantly, which may occur during a pandemic, or even cease to function in certain parts of the country due to unexpected traffic patterns, coupled with denial of service attacks, business and governments need to be prepared. This will not be an easy task.

GENERAL DISCUSSION

The sections that follow discuss in detail the answers to the questions that were posed to symposium attendees through the panel discussion and the subsequent TTX. Each section provides planning guidance to both organizational planners and organizational emergency management/security functions.

Business Continuity Effects Due to Internet Reduced Availability with Examples of Healthcare and Education.

The symposium data suggested that healthcare and education would be greatly impacted over the long term during periods of reduced availability. In 2006, healthcare approached one-sixth of the gross domestic product (GDP), inferring that the economic impact during periods of reduced Internet availability would be significant. The amount of communication being passed over the Internet due to patient electronic records, clinical data being shared geographically, and the bandwidth of clinical data, especially those requiring visualization, would all suffer time lags and delays with the ultimate potential of affecting patient diagnostics and treatment protocols.

A significant percentage of education from K-12 is still done face-to-face (F2F), suggesting that during periods of social distancing, essential delivery of education material would not occur. When education delivery is viewed at the community college or college level, we do see a movement toward both distance learning and hybrid (blended learning) course delivery. However, the majority of distance learning courses are delivered over home-to-school Internet connections, suggesting that some delays in the delivery of course content would occur during periods of reduced Internet availability.

In addition, over the short term, e-mails — which in 2006 averaged 84 billion per day — voice over Internet protocol (VOIP), and instant messaging would be affected. This will leave those people whose social networks are tied to a virtual space to seek out different forms of social networking. It might be very difficult during periods of social distancing for those individuals and collectives that rely on virtual communication to adapt to both physical and virtual isolation.

Service Provider Collaboration for the Collective Good.

The symposium discussed whether existing protocols for providing collaboration and coordination between U.S. service providers (cable, telephone, and "last mile" providers) are sufficient enough to preserve Internet access and limit overload. Discussion for this topic was robust. It is clear that the ownership of the Internet resides with the private sector and, in that vein, there is some but not a lot of coordination between Internet "backbone" providers to ensure that infrastructure "build-outs" keep up with capacity demands. However, during a pandemic or any emergency situation which may require a reduction of Internet traffic, existing protocols are either insufficient or do not exist. Furthermore, the symposium data suggested,

> To date the private sector has established no definitive industry standards governing Internet user priorities and preferences in the event of a catastrophic event or an 'incident of national significance.'[7]

This gets into the entire notion of establishing priorities during periods of reduced Internet availability. Recommendations emerging from the symposium include the following:

- In emergency situations; forming an advisory group comprising Internet Service Providers and Government representatives to address key issues;
- Expanding the role of existing ISP groups (FIS-PA) to include formulating policies.

As the discussion moved forward, a further suggestion was that, during a pandemic or a national emergency, each organization should "voluntarily" reduce their Internet traffic by 10 percent below peak levels. Additional symposium recommendations in this area were:

- limiting video streaming and VoIP;
- adopting off-hour business solutions;

- prioritizing business applications;
- blocking noncritical Internet traffic.[8]

This is certainly an area open to more debate, such as addressing the role government should play in Internet traffic regulation during emergency situations and/or periods of reduced Internet availability. The consensus was that the government should be a partner with the private sector with limited intervention.

Points of Internet Failure.

The symposium data indicated that planners must consider access infrastructure and bandwidth as they develop business practices that focus on their continuity of operations. Access infrastructure must be planned from business locations to the first ISP and also from a "critical" employee location to that employee's primary ISP. Businesses for the most part do a good job in monitoring their network traffic to include their Internet access points. There are often "first" and "last mile" issues which suggest that redundancy of access becomes a critical part of the plan. However, what is often overlooked is the access that critical employees should have from their home location. This becomes an important planning consideration during social distancing when the tacit expectation is that an employee can access organizational applications from their home location as they would from their work location. For employees, the issue of "first" and "last mile" redundancy becomes salient as well. This suggests that organizational planners should possess an inventory of critical employee home access capabilities which might suggest redundant Internet access from a home location.

Bandwidth is the second item that planners must consider. Again, this is important at business locations, but becomes more important when employees work at home. We are in an era where audio, video, and graphics are transmitted over Internet infrastructures. Many organizational applications are developed for a thin client architecture where most of the processing is performed on organizational servers. This architecture suggests that significant bandwidth capacity may be required to access web-based organizational applications.

The symposium data indicated that the following are the least likely points of failure: "Among the least likely points of failure are Domain Name Servers (DNS), corporate high-capacity bandwidth, local exchange carrier, and redundant corporate routing."[9]

The Effects on Computer Applications and/or Protocols.

What are the effects on applications and/or protocols if the Internet slows down rather than halting during a pandemic, as well as mitigation strategies? Symposium data suggested that this question is tightly coupled to the role that the Internet plays within organizational supply and value chains.[10] Much of organizational supply and value chains are outsourced to different organizations (vendors or partners) requiring "tight coupling"[11] from a communication perspective. This suggests that access and bandwidth considerations that were previously addressed take on a significant level of importance.

In conjunction with supply and value chain considerations unique to the specific organization, there is the entire issue of supply/value chain interdependencies and critical application access.[12] Business environments where a "just in time" mentality has developed suggests a business continuity focus on stabilizing the supply chain during a pandemic or incident of national significance. The symposium indicated that the supply/value chain issue should be stabilized first before employee essential needs of "food, water, and healthcare" should be addressed.[13]

Increased Internet Demand.

In the face of heavy demand on the Internet, which features or services should contingency planners expect to shut down or redirect to conserve or preserve bandwidth? The Internet has become less of an "amenity" and more of an "expectation."[14] Witness that what began as a service that hotels would offer to gain a competitive advantage has now become a common expectation of business travelers. Since the expectation for robust and ubiquitous Internet services has been set, restricting usage would be met by a general resistance from the public writ large. This resistance could be somewhat overcome by requesting the public to engage in behavior directed toward voluntary restrictions on their Internet use. However, the symposium indicated that "Voluntary restrictions would have to be imposed for limited periods, applied equitably, and based on established priorities."[15] It was recommended that the public sector, especially the individual states, develop a list of priority users and suggested the following:

- "Urgent (utilities, public service networks, government),
- Priority (commodity transportation, food, medicine, relief supplies),
- Normal (those not listed above)."[16]

What was not mentioned at the symposium but has relevance here is the development of a priority switching scheme for critical Internet services. At present there is "Internet 2"[17] and "The National Lambda Rail."[18] Both are services that possess fiber backbones which are separate from the basic backbone infrastructure of the commodity Internet. Once developed, urgent and priority services could benefit by being switched during an emergency to one of these high bandwidth, high capacity services.

Hacker Attacks.

Should contingency planners expect attacks from hackers during a state when the Internet is weakened? The symposium data indicated that the cyber infrastructure used by organizations is always at risk from hackers and from a variety of sources initiating unwanted intrusions. During a pandemic, it was agreed that the weakened state of the commodity Internet has the potential of putting organizations at a higher level of risk. The greatest vulnerabilities will be in the areas of online banking and the movement of critical operations to the commodity Internet.

It is expected that during periods of social distancing, online banking activity will increase significantly which would open up opportunities for hacking. Additionally, as more organizationally "critical" application functions move to the Internet due to employees performing telework, this will become a target for hacking activity as well. Hackers are not averse to taking advantage of other vulnerabilities. It was agreed that identify theft activities would increase significantly, especially targeting people who died as a result of the pandemic. Finally, the weakened state of the Internet could spawn denial of service activity. The white paper suggested the following as potential remedies:

> Businesses should consider adding varying degrees of redundancy and security during their preparations. They can improve the security of online, networked operations during the mass migration of critical functions and services, including telecommuting, to the Internet. Specifically, companies can step up enforcement of standard security controls and policies (e.g., firewalls).

> They also can install encryption software, limit employee access and privileges to e-mail, and control access to major non-mission-critical business processes. They can increase the frequency of mandatory password resets, require two-factor authentication, set tighter controls over extra-net partners, implement more aggressive patch management, and increase monitoring of the cyber or virtual environment.[19]

Growing Internet Reliability.

Are we as a nation becoming too dependent on the Internet and underestimating its risks for the sake of cost, convenience, and efficiency? Internet dependency has been growing since the National Science Foundation allowed the commercialization of the Internet backbone in 1993. E-mail communication has increased significantly each year, and services like "Facebook"[20] and "Twitter"[21] are beginning to redefine technology based "social networking." Blogging activity is increasing, as well as online shopping. So we as a nation and as a society have become very dependent upon the Internet and have incorporated its use into everyday life. The Internet has become extremely convenient.

The convenience of the Internet needs to be balanced against potential risks. An understanding of this balance and the steps that should be taken by people in general, and organizational employees specifically, suggest focus and constant reinforcement on education. This education should address and develop an understanding of the risks of the Internet and its counterbalance — the rewards of Internet use.

A list of planning guidelines that organizations should follow for both educating themselves as well as educating their employees is included in the appendix. During the symposium, the value of developing a risk–reward education program was stressed in order to further develop an understanding of the risks and vulnerabilities of Internet use and access.

Internet Resilience.

Will the Internet and ISPs be resilient enough to hold up under the onslaught of school, business, home enterprise, emergency management, and recreational users during a pandemic?[22] The ability for ISPs to engineer their capacity in such a way where they are able to accommodate this surge becomes important. It is expected that the Internet will not "break" during a pandemic, but it will certainly "bend" under the surge in expected use.

The white paper suggested areas that need to be addressed to begin to ensure that the Internet is as resilient as possible. These are:

> The goal would be to avoid or eliminate single points of failure; establish reliability standards; have multiple geographically isolated Post Office Protocal (POP)

servers; and ensure redundancy using non-terrestrial communications to geographically diverse ground stations. In addition, Tier 1 and 2 providers could manage bandwidth for Tier 3 and 4 providers, allowing maximum efficiency in meeting the expected surge in demand for Internet bandwidth.[23]

CONCLUSION

In general, it was concluded that the backbone of the Internet is fairly "robust" and should be capable of withstanding the surge that would be expected during the initial stages of a pandemic declaration. However, the points of backbone access and the ability to address local surge issues may cause the Internet to bend to levels that may be unacceptable to local users. The white paper that followed the symposium concluded with the following recommendation, included here in its entirety:

> In the U.S., the Internet is analogous to private and commercial cars and trucks, i.e., it is indispensable. Continuity of Operations (COOP) planners must take threats to Internet availability as seriously as they would take threats to the availability of gasoline.
>
> The direct and indirect threats a pandemic would pose to the Internet are genuine.
>
> The potential for hostile human interference — for example, terrorist attacks or other disruptive behavior — during a pandemic should be factored into continuity plans. The U.S. economy remains a high-value target, and America's enemies probably would attempt to exploit a pandemic through asymmetrical warfare (e.g., cyber attacks) to further weaken the economy and therefore the country.

Degradation or loss of Internet service during a pandemic may reduce businesses to a state Herbert Spencer described as 'survival of the fittest.' In this environment, organizations that were well prepared beforehand will have the best chance of prevailing. To improve their chances, companies can:

- Engineer systems for peak usage by expanding capacity or reserving additional bandwidth,
- Eliminate or reduce vulnerabilities, and
- Educate employees to take care of themselves.

Internet Service Providers (ISPs) and government representatives should form a joint task force to develop an Internet assurance strategy and voluntary guidelines for implementation during a pandemic. However, while the private sector probably would accept voluntary controls over Internet use during a pandemic, as long as limitations and restrictions are justifiable and equitably applied, government-directed mandates could be opposed as Marshall Law.

Identify potential problems now by conducting comprehensive exercises that would stress IT systems. Companies could conduct tests locally at first, adopting a process of continuous review that would integrate technology issues into overall planning efforts, incorporate the legal and human resources functions into the planning process, ensure that critical employees have primary and secondary means of communication, develop policies and standard operating procedures for mission critical functions, and establish a worst-case scenario as a baseline for testing. Companies could then coordinate regional exercises with government and other businesses.

The supply chain is a national center of gravity, and the Internet is an integral component of America's economic engine. These are a foundation of business and workforce survival; therefore, protecting them is essential for Continuity of Community and economic recovery. Because the 'social fabric' may unravel in the event of a supply chain meltdown, companies should organize mitigation measures around supply chain failures and the reduced availability of critical workers. These Page measures are an essential underpinning for successful voluntary home isolation policies.

There are non-intrusive steps the private sector can take to prevent Internet overload and preserve capacity. These include voluntary conservation guidelines, in-house measures and protocols to limit consumption of bandwidth, and employee understanding and compliance.

Companies and government should prepare the general public for Internet disruptions. This preparation can include promoting civic responsibility to gain cooperation for Internet emergency measures, explaining Internet prioritization schemes, and trying to take the mystique out of information technology (i.e., persuade people that IT is a utility or resource, not much different from electricity or transportation).

Companies, government, and the general public should strive to understand a pandemic's physiological and technological challenges, and then adopt multi-faceted approaches to physical, cyber, and personnel protection.[24]

These recommendations frame the type of "preparedness" thinking that should go into the development of plans due to a pandemic declaration (we are now in WHO, phase 6). The appendix provides important and specific guidance to planners given the uncertainty of H1N1.

ENDNOTES - CHAPTER 3

1. SunGard, available from www.*sungard.com/*.

2. New Jersey Business Force, *www.njbusinessforce.org/*.

3. New Jersey Business Force/SunGard White Paper, "Will the Internet Be There When You Really Need It?" Pandemic Symposium sponsored by the New Jersey Business Force and SunGard, 2007.

4. World Health Organization, *www.who.int/en/*.

5. New Jersey Business Force/SunGard White Paper.

6. *Ibid.*

7. *Ibid.*, p. 4.

8. *Ibid.*

9. *Ibid.*, p. 4.

10. M. E. Porter, "How Competitive Forces Shape Strategy," *Harvard business Review*, March/April 1979; M. E. Porter, *Competitive Strategy*, New York: Free Press, 1980; M. E. Porter, *Competitive Advantage*, New York: Free Press, 1985.

11. M. J. Chumer and M. Turoff, "Command and Control (C2): Adapting the Distributed Military Model for Emergency Response and Emergency Management," 11th ICCRTS, 2006, available from *www.dodccrp.org/events/11th_ICCRTS/html/papers/005.pdf*.

12. Porter, "How Competitive Forces Shape Strategy"; Porter, *Competitive Strategy*; Porter, *Competitive Advantage*.

13. New Jersey Business Force/SunGard White Paper, p. 5.

14. *Ibid.*, p. 7.

15. *Ibid.*, p. 7.

16. *Ibid.*, p. 7.

17. Internet 2, available from *www.internet2.edu/*.

18. National Lambda Rail, available from *www.nlr.net/*.

19. New Jersey Business Force/SunGard White Paper, p. 8.

20. Facebook, available from *www.facebook.com/*.

21. Twitter, available from *twitter.com/*.

22. Robert Stephan, Statement for the Record, 2008, available from *homeland.house.gov/SiteDoments/20080514143442-12325.doc*.

23. New Jersey Business Force/SunGard White Paper, p. 10.

24. *Ibid.*, pp. 11-12.

APPENDIX

The 10 items listed in this appendix are drawn directly from the white paper and are offered here as guidance for all organizations to follow in developing a resilient COOP that focuses upon Internet vulnerabilities.[1]

Planning Guidelines.

1. System and staff redundancy, enhancing redundancy by purchasing diverse equipment and systems.

2. Survivability based on the Continuity of Community concept.
   a. Plans, policies & procedures to ensure the resiliency of:
      i.   Economy
      ii. Government
      iii. Society
      iv. Family
      v.   Nuclear and Extended
      vi. The Individual
   b. Information technologies take on increasing importance when employing emergency measures to contain pandemic outbreaks,
   c. Quarantines,
   d. Social distancing.

3. Preparation combined with prevention,
   a. Ensuring multiple means of Internet access, and,
   b. Assessing existing bandwidth against potential surge requirements.

4. Identification of essential systems and people.

5. Education, training, exercising, and testing of IT systems in concert with continuity plans.
   a. Preparing employees to telecommute, including encouraging them to embrace mobile (i.e., handheld) and personal computing platforms,
   b. Educating, training, and testing employees on recovery responsibilities,
   c. Examining security issues.

6. Staffs that are important to the continuity effort, including Human Resources, Legal, and Information Technology.

7. Cascading impacts.
   a. Looking at service provider plans and the capacities and capabilities they possess,
   b. Determining whether first- and last-mile connections are potential points of failure.

8. Systems security in all facets of operations.
   a. Checking personnel, firewalls, passwords, etc.,
   b. Maintaining security's priority over urgency,
   c. Enforcing rules/procedures across all organizational levels,
   d. Remaining vigilant against cyber threats.

9. The balance between mitigation measures and demand for IT and Internet services.
   a. Reducing non-essential usage to prevent overloading,

b. Addressing problems at the source to lower unrealistic expectations,

c. Making concerted public relations and customer relations effort.

10. Realistic expectations.

a. Planning and reinforcing what you can control,

b. Accepting and trying to influence what you cannot,

c. Proceeding without waiting for government or anyone else to tell you what to do.

ENDNOTES - APPENDIX

1. New Jersey Business Force/Surguard White Pages, pp. 9-10.

REFERENCES

Chumer, M. J., and M. Turoff, *Command and Control (C2): Adapting the Distributed Military Model for Emergency Response and Emergency Management, 11th ICCRTS*, 2006, available from *www.dodccrp.org/events/11th_ICCRTS/html/papers/005.pdf.*

Facebook, available from *www.facebook.com/.*

Internet 2, available from *www.internet2.edu/.*

National Lambda Rail, available from *www.nlr.net/.*

New Jersey Business Force, available from *www.njbusiness-force.org/.*

New Jersey Business Force/SunGard White Paper, "Will the Internet Be There When You Really Need It?" Pandemic Symposium Sponsored by the New Jersey Business Force and SunGard, 2007.

Porter, M. E., "How Competitive Forces Shape Strategy," *Harvard Business Review*, March/April, 1979.

_____, *Competitive Strategy*, New York: Free Press, 1980.

_____, *Competitive Advantage*, New York: Free Press, 1985.

Stephan, Robert, Statement for the Record, 2008, available from *homeland.house.gov/SiteDocuments/20080514143442-12325.doc.*

SunGard, available from *www.sungard.com/.*

Twitter, available from *twitter.com/.*

World Health Organization (WHO), available from *www.who.int/en/.*

CHAPTER 4

ARE LARGE-SCALE DATA BREACHES INEVITABLE?

Douglas E. Salane

INTRODUCTION

Despite heightened awareness, large-scale data breaches continue to occur and pose significant risks to both individuals and organizations. An examination of recent data breaches shows that fraudsters increasingly are targeting institutions that hold large collections of credit card and social security numbers. Particularly at risk are card payment processors and retailers who do not properly secure their systems. Frequently, breached data winds up in the hands of overseas organized crime rings that make financial data available to the underground Internet economy, which provides a ready market for the purchase and sale of large volumes of personal financial data. This chapter concludes that strong data breach notification legislation is essential for consumer protection, and that the direct and indirect costs of breach notification provide significant economic incentives to protect data. Also needed are standards for end-to-end encryption, enterprise level methods for quickly patching and updating information systems, and enhanced privacy standards to protect sensitive financial information.

A data breach occurs when an organization loses control over who has access to restricted information. The Privacy Rights Clearing House, a nonprofit privacy advocacy organization, maintains a partial list of the breaches reported since 2005.[1] Losses of tens of thousands of records now occur almost on a weekly basis. Large-scale breaches at data aggregators, credit card payment processors, and national retail chains have compromised the sensitive personal and financial data of millions individuals. Currently, 44 states have data breach notification laws that require organizations to notify the individuals affected by a breach. For organizations holding data on individuals, breaches are no longer an internal matter and can be quite costly, both in terms of breach notification costs and the loss of confidence of customers and business partners.

Data breaches exposing information that can be used to commit fraud are of particular concern. Such breaches typically involve sensitive financial information such as credit card and bank account numbers. Often causing even greater harm, however, is the loss of personally identifiable information (PII) such as driver license or social security numbers. Unlike compromised credit card and account numbers, it is difficult to know how thieves will use a social security number or other PII to commit fraud. A growing demand for the stolen PII now provides a ready market for both types of information, and data thieves have ample incentive to steal both.

The scale and scope of data breaches during this decade has been alarming. From 2003 to 2005, each of the three leading data aggregation companies, Acxiom,[2] LexisNexis,[3] and ChoicePoint,[4] suffered serious data breaches by failing to control business partners who had access to their databases.[5] In 2005, Choice-Point inadvertently released the financial records of 163,000 persons by making the data available to identity thieves who posed as legitimate clients. In 2003 and 2004, in two separate incidents, Acxiom subcontractors stole information in the company's databases. In one case, the subcontractor stole over one billion records. From 2003 to 2005, LexisNexis found that unauthorized persons used identification of legitimate users to obtain social security numbers, driver's license numbers, and the names and addresses of over 310,000 individuals in its databases. In a May 2009 announcement, the company notified over 40,000 individuals that credit card data that it held may have been compromised in 2007.

During the past 4 years, several major retailers and card payment processing companies have had extremely large data breaches. In June 2005, Master Card disclosed that a card processor, CardSystems Solutions, suffered a data breach that compromised the credit card information of over 40 million card holders.[6] In the widely publicized TJX Companies breach that occurred from 2005 to 2007, thieves stole over 45 million credit card numbers.[7] According to the Massachusetts Bankers Association, the breach affected the credit records of over 20 percent of New Englanders. In March 2008, Hannaford Brothers Co. disclosed that malicious software in its payment systems compromised at least 4.2 million credit and debit card accounts.[8] In December 2008, payment processor RBS Wordplay said a breach of its payment systems affected more than 1.5 million people.[9] Security and law enforcement experts are still trying to determine the extent of the Heartland Payment System Breach discovered in December 2008. Heartland processes over 100 million credit/debit transactions per month and is one of the top 10 payment processors. For over 18 months, malicious software on a Heartland server intercepted unencrypted Track 2 (information on the magnetic strip of a credit or debit card). The company became aware of the breach when Visa reported excessive fraudulent activity in credit card transactions processed by Heartland.[10]

Although large-scale breaches attract the most attention, smaller targeted breaches can result in significant losses since they often provide thieves with the information needed to commit fraud. Recently thieves installed skimmers on automatic teller machines (ATMs) in New York City and positioned concealed cameras near the machines to record Personal Identification Numbers (PINs). After fabricating credit cards with the stolen information, the thieves were able to steal over $500,000 from about 200 victims.[11] Thieves then attempted to withdraw the maximum allowable amount from each account for as many days as possible. Skimmers for capturing the card's Track 2 data and devices for fabricating cards are available on the Internet. This type of crime no longer requires exceptional technical skills, and ATM frauds that use this equipment are becoming increasingly common.

Due to the potential impact of breaches on consumers, organizations, and commerce, data breach research is an active area. Two organizations that provide breach information are the Open Security Foundation, through its DataLossDB Project, and the previously mentioned Privacy Rights Clearing House.[12] The DataLossDB Project maintains a downloadable database of incidents and provides aggregate statistics on breaches since 2005. The primary sources of information on data breaches are breach notification letters sent to state attorneys general, which typically are required under state breach notification laws. Copies of breach notification letters are then sent to individuals whose information has been compromised. Press reports, SEC filings, and company statements are other important sources. Despite California's landmark breach notification legislation in 2003 and the adoption of breach notification legislation in 44 states, detailed information on a data breach is seldom made public or shared with the larger security community at the time of a breach.

Data breaches, particularly large-scale breaches involving PII, raise many questions. Unfortunately, the secrecy that typically surrounds a data breach makes answers hard to find. Detailed information, which may be essential for threat detection throughout a particular industry, is seldom made available at the time a breach occurs. In fact, the details surrounding a breach may not be available for years since large-scale breaches usually result in various legal actions. The parties involved typically have no interest in releasing any more information than the law requires. Ironically, detailed breach information often becomes available in the course of a legal action when it becomes part of the public record. Thus the exact means by which a breach occurred often is not known until long afterward, if ever. Moreover, information about perpetrators and what exactly they do with the information is difficult to obtain. Such information may only come to light years later, if at all, in the course of criminal prosecutions. In addition, it is often not clear how to quantify the harm that may be caused by a breach—if 40 million records are compromised, how many of those records will likely to be used to commit fraud? What information should be made available to affected individuals, and how should they be instructed to protect themselves? Who bears the costs? In industries where multiple parties process data, who should be held responsible for a breach?

The remainder of this chapter examines notable large-scale breaches in the data aggregation, card payment processing, and retail industries. It explores remedies and practices that have been suggested to mitigate breaches, particularly in the card payment industry. The chapter also discusses the costs of notable large breaches, both to individuals and the companies involved. It describes the research and developments needed to improve data breach detection, deterrence, and response.

NOTABLE BREACHES: INSTITUTIONS, CAUSES, AND COSTS

By 2005, largely through acquisitions of smaller data management companies, Acxiom, ChoicePoint, and LexisNexis had grown to be the world's three largest aggregators and providers of individual, data, each with revenues of over $1 billion annually. These organizations leveraged their significant analysis and processing capabilities, gleaned over many years of managing data for large corporate clients, to provide detailed information on, and profiles of, individuals to insurers, collection agencies, direct marketers, employment screeners and government agencies, including state and local law enforcement agencies. The website of Accurint, the information subsidiary of LexisNexis, indicates the detailed information held and made available.[13] For example, one product provided by the company, "People at Work," holds information on 132 million individuals including addresses, phone numbers, and possible dates of employment. The site advertises the ability to find people, their relatives, associates, and assets. Large-scale breaches at each of these data aggregators earlier in this decade raised a great deal of attention among privacy advocates and prompted calls for regulation of the activities of the data aggregation industry.[14]

During 2002 and 2003, Acxiom suffered two separate serious data breaches that involved Acxiom business partners who had legitimate password access to the company's databases.[15] The first involved the system administrator of a small company who provided services to Acxiom and who routinely downloaded files from an Acxiom FTP server. The administrator exceeded his authority on the server and was able to download and decrypt a file containing passwords. He obtained a master password that allowed him to then download files belonging to other companies. The administrator sealed his fate when he told a hacker friend in a chat room that he had been able to obtain access to a local telephone company database. A subsequent investigation of the hacker friend led to the administrator. As part of the same investigation, Acxiom technicians came upon a second more serious breach that involved theft by a subcontractor to an Acxiom contractor. From January 2001 to June 2003, the subcontractor, who owned a firm that provided e-mail advertising services, accessed over one billion records in Acxiom's databases by extending his authorized access. The individual was later arrested and convicted on various federal charges that included 120 counts of unauthorized access of a protected computer.[16] Prosecutors claim he used the data in his own e-mail advertising business and eventually planned to sell his company and its newly expanded database to a credit rating company.

The ChoicePoint breach occurred in the fall of 2004 and involved the theft of 145,000 consumer records — the number was later revised upward to 163,000 records.[17] Under California's breach notification law, ChoicePoint had to disclose the breach to California residents. Shortly afterward, attorneys general in 38 states demanded that ChoicePoint disclose the breach to victims in all states.[18] The breach led to numerous calls for an investigation of how information held by aggregators might be used to harm individuals.[19] The breach cost ChoicePoint $2 million just in notification fees and over $10 million in legal fees. In February 2005, the Company said about 750 individuals had been victims of identity theft. The company stated at the time that the breach did not involve a compromise of its networks or hacking, but was carried out by a few individuals who posed as legitimate business customers and were given access to the data, which included personal financial information. The company stated that financial fraud conducted by seemingly legitimate businesses is a pervasive problem. The Federal Trade Commission (FTC) later determined that ChoicePoint was in violation of the Fair Credit Reporting Act. The company settled with the FTC by paying $10 million in fines and $5 million for consumer redress. One of the perpetrators, a Nigerian national living in California, was later arrested and tried under California law on charges of identity theft and fraud. He was sentenced to 10 years in prison and ordered to make restitution of $6 million. The incident led to dramatic changes in the way ChoicePoint safeguards sensitive personal information and how it screens potential business customers.

In 2005, LexisNexis, another leading data aggregator, announced a major breach that exposed the personal information of 310,000 individuals.[20] LexisNexis found after analyzing data over a 2-year period that unauthorized people used identification and passwords of legitimate customers to obtain consumer social security numbers, driver's license numbers, names, and addresses. The company stated that the breach involved 59 incidents of improper access to data. The company added that various techniques were used to gain access to the data, including, collecting identification and passwords from machines infected with viruses, using computer programs to generate passwords and identification that matched those of legitimate customers, and unauthorized access by former employees of companies with legitimate access to LexisNexis data. The incident appeared to be not one breach, but a series of breaches that occurred over a multi-year period and involved several different groups.

In May 2009, LexisNexis disclosed a breach that exposed the personal information of 40,000 individuals and compromised names, birthdates, and social security numbers.[21] The breach appears to have taken place from June 2004 to October 2007. The company breach letter said the thieves, who were once legitimate LexisNexis customers, used mailboxes at commercial mail services and PII taken from LexisNexis to set up about 300 fraudulent credit cards. The breach letter indicated that LexisNexis learned of the breach from the U.S. Postal Inspection Service, which was investigating the fraudulent credit cards.[22]

In congressional testimony in 2005, Acxiom's chief privacy officer discussed the company's data breaches.[23] She claimed that most information obtained was of a nonsensitive nature, and none of it was used to commit identity fraud. She noted that the company would henceforth require stronger passwords and keep data on servers only for the period for which it is needed. She mentioned that Acxiom had decided to appoint a chief information security officer, a position now common in most large organizations. From her testimony, it was obvious that this breach was an embarrassment for a company that obtains over 80 percent of its revenues from managing data for large corporations and large public agencies. She indicated that Acxiom was in the process of participating in dozens of audits by clients, whose trust in the company had certainly been diminished. The privacy officer reflecting the words of the then FTC commissioner said there is no such thing as perfect security and that breaches will happen even when all precautions are taken. The privacy officer's testimony underscored the importance of removing data when it was no longer needed and effectively monitoring contractors and vendors with access to company data. At a recent presentation at John Jay College, the chief security officer of Time Inc. indicated that vendor management now was one of his major responsibilities.[24]

The retail and card payment processing industries have suffered a number of large-scale breaches during the past 5 years. Unlike the data aggregation industry, breaches in these industries appear to have involved malware on servers that collected data and transmitted it outside the company. These breaches, however, also involved individuals with detailed insider knowledge of the systems that were compromised. Although the credit card industry and retail industries have not reported significant rises in the rates of credit card fraud, the scope of recent payment card breaches, the rapidity with which stolen credit information was used, and the geographical scope of the fraud, raise concerns that data thieves are now taking advantage of the capabilities afforded by worldwide crime organizations to monetize vast collections of breached financial information.[25]

One of largest breaches of a payment processor occurred at CardSystems Solutions, a company that processed both credit and debit credit card transactions. According to the FTC,[26] in 2005 the company handled over 210 million card purchases worth $15 billion for more than 119,000 small and mid-size merchants. The company's CEO admitted in congressional testimony that the data thieves captured Track 2 information belonging to 263,000 individuals.[27] Security experts later determined that credit and debit information of over 40 million customers may have been compromised. Despite the incredible volume of transactions processed by the company, at the time, the company had only 115 employees. The breach was not discovered by CardSystems, but by MasterCard security while tracking fraudulent card activity.[28]

The FTC charged CardSystems Solution with violation of Section 5 of the FTC Act, which prohibits unfair or deceptive business practices.[29] The FTC claimed that the company violated the Act by failing to adopt widely accepted, easily deployed security standards that would have prevented the exposure of the sensitive financial data of tens of millions of individuals. The FTC further charged that the company neglected industry security polices with respect to the type of data it collected and the amount of time it held the data.

A forensic investigation of the breach found numerous security lapses both in the company's systems and procedures. The company violated it own industry security polices by storing data in unencrypted format on a server accessible from a public network. Data thieves were able to execute a Structured Query Language (SQL) injection attack that allowed an unauthorized script to be placed on a WebFacing server.

The script exported data to an external FTP site every 4 days. In addition, data was retained for purposes other than payment processing, another violation of industry policy. Furthermore, the company did not adequately assess its system vulnerabilities to commonly known attacks, did not use strong passwords, and did not implement simple, widely used defenses to thwart SQL attacks. The CEO also added in congressional testimony that the company stored Track 2 data for later analysis, another violation of industry security standards.[30]

The breach raised new levels of security awareness within the card payment processing industry and provided significant impetus for compliance with the industry's newly developed Payment Card Industry Data Security Standard (PCI DSS or simply PCI).[31] Today, loss of PCI certification can put a payment processor out of business, because it means that the company failed to comply with information security standards, which undermines the confidence of customers and partners. Shortly after the CardSystems breach, Visa and American Express stopped processing with the company. After revising security policies, upgrading systems, and implementing end-to-end encryption on its backend systems and networks, the company eventually gained PCI certification. PayByTouch, another payment processor, then purchased the company at a steep discount.[32] The largest breach of a retailer's payment processing systems occurred at TJX Companies from 2005 to 2007.[33] Intruders had access to the systems for over 18 months. In filings with the SEC, the company said 45.6 million card numbers may have been taken. Card issuing banks later raised the total to 94 million. In addition, thieves captured personal information such as driver's license numbers, which was used to track merchandise returns.[34] According to industry estimates, a card replacement can cost between $5 and $15 dollars, and a breach notification may cost up to $35 per notification. Shortly after the compromise, thieves used the card numbers to make purchases in Georgia, Florida, and Louisiana in the United States, as well as in Hong Kong and Sweden. By September 2007, the breach had cost the company over $150 million, and the company still faced numerous class action law suits.

TJX believes a flaw in its wireless networks may have allowed malware to be placed on one of its Retail Transaction Switch Servers (RTS) that processes and stores information on customer purchases and charge backs for its stores throughout North America. At the time TJX was in the process of upgrading its wireless security from the weaker Wired Equivalent Privacy (WEP) standard to the stronger WiFi Protected Access (WPA) standard.[35] TJX admits that intruders had accessed the system at times from July 2005 to January 2007.

A report by the Office of the Privacy Commissioner of Canada[36] provides a summary of the security lapses of TJX Companies that led to the breach. The privacy commission found that the TJX intruders gained access to the names, addresses, driver's license numbers, and provincial identification numbers of over 330 persons with addresses in Canada. According to Canadian privacy law, TJX should not have collected this information in card transactions. Citing analyses of the incident, the commission found that the company did not have in place adequate logging procedures to do a proper forensic analysis of the incident. The data thieves actually deleted information so it was difficult to tell what information was compromised.

The commission also faulted the company for not being fully compliant with industry standards and practices such as PCI. The commission noted that as far back as 2003, the Institute of Electrical and Electronics Engineers (IEEE) standards committees had recommended migration from the WEP security standard to the stronger WPA standard, yet the company had at the time of the breach failed to complete the migration. Even though the commission found that TJX had an adequate organizational security structure in place, it faulted the company for collecting too much data, holding it too long, using a weak security protocol, and not having adequate monitoring in place to detect a breach in progress or to determine the extent of the breach after the fact.

Another payment processor, RBS World Pay of Scotland, suffered a serious breach in December 2008 that involved over 1.5 million financial records.[37] According to the Federal Bureau of Investigation (FBI), thieves stole Track 2 data from debit cards that were used to pay employees. They also may have accessed the social security numbers of one million customers. The FBI said the thieves worked with cashiers in 49 cities, including Atlanta, Chicago, New York, Montreal, Moscow, and Hong Kong, to withdraw over $9 million from accounts. The cashiers locally fabricated cards and made withdrawals from local ATMs. Timing is critical in these frauds. If good fraud monitoring is deployed, the information has to be monetized quickly before cards are cancelled.

In January 2009, Heartland Payment Systems Inc. announced the largest data breach to date of a payment processor, over 100 million cards compromised. Heartland is among the top 10 card payment processors and handles over 100 million credit and debit card transactions per month. The breach was detected not by Heartland, but by VISA's security organization, which noticed an increase in fraudulent activity on cards processed by Heartland. The source of the breach was malware on a Heartland system, which intercepted payment information sent to Heartland from thousands of retail merchants. At the time of the breach announcement, Heartland claimed no social security numbers, unencrypted PIN numbers, addresses, or telephone numbers were revealed.[38] Thieves, however, were able to intercept the Track 2 information, which is sufficient to fabricate a duplicate credit card. At the time, the company said it did not know how long the malware was in place, how it got there, or how many accounts were compromised. A security analyst at Gartner Inc. noted that the company was probably not doing file integrity monitoring to detect unauthorized changes in files and directories.[39]

The losses in this breach are significant. Thus far, the breach has cost the company $12 million, including a $7 million fine imposed by MasterCard. Given the number of compromised cards, banks would be unlikely to cancel and reissue all of them since the costs could be between $600 million to $1 billion, which is bigger than any anticipated fraud. Heartland, however, faces a class action lawsuit filed on behalf of financial institutions that have reissued credit and debit cards and now are attempting to recover these and other expenses associated with the breach. The loss of confidence on the part of customers and partners is also a major issue the company is attempting to address.[40]

Thus far, this report has focused on breaches by companies in the data aggregation and payment processing industries. Large-scale breaches, of course, can occur in any organization that maintains large data repositories or does high volume transaction processing. The Open Security Foundation DataLossDB website shows a dramatic increase in the number of breach incidents since 2000, which is most likely due to the widespread adoption by states of breach notification laws beginning in 2005.[41] Statistics available on that the DataLossDB site show that educational institutions and government agencies account for 42 percent of reported incidents, while nonmedical businesses account for about 46 percent. Rather than malicious attempts to steal data, many breaches, about 29 percent of those reported, are simply the result of lost or stolen storage media (tapes, jump drives, and laptops). The site also shows that breaches involving third parties, common in the payment processing industry, often result in a greater numbers of records lost than those that do not involve third parties.

MONETIZING THE CRIME

What makes large-scale data breaches so dangerous is that modern organized crime has developed efficient mechanisms for the sale and widespread distribution of large collections of identities and personal financial information.[42] So-called carding forum websites provide repositories for credit information for cyber thieves around the world. These sites often make available both Track 1 and 2 data from a card. In addition, there are sites that include full information about a victim, so-called "fulls," which include name; address; telephone, social security, credit, or debit card numbers; PINs; and a possible a credit history report. This information is, of course, more costly than just credit card or account numbers. Thieves know that there is a ready market for the proceeds of a large-scale breach of financial information or PII that can be used to commit fraud.

Carders (those who run carding sites) typically buy information from hackers who are responsible for the breach. Carders can break the data into smaller packages and distribute it to lower level carders who may assume the more risky task of making the card's information available to end users. End users, sometimes known as cashers, ultimately monetize the stolen information, which involves the most risk and difficulty (fabricating a card, changing an address, etc.). In some card account heists, a worldwide network of cashers fabricates cards and makes withdrawals at ATMs around the world shortly after the breach. The Shadow Crew site, for example, which was dismantled by the U.S. Secret Service in 2004, had over 4,000 members throughout the world, trafficked in at least 1.7 million credit cards, and caused losses estimated at $4.3 million.[43] Many considered the Shadow Crew to be a loose configuration of cyber criminals, not a highly organized crime group.

A ready market for a large collection of account information creates serious response issues for financial institutions. In a small-scale breach that involves 200 accounts, banks can simply reissue cards with new account numbers. The cost to reissue 45 million compromised cards, however, is probably going to be more than any credit fraud so banks will not reissue cards in such a large breach. Thus compromised cards may stay active and available at carding sites long after the breach. Losses to individuals, merchants, and banks may continue for some time. ID Analytics, a firm that investigates credit fraud, found in one breach they studied that breached information was used sparingly at first, probably to avoid fraud detection.[44] Soon after the breach was discovered, however, there was an immediate increase in activity in the use of breached identities, followed by a sharp drop off in use after the breach was publicly announced.

Recently, a site known as Dark Market was closed down by its alleged operator. Besides credit card information, the site offered ATM skimmers and other hardware needed for fraud operations. The site's operator said he was closing it because too many law enforcement agents and reporters had gained access to the site, and it was proving difficult to be sure that their accounts had been eliminated. Dark Market even provided review mechanisms that allowed users to evaluate merchandise and weed out so-called "rippers," or those who rip off other fraudsters. In recent congressional testimony, Rita Glavin, Acting Assistant Attorney General, expressed concern that international carding forums provided a ready market for large-scale data breach contraband.[45] She noted that at its height, Dark Market had 2,500 members worldwide. Late in 2008, in connection with the Dark Market site, the FBI announced the arrests of 60 people from six different countries including the United States, Estonia, and the People's Republic of China. Investigators found more than 40 million credit cards, including some from the TJX breach. An FBI undercover agent who penetrated the site provided further details of the Dark Market operation at the April RSA security conference.[46]

CHALLENGES AND REMEDIES

Each industry presents its own data security challenges. Notable large-scale breaches in the data aggregation industry indicate the need to prevent insiders from exceeding authorized access, this is a challenge in an industry where revenue comes from making data available to partners and clients. In the card payment processing industry, the complexity of the data flow and systems in use make securing data a vexing task. In this section, we focus primarily on remedies proposed and existing challenges in the payment processing industry, which has experienced the largest breaches of sensitive financial information.

In 2006, the payment processing industry adopted the Payment Card Industry Data Security Standard.[47] The standard addresses the following areas: network security, protection of card holder data, management of vulnerabilities in system and application software, access control measures, monitoring and testing of network resources, and organizational information security policies. The goal is that all organizations involved in the processing of payment transactions, i.e., card issuing banks, merchants, acquiring banks, and card brand associations, will eventually comply with the PCI standard. An industry supported council oversees continued development of the standard, certifies organizations as compliant, and certifies PCI auditors who monitor compliance.

Recent congressional testimony on PCI standards by representatives of the card associations, a major retailer, and the National Retailers Association indicate the difficulty of establishing, implementing, and monitoring compliance of security standards in an industry as complex as the payment processing industry.[48] For example, the head of fraud control at Visa pointed out that the company serves as the connection point between 1.6 billion payment cards, 16,600 financial institutions, and 29 million merchants in 170 countries.

He could have also added that this system includes hundreds of payment processors such as Heartland and RBS who provide the electronic delivery path that connects merchants, card organizations like Visa and MasterCard, and the financial institutions who provide the funds. In addition, these payment processors also handle ATM card and debit transactions for financial institutions. In these transactions, they hand data over to organizations such as NYCE, which acts as a clearing house for ATM transactions.[49] The card payment system includes larger retailers such as Wal-Mart, with adequate budgets for data security, as well as small corner stores that have very limited resources. It is not surprising that rates of PCI compliance vary considerably throughout the industry.[50]

One frequent criticism of the PCI standard is the requirement for data to be encrypted only on public networks, or if stored on devices accessible from public networks. Data on private networks does not need to be encrypted. In fact, typically Track 2 data delivered by retailers to payment processors is not encrypted. In recent congressional testimony, the head of the National Retailers Association and the CEO of a major retail chain both stated that their organizations would prefer to deliver data in encrypted format. Currently, this is not feasible since there is no industry-wide encryption standard. After the CardSystems breach and the more recent Heartland breach, both organizations proposed either encryption in back end systems or end-to-end encryption as solutions. The Accredited Standards Committee X9 (ASC X9) of the American National Standards Institute (ANSI) is currently working with payment processing industry to develop the end-to-end standard.[51] The cost would be considerable since merchants would have to upgrade all point of sale equipment to comply with the standard. Some large retailers, however, believe that the cost of large-scale breaches makes the case that there is a potentially significant return on investment as a result of acquiring the required equipment upgrades.[52]

Retailers criticize the card payment system because it requires them to retain too much data on their systems. Charge-backs present a difficult challenge for the industry since retailers must retain PII in addition to credit card data to uniquely identify transactions and prevent charge-back fraud. Frequently, retailers retain a card number and an address, which might provide credentials for a purchase. Rather than maintain data to track the transaction, retailers would like the payment processor and the card association to have systems that can provide them with records of the transaction so they only have to store a signature and a number that identifies the transaction. The Canadian Privacy Commission examination of the TJX Companies breach faulted the company for storing driver's license numbers and provincial identification numbers, which were taken from about 300 people in Alberta, Canada, during the breach and used to commit fraud.[53]

To prevent and respond to data breaches on an industry-wide level, the security community in an industry must have detailed knowledge of incidents and vulnerabilities as soon as possible. For most commercial and open source software, information sharing and collaboration regarding software vulnerabilities and available patches have been the norm for some time.[54] In the payment processing industry, where a vulnerable software component could be in use throughout the industry, such information sharing and response capabilities are only beginning to be considered. In March 2009, The Financial Services Information Sharing and Analysis Center (FS-ISAC) formed the Payments Processing Information Sharing Council (PPISC), a forum for sharing information about fraud, threats, vulnerabilities, and risk mitigation practices.[55] At the council's first meeting in May 2009, the CEO of Heartland handed out USBs with the malware found on Heartland's systems so other payment processors could try to determine if it was on their systems.[56] Effective deterrence and response require that knowledge of software vulnerabilities and malware be made available, at least to the security community, as soon as it is available.

Card companies increasingly are promoting optional passwords to use with cards.[57] Only a few participating merchants now accept password protected cards, but the number of merchants is increasing. Password protected cards may be particularly attractive to merchants who accept online purchases and international transactions. Unlike card present transactions where fraud rates have dropped during the past 10 years, credit card fraud associated with online and international purchases is a continuing problem for the industry.

The card associations MasterCard and Visa have long used fraud detection systems based on usage patterns to detect anomalous transactions. Their systems store examples of valid transactions and constantly update cardholder data to create a current usage profile. Each new transaction is evaluated against the individual's transaction history. For example, card present purchases of certain types of items outside of an individual's geographic region trigger an alert. These anomalous detection systems have to be consistently updated as thieves consistently find ways to circumvent them. A recent trend is the use of a botnet computer to make an online purchase from an IP address that is within the card holder's geographical region.[58]

Breach prevention, detection, and response present challenges to law enforcement agencies, the IT industry, and those charged with formulating information security policy. Based on the breaches examined here, the following is a brief summary of the challenges:

Law Enforcement: (1) Immediate notification in the event of a breach. (2) Enhanced knowledge of carding sites and the role that organized criminal activity plays in monetizing large-scale breaches. (3) Cooperation among law enforcement agencies and governments throughout the world to facilitate breach investigations.

IT Industry: (1) Tracking data in large complex systems. (2) Capabilities for rapid system wide updating and patching. (3) Automated fraud detection tools. (4) Maintaining the integrity of software and systems. (5) Standards for end-to-end encryption in complex distributed systems. (6) Industry-wide clearing houses to share breach information and coordinate an industry wide response to a breach.

Information Security Polices: (1) Limiting data collection and retention versus maintaining data for marketing and other activities. (2) Protecting data when there is commingling of proprietary systems and networks with those attached to the Internet. (3) Authorization and auditing polices that address the ease with which large data repositories can be copied.

National breach notification legislation is now before Congress.[59] In addition to notification, the bill would force companies holding PII to follow data privacy policies established by the Federal Trade Commission. Proponents claim several advantages of the proposed law: (1) It simplifies breach notification requirements for organizations; (2) It establishes standards for protecting data; and (3) It provides uniform standards by which individuals could check data held for accuracy. Previous attempts at national breach notification legislation raised concerns among privacy advocates because the proposed federal legislation had a lower threshold for breach notification than most state laws, which the bill would have preempted.

The Federal Stimulus bill passed in February 2009[60] requires notification of health care data breaches. The bill requires all medical providers, health plan administrators, and medical clearing houses covered by HIPPA, and even organizations not covered by HIPPA, e.g., the online health record services proposed both by Google and Microsoft, to provide information on breached medical data. Moreover, the law requires the Department of Health and Human Services to issue guidelines for protection of sensitive medical data. Given the rash of large-scale data breaches during the past decade, it is not surprising that recent national breach notification legislation includes provisions for increased government oversight of the use of PII.

CONCLUDING REMARKS

Data breaches must be understood within the industries and organizations within which they occur. Notable breaches in the data aggregation industry involved insiders such as contractors who extended their authorized access. Breaches in the payment processing industry made use of malware that relayed sensitive personal financial information to data thieves. Regardless of the industry, however, basic privacy policies that; (1) limit the amount of data collected, (2) limit where data is stored and the time for which it is stored, and (3) restrict the use of data to the task for which it was collected, play a critical role in preventing breaches. Large-scale breaches are expensive, especially if the lost information involves sensitive personal financial data. Breaches in the payment industry can exact extremely high costs, particularly to organizations such as card processors whose businesses depend on the trust of partners and customers. Breach notification laws, which keep both consumers and business partners aware of what is happening with their data, are changing the way all industries and organizations view information security·

ENDNOTES - CHAPTER 4

1. Privacy Rights Clearing House, available from *www.privacyrights.org/*.

2. About Acxiom, available from *www.acxiom.com/about_us/Pages/AboutAcxiom.aspx*.

3. LexisNexis – About Us, available from *www.lexisnexis.com/about-us/*.

4. ChoicePoint, available from *www.choicepoint.com/*.

5. Reed Elsevier, the parent company of LexisNexis, purchased ChoicePoint in 2008.

6. T. Zeller, "MasterCard Says Security Breach Affects Over 40 Million Cards," *The New York Times*, June 5, 2005.

7. J. Vijayan, "TJX data breach: At 45.6 million card numbers, it's the biggest ever," *Computerworld*, March 29, 2007.

8. J. Vijayan, "Hannaford says malware planted on its store servers stole card data," *Computerworld*, March 28, 2008.

9. B. Krebs, "Data Breach Led to Multimillion Dollar ATM Heists," Security Fix, *The Washington Post*, February 5, 2009.

10. B. Krebs, "Payment Processor Breach May be Largest Ever," Security Fix, *The Washington Post*, January 20, 2009.

11. A. Gendar, "ATMs on Staten Island rigged for identity theft; bandits steal $500G," *The Daily News*, May 11, 2009.

12. Open Security Foundation, DataLossDB Project, available from *datalossdb.org/*.

13. Accurint, available from *www.accurint.com/*.

14. D. Solove and C. J. Hoofnagle, "A Model Regime of Privacy Protection," *University of Illinois Law Review*, February 2006, pp. 375-404.

15. K. Poulsen, "Chats led to Acxiom hacker bust," *SecurityFocus*, December 19, 2003, available from *www.securityfocus.com/news/7697*; B. J. Gillette, "Data thief exposes flimsy security, nets 8 years," *Email Battles*, February 24, 2006, available from *www.emailbattles.com/*.

16. United States Code, Section 1030 (a) (2) (c), available from *www.law.cornell.edu/uscode/18/1030.html*.

17. L. Rosencarnce, "ChoicePoint says data theft cost is $6 Million," *Computerworld*, July 21, 2005.

18. T. R. Weiss, "State officials push choice point on ID theft notifications," *Computerworld*, February 18, 2005.

19. G. Gross, "Lawmakers call for ChoicePoint investigation," *Computerworld*, March 3, 2005.

20. J. Krim, "LexisNexis data breach bigger than estimated," *The Washington Post*, April 13, 2005.

21. A. Westfeldt, "LexisNexis warns 32,000 people about data breach," *SanFrancisco Chronicle*, May 1, 2009.

22. LexisNexis Breach Notification Letter, available from *privacy.wi.gov/databreaches/pdf/LexisNexisLetter050509.pdf*.

23. J. Barret, Acxiom Corporation, Testimony before House Committee on Energy and Commerce, Subcommittee on Commerce, Trade and Consumer Protection, May 11, 2005, available from *archives.energycommerce.house.gov*.

24. R. Duran and F. Garcia, "Information Security and Privacy: Challenges in a Bad Economy and Difficult Legislative Environment," presentation at the Center for Cybercrime Studies, John Jay College of Criminal Justice, March 10, 2009.

25. CyberSource Corporation, "Online Fraud Report: Online Payment Fraud Trends, Merchant Practices and Benchmarks," available from *www.cybersource.com*.

26. Federal Trade Commision, "CardSystems Solutions Settles FTC Charges," February 23, 2006, available from *www.ftc.gov/opa/2006/02/cardsystems_r.shtm*.

27. J. Perry, CardSystems Solutions, Testimony before House Subcommittee on Oversight and Investigations of the Committee on Financial Services, July 21, 2005, available from *www.house.gov*.

28.T. Krazit, "MasterCard Blamed a Third Party Processing Firm," *Computerworld*, June 17, 2005.

29. Federal Trade Commission, "Enforcing Privacy Promises: Section 5 of the FTC Act," available from *www.ftc.gov/privacy/privacyinitiatives/promises.html*.

30. Perry.

31. PCI Security Standards Council, "About the PCI Data Security Standard (PCI DSS)," available from *https://www.pcisecuritystandards.org/security_standards/pci_dss.shtml*.

32. M. Mimoso, "Cleaning up after a data attack," *Information Security*, April 14, 2006.

33. Vijayan, "TJX Data Breach at 45.6M card numbers."

34. J. Vijayan, "Breach at TJX puts card info at risk," *Computerworld*, January 22, 2007.

35. Sans Institute, "The Evolution of Wireless Security Standard in 802.11 Networks: WEP, WPA, and 802.11 Standards," 2003, available from *www.sans.org*.

36. Office of the Privacy Commissioner of Canada, "Report of an Investigation into the Security, Collection, and Retention of Personal Information: TJX Companies," September 25, 2007, available from *www.priv.gc.ca/cf-dc/2007/TJX_rep_070925_e.cfm*.

37. Vijayan, "Hannaford Says Malware..."

38. E. Mills, "Payment Processor Heartland Reports Breach," CNET News, January 20, 2009, available from *news.cnet.com/8301-1009_3-10146275-83.html*.

39. J. Vijayan, "Heartland Data Breach Sparks Security Concerns in Payment Industry," *Computerworld*, January 22, 2009.

40. Heartland Payment Systems, "Heartland Payment Systems Returns to Visa's list of PCI-DSS Validated Service Providers," May 1, 2009, available from *www.iteotlandpaymentsystems.com*.

41. Open Security Foundation DataLossDB Project, Data Loss Statistics, available from *datalossdb.org/statistics*.

42. K. Perreti, "Data Breaches: What the Underground World of Carding Reveals," *Santa Clara Computer and High Tech Law Journal*, Vol. 25, No. 2, 2009, pp. 375-413.

43. D. Gage, "Head of Shadowcrew Identity Theft Ring Gets Prison Time," *Security Baseline*, June 30, 2006, available from *www.baselinemag.com*.

44. ID Analytics, Inc., available from *www.idanalytics.com/*.

45. U.S. House of Representatives, "Do Payment Card Industry Data Standards Reduce Cybercrime?" Hearing of the Committee on Homeland Security, Subcommittee on Emerging Threats, Cybersecurity, Science and Technology, March 31, 2009, available from *www.usdoj.gov*.

46. S. Nicholas, "FBI Agent discusses big cybercrime bust," *iTnews*, April 23, 2009, available from *www.itnews.com.au*.

47. PCI Security Standards Council.

48. Nicholas.

49. NYCE Payments Network, LLC, available from *www.nyce. net/about.jsp*.

50. A.Conry-Murray, "PCI and The Circle of Blame," *Information Week*, February 25, 2008, pp. 31-36.

51. Heartland Payment Systems, "Accredited Standards Committee X9 Developing New Merchant Data Security Technology Standards," April 29, 2009, available from *www.heartlandpaymentsystems.com*.

52. L. McGlasson, "Heartland Databreack: Is End-to-End Encryption the Answer?," *BankInfo Security*, May 11, 2009, available from *www.bankinfosecurity.com/articles.php?art_id=1455&pg=1*.

53. Office of the Privacy Commissioner of Canada, "Report of an Investigation into the Security, Collection and Retention of Personal Information: TJX Companies, Inc.," September 25, 2007, available from *www.priv.gc.ca/cf-dc/2007/TJX_rep_070925_e.cfm*.

54. Financial Services Information Sharing and Analysis Center, "Payments Processing Information Sharing Council Forms to Foster Information Sharing among Payment Processors," available from *www.ppisc.com/InTheNews.asp*.

55. U.S. CERT, "Technical Cybersecurity Alerts," available from *www.us-cert.gov/cas/techalerts/index.html*.

56. R. Vamosi, "Heartland Comes out swinging after databreach," *Computerworld*, May 12, 2009.

57. A. Mahtab and M. Bokhari, "Information Security Policy Architecture," International Conference on Computational Intelligence and Multimedia Applications, Vol. 4, December 13-15, 2007, pp. 120-122.

58. Brett Stone-Gross *et al.*, "Your Botnet is My Botnet: Analysis of a Botnet Takeover," Technical Report, Santa Barbara, University of California, Department of Computer Science, available from *www.cs.ucsb.edu/~seclab/projects/torpig/torpig.pdf.*

59. Data Accountability and Trust Act, H.R.2221, 111th Congress, 2009.

60. B. Bain, "Law Requires Health Data Breach Notifications," Federal Computer Week, February 27, 2009, available from *www. fcw.com/Articles/2009/02/27/Health-Data-Breach-Notification.aspx.*

CHAPTER 5

THE ROLE OF CYBERPOWER IN HUMANITARIAN ASSISTANCE/DISASTER RELIEF (HA/DR) AND STABILITY AND RECONSTRUCTION OPERATIONS*

Larry Wentz

INTRODUCTION

Cyber in the context of this chapter is used in its broadest definition. It includes aspects of both information and information communications technology where information and communications technology (ICT) is defined as the convergence of telecommunications and information technology. Aspects of the ICT encompass the range of technologies for gathering, storing, retrieving, processing, analyzing, and transmitting information that are essential to prospering in a globalized economy and establishing a knowledge culture. Additionally, ICT includes policies, processes, infrastructure, systems, services, education, and people and, most importantly, discussions of ICT need to consider the associated information and messaging activities and their impact on the society and its functions.

This chapter explores the role and challenges of cyberpower (information and ICT) in humanitarian

---

*The views expressed in this article are those of the author and do not reflect the official policy or position of the National Defense University, the Department of Defense or the U.S. Government. All information and sources for this chapter were drawn from unclassified materials.

assistance/disaster relief (HA/DR) and stability and reconstruction operations. It examines whether a strategic use of cyber in U.S. Government (USG) engagement and intervention activities such as HA/DR and stability and reconstruction operations could lead to more successful results. Certainly, the information revolution has been a dynamic and positive factor in business, government, and social arenas in the Western world. The combination of technology, information content, and people schooled in the use of each has reshaped enterprises and activities of all types.

Complicating the challenges of HA/DR and stability and reconstruction operations related to failed-state interventions is the local situation that typically consists of: spoilers interfering with the intervening forces; refugees and internally displaced persons requiring humanitarian assistance; buildings requiring reconstruction; roads, power, water, telecommunications, healthcare, and education systems disrupted or dysfunctional; absence of a functioning government and laws, lack of regulations and enforcement mechanisms; widespread unemployment and poverty; and a shortage of leaders, managers, administrators, and technical personnel with 21st century technical and management skills. Additionally, there is a lack of a USG whole of government approach, a lack of trust among stakeholders, and policy, procedures, business practices, and people and organization culture differences. It is not a technology challenge per se. Generally, technology is an enabler if used properly.

This chapter concludes that civil-military collaboration and information sharing activities and smart use of information and ICT can have decisive impacts if they are treated as a core part of the nation's overall strategy and not just as "nice to have" adjuncts to responses to HA/DR or to the kinetic phases of warfare and stability and reconstruction operations. It is further suggested that utilizing the elements of the information revolution and the whole of government in a strategic approach to HA/DR and stability and reconstruction operations can have positive results and sets forth the strategic and operational parameters of such an effort. Finally, enhancing the influence of USG responses to HA/DR and interventions in stability and reconstruction operations will require a multifaceted strategy that differentiates the circumstances of the messages, key places of delivery, and sophistication with which messages are created and delivered, with particular focus on channels and messengers.[1]

ROLE OF CYBER AND CHALLENGES

Lack of effective communication, coordination, collaboration, and information sharing among military, civilian government elements, international organizations (IO), intergovernmental organizations (IGO), nongovernmental organizations (NGO), private sector, and affected/host nation elements that form the network of partners and stakeholders involved in complex operations such as humanitarian assistance, disaster relief, security, stability, and reconstruction are consistent factors impacting the ability to conduct more successful operations. There are a number of reasons for this, the most common ones being the lack of a whole of government approach, a lack of trust among stakeholders, differences in policies, procedures, and business practices, and people and organization culture differences. It is not a technology challenge per se. Generally, technology is an enabler if used properly.[2]

A recent workshop co-hosted by the Asia Pacific Center for Security Studies, the Center of Excellence in Disaster Management and Humanitarian Assistance, and the Pacific Disaster Center focused on information sharing for crisis resilience—beyond response and recovery. The workshop out brief identified the following information sharing gaps:

- Lack of a tradition of sharing info within organizations/nation/internationally
- No incentive for organizations/nations to share information/cooperate
- Knowledge: governments do not know where to get info/funding, baseline information/education/training
- Lack of overarching coordinating body
- National realization that info sharing is a priority and commitment to follow-up
- Resiliency/redundancy of systems
- Political will and leadership
- No agreed upon standard set of collaboration tools
- Lack of confidence building measures
- Lack of forums for face to face networking/dialogue
- Lack of understanding between sectors
- Insufficient human resource capacity
- Lack of taking into account local conditions/cultures
- Lack of liaisons
- Information overload (condense and concise): double edged sword
- Lack of standard lexicon/terminology
- Understanding different cultures (military, government, civilian)
- Technology gaps: sending alert but a delay in response from supporting agencies

- Insufficient funds for risk reduction and resiliency
- Assessment of current condition (need to agree on where we are and where we want to be)
- Ability of government to disseminate information internally and to receive from outside
- Lack of standards and data compatibility (not geospatial referenced)
  - No central repository
  - Need better knowledge management
  - Example of a solution: Aid Management Platform and AiDA (accessible database of activities and programs)
  - Development Gateway
  - Reliability and validity
- Too much data (yellow pages on data about data) and information saturation of users
- Gaps in ability for decision makers to focus on the appropriate information
- Ability to identify and communicate with highly vulnerable groups
- Models are insufficient for leaders to make decisions before, during and after a disaster
- Language gaps
- Understanding culture and policy effects on disaster preparedness
- Ownership of information
- Building relationships between private and public sectors
- Gaps in how society responds to the information given
  - Trust in government/sector
  - Education
  - Cultural reasons

The gaps noted above should not come as a surprise and illustrate that much work still needs to be done to create and deploy collaborative information environments to achieve "unity of effort" across the civil-military boundaries. The underlying issues are intellectual, cultural, and social, not technical. Information-rich, easily accessed networks have become a critical commodity—essential service. Today the responder community increasingly demands that all stakeholders in complex operations be able to share situational awareness, reach back in time and distance for unforeseen data requirements, create and exchange data, and collaborate virtually across domains and boundaries.

Prior to a crisis, ICT and related networks need to be self-organizing, flat, robust, and open in order to maintain awareness, develop proactive responses, provide ground truth, and amplify social networks. During a crisis, these same networks need to be deployable in an ad hoc fashion, hastily pushed out or set up in areas that may have been ravaged by war or natural disaster. Networks with nontraditional partners need to be set up and function in the most adverse conditions, using come with what you have ICT or assets indigenous to the crisis area. The information content will no longer be determined by a small handful of experts but by the users themselves. The complexity will drive the practitioners to settle for networks that will simply help them make sense of the situation—sense making—rather than seeking to gain information dominance and clarity. The new information age means ICT is no longer just good to have but essential. The emerging architecture is one of participation, strong social and knowledge networking, and agility to use all available means to communicate—

connectivity increases effectiveness, free revealing makes sense, the community generates content, and the lead user drives the market.

Experience from recent real world operations suggests there is an urgent need to review and revise existing policies, doctrine, procedures, and business practices, and to explore more effective use of information and ICT as an enabler. ICT can be used to overcome current short falls in order to improve the ability of stakeholders to more efficiently and effectively respond, to build trust among diverse groups, to promote unity of effort across civil-military boundaries, and to develop and leverage ICT tools and systems. ICT as an enabler can facilitate seamless information flow to support shared situational awareness, collaboration, coordination, and information sharing as needed.

There are a number of Department of Defense (DoD), Department of State (DoS), U.S. Agency for International Development (USAID), and policy, doctrine, and guidance documents from other organizations that need to be considered in the process of institutionalizing change in how the U.S. military and civilian elements view and integrate ICT into warfighting operations and support of HA/DR and stability and reconstruction operations. Figure 5.1 is an attempt to identify and map the relationship of the existing policy, doctrine, and guidance documents that form the basis for guiding the planning for, and execution of, HA/DR and stability and reconstruction operations. It should be noted, the documents identified do not specifically refer to ICT as an "essential service," although some, such as DoD Directive (DoDD) 3000.05, "Military Support of Stability Operations"; DoD Instruction (DoDI) 8220.02, "ICT Support to Stability Operations"; and *Field Manual (FM) 3-07, Stability Operations*, certainly imply its importance. None address ICT as a "smart power" tool and as an enabler for HA/DR and stability and reconstruction operations. The National Security Strategy Directive (NSPD)-44, "Management of Interagency Stability Operations"; DoDD 3000.05; DoDI 8220.02; and FM 3-07 are significant steps forward and give ICT much needed attention, but much remains to be done to provide the necessary policy and doctrine guidance required to use ICT operationally as a "smart power" enabler of stability and reconstruction operations. ICT also is a critical enabler of other "smart power" missions such as HA/DR and building partnership capacity (BPC) overseas and defense support to civil authorities (DSCA) at home.

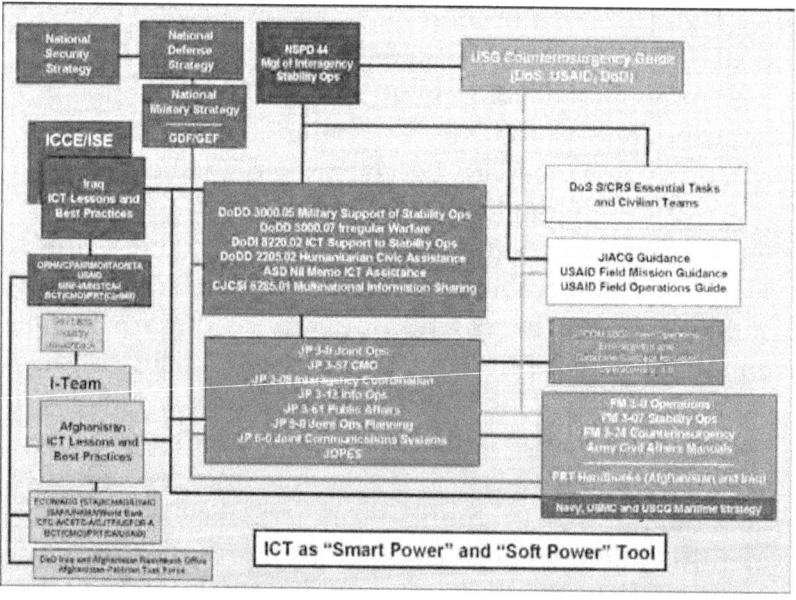

Figure 5.1. Mapping of Policy and Doctrine Documents and Ad Hoc Solutions.

The net effect of shortfalls in policy and doctrine guidance has been the need to use ad hoc approaches tailored to fill real world operational gaps. Examples include creation of various USG ad hoc reconstruction-oriented organizations (a combination of DoS and DoD personnel) in both Iraq (e.g., Iraq Reconstruction Management Office) and Afghanistan (e.g., Afghan Reconstruction Group) and the DoS's employment of senior telecom advisors (STA) at the embassies as a temporary measure to provide senior leadership in the use of commercial ICT, to provide advice to in-country USG civilian and military elements, and to deal with affected nation counterparts— there is a need to have senior civilian professionals dealing with professionals. In the absence of a coordinated USG approach, DoD implemented special arrangements, such as the Multi-National Force-Iraq (MNF-I) Communications and Information Systems (OIS) Iraq Communications Coordination Element (ICCE), created to facilitate co-ordination and information sharing among civilian-military ICT stakeholders, to provide ICT advice and planning focus for the use of ICT including the U.S. military use of Iraqi ICT, and to work with the Iraqi ICT counterparts. In Afghanistan, the first STA at the Kabul Embassy established an Integration-Team (I-Team) that was used to facilitate coordination and information sharing among civilian and military ICT stakeholders. He also created two reachback arrangements, one USG-focused and the other U.S. ICT industry-focused. DoD also created an Iraq and Afghanistan Reachback Office in the Pentagon to provide reconstruction assistance to all sectors. Some of the various ad hoc arrangements used in Iraq and Afghanistan are illustrated in Figure 5.1 (shown in shades of gray). Experience suggests that all of these ad hoc efforts had varying degrees of success, and their best practices need to be captured, documented, assessed, and then applied as appropriate in future operations.

A related important task at hand that is being actively worked is to incorporate ICT as an "essential service" and as "critical infrastructure" in the appropriate policy and doctrine guidance. Additionally, efforts have been initiated to capture the best practices and key lessons from experiences in Iraq and Afghanistan and to codify and insert those lessons into appropriate policy, doctrine, planning, and operational guidance documents. While this would drive immediate effects in both of these areas of responsibility (AORs), the more important effect is to embody this policy and doctrine at the departmental level and more specifically, the Services and the combatant commands. We need to change the way we do business in the future.

Over the past 30 years, the information revolution had an important impact on the conduct of military operations. In the United States, it produced what is often called "netcentric warfare" or "netcentric operations" — the combination of shared communications, key data, analytic capabilities, and people schooled in using those capacities — that has enabled enhanced joint activities, integrated distributed capabilities, supported greater speed, and more effective maneuver. The result has been that the United States and its allies have been able to conduct very effective combat operations under a range of conditions, including quick insertion (Panama), maneuver warfare (major combat operations in Iraq), an all-air campaign (Kosovo), and a Special Forces–led effort (Afghanistan).

At the same time that major combat operations have proceeded so successfully, the United States and its allies have undertaken a variety of humanitarian assistance, disaster relief, stability, and reconstruction operations in Somalia, Haiti, Bosnia, Kosovo, East Timor, several African countries, Afghanistan, and Iraq. These operations generally have included both economic and governance reconstruction and have spanned the full security gamut from nonviolent humanitarian assistance and peacekeeping to full-blown counterinsurgency. Not one of these operations has approached the success achieved in combat operations undertaken during the same period.

U.S. military doctrine recognizes the importance of building broad coalitions of stakeholders in complex contingencies. But, in practice, the focus of military communicators usually is on the needs of the joint or coalition force rather than on external links with civilian participants in the operation. Such external links demand that unclassified information be shared in both directions. Thus, the challenge is twofold: (1) How to encourage the military to engage more with civilians, and (2) how to encourage civilians to link better to the military or local stakeholders? However, there are other factors that need to be considered. In humanitarian operations, there are the guiding principles of impartiality, neutrality, humanity, and independence from political considerations and associated sensitivities to military involvement and intent that need to be carefully considered and managed. Caution needs to be exercised in circumstances where there is a risk that military actions may be perceived as reflecting political rather than humanitarian considerations.

Civilian organizations, including the U.S. DoS and USAID elements, believe rather strongly that the military should not be the first choice option for intervention when civilian relief activities are already there or are being put in place. International organizations such as the United Nations (UN) and NGOs also question whether under the Oslo guidelines, the military should be involved at all in disaster relief activities.[3] Most view the use of the military as complementing civilian relief activities and should be requested only where there is no comparable civilian alternative. They argue that it is capabilities versus needed capabilities, and in the latter case, civilian assets may be adequate to get the job done. There are also concerns about mixing the use of the terms stability and humanitarian operations and in turn doing things under the banner of stability operations that are humanitarian assistance, creating misperceptions and unnecessary confusion about the purpose or the use of military assets.

There is a strong view within the civilian community that the military needs to be better informed of civilian roles, responsibilities, and capabilities, and that ambassadors need to be better informed about when it is appropriate to request military assistance. Use of the military is a more costly option. Catastrophic disasters obviously require military assistance since they are the only responder element that has the means. There is also a need to educate the civilian community about military roles, responsibilities, capabilities, and business processes. A lack of shared understanding about the civil-military stakeholder roles, responsibilities, capabilities, and limitations is a key factor that needs to be addressed through improved education and training programs and exercises that involve both military and civilian element participation—this will build a more informed and shared understanding of each other and create trust relationships before they will have to work together in a real disaster response.

Historically, ICT has proven to be a basic enabler of informal social and economic discourse, leading to a strengthening of civil society and the promotion of security, internal stability, job creation, and economic solidity in affected nations. It is a demonstrated enabler of national transformations. There is little doubt that ICT is an engine for economic growth, a means to shape the information environment, and a means to improve social wellbeing. Advances have progressively reduced the costs of managing information, enabling individuals and organizations to undertake information-related tasks much more efficiently and have introduced innovations in products, processes, and organizational structures. ICT enables the generation of new ways of working, market development, and livelihood practices. Additional arguments as to why ICT, and host nation ICT in particular, is important in stability and reconstruction operations include but are not limited to:

- ICT can be used to help create a knowledgeable intervention, organize complex activities, and integrate stability and reconstruction operations with the affected nation.
- Affected nation ICT provides an alternative source of ICT capabilities for use by U.S. Government and coalition partners.
- ICT provides opportunities to shape the environment for stability and reconstruction operations.
- ICT is essential for prospering in a globalized economy and for establishing a knowledge culture.
- ICT can significantly change key parts of affected nation society, particularly providing young people access to global knowledge that changes sectarian attitudes and behaviors.
- ICT provides affected nation transparency to

help reduce corruption and enhance government legitimacy.

- ICT provides the best way to help every sector at once through realistic and modern e-Gov methods (security, governance, distance learning, telemedicine, geographic information system (GIS)-based agriculture, finance, power and water management, and e-commerce).
- ICT allows the U.S. Government to positively influence attitudes of the leadership and the general population of the affected nation.
- ICT is demonstrated to be one of the best generators of jobs and revenues for the affected nation.
- ICT gives situational awareness of the affected nation's forces, capabilities, and threats, which can save lives.

Numerous studies of the HA/DR and stability and reconstruction operations suggest that the strategic use of information and related technology can significantly increase the likelihood of success in affected nation cross-sector reconstruction and development. This is possible if information and ICT are engaged at the outset as part of an overall strategy that coordinates the actions of outside interveners and focuses on generating effective results for the affected nation. This has certainly been the case in business, government, and social arenas in the Western world where the information revolution has been a dynamic and positive factor. The combination of technology, information content, and people schooled in the use of each has reshaped enterprises and activities of all types around the world.

An ICT business model like that suggested in Figure 5.2, coupled with the smart use of information and

ICT, could be employed to help create a knowledge-able intervention; facilitate appropriate integration of intervener ICT reconstruction and development initiatives with the affected nation ICT strategy and plans; help organize complex activities; and enable coordination, information sharing, and implementation activities among interveners and with the affected nation, making the latter more effective. Additionally, ICT can be used to link constituent parts of an integrated multinational reconstruction and capacity-building effort, can help multiple sectors simultaneously (e.g., security, governance, education, health, agriculture, finance, and commerce) and can be used to enhance situational awareness of cross-sector reconstruction and development activities.

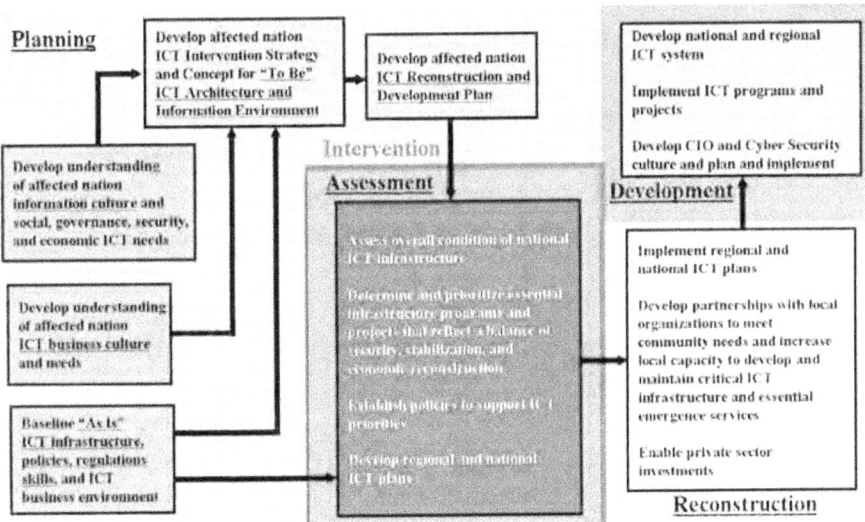

Figure 5.2. ICT Business Model.

Experiences from recent U.S. Government and co-alition interventions in the Balkans, Afghanistan, and

Iraq have repeatedly demonstrated that ICT activities supporting stabilization, reconstruction, and development operations in the affected nation can be problematic. These activities suffer from a lack of adequate understanding of the affected nation information culture and related ICT business culture. There is no clear mapping of the organizational roles and responsibilities of the responding stakeholders. Program development, project coordination, information sharing, and ICT implementation are largely uncoordinated and nonstandard. There is no agreed architecture and plan for affected nation ICT reconstruction. A coherent ICT-oriented civil-military strategy and plan for intervening nations and responding IO and NGO organizations is lacking as well, and there are no agreed mechanisms and procedures to enable effective civil-military coordination and information sharing among participants and with the affected nation. Finally, donors and interveners do not consistently view ICT as a high priority need to be addressed early and as an enabler of cross-sector reconstruction and development.

New metrics are needed for measuring progress in complex operations. The U.S. Army Corps of Engineers project, Measuring Progress in Conflict Environments (MPICE), is a good start but needs to more effectively incorporate the ability to measure the impact of information and ICT as an enabler of sector reconstruction. MPICE is based on the methodology and framework proposed in the United States Institute of Peace (USIP) book, *The Quest for Viable Peace.*[4] Other tools are needed for collecting and analyzing information exchange data. For example, modeling and simulation tools to support planning and training (e.g., DARPA's Conflict Modeling, Planning, and Outcomes Experimentation [COMPOEX] program that is a suite of tools to help military commanders and their civilian counterparts to plan, analyze, and conduct complex operations), improved processes and tools for imagery sharing (products versus raw data), and visualization tools for displaying analysis and shared situational awareness such as GIS, imagery products, and annotation, and mapping tools.

COMMERCIAL ICT CAPABILITY PACKAGES[5]

The efficient and effective deployment of communications assets into austere environments continues to be a key aspect and an important challenge of crisis response. Rapidly deployable ICT capabilities such as very small aperature terminals (VSAT) like the ground-to-air transmit and receive (GATR) and broadband global area network (BGAN) terminals, satellite phones, cell phones, voice-over Internet protocol (VoIP) phones, hand-held radios, and devices that allow disparate communications equipment to interoperate (such as the AC-1000 IP bridge) are readily available to assemble as ICT fly-away kits. However, there is no agreed upon architecture and strategy that can be used to guide responders on how to assemble deployable ICT packages and build hastily formed networks in the crisis area. It is largely an ad hoc plug and play exercise. Hence, there remains the need to help responders determine the right set of items to include in their fly-away ICT package that are simple to use and will interoperate with the ICT that others bring to the crisis.

New collaboration tools are needed that can be employed in disadvantaged information and ICT environments to facilitate collaboration (inexpensive, simple to use, and low bandwidth) and asynchronous information sharing (need to have tools that do not overload limited bandwidth data links when synchronizing databases). Some of the existing tools include Groove, Sahana, and WebEOC. Other tools are needed that can be used to help breakdown organizational culture, business processes, and technology barriers by creating virtual communities of interest (including language translation) and open collaborative information environments. Web 2.0 tools such as wikis, blogs, Facebook, LinkedIn, Twitter, and YouTube need to be more broadly adopted by civil-military crisis responders. Other off-the-shelf tools to be considered include Toozl (open office on a memory stick) and smart phones (such as the iPhone and the BlackBerrys), and global positioning systems (GPS). Presently, there are numerous Internet websites employed during a crisis response, such as the U.S. Pacific Command (USPACOM) Asia-Pacific Advanced Network (APAN), and UN OCHA websites, such as ReliefWeb and the Virtual On-Site Operations Coordination Center, but there are no agreed guidelines for developing and populating these websites or related database standards. UN OCHA has also created an Emergency Telecoms Cluster to facilitate the deployment of ICT capability packages in disaster areas. Telecom NGOs such as NetHope and Telecoms sans Frontiers have emerged to help provide ICT capabilities in disaster areas for NGO use. All of these ICT capability packages are based on off-the-shelf commercial products and open source products on the Internet.

There is a need to develop a knowledge repository of these capabilities and best practices that can be openly shared with the broader community and is kept current with changing technology. The National Defense University (NDU) Center for Technology and National Security Policy-led project STAR-TIDES has as part of its research program the development of a knowledge repository for ICT and the plan is to post it on the project website.[6]

ICT STRATEGY FOR STABILITY AND RECONSTRUCTION OPERATIONS-AFGHANISTAN EXAMPLE[7]

The fundamental task of an ICT strategy is to enhance affected nation capacity. That is the critical result for which the complex operation is undertaken. To achieve that result in an effective fashion, the strategy needs to accomplish two tasks, each is familiar to the international community: first, assess the affected nation and, second, establish a goal toward which to build. To put it more in the vernacular, a cure without a diagnosis will be improbable; directions without destination will be random. In short, an effective approach will require an information business plan for the affected nation. Unfortunately, the reality is that there is no agreed international or USG ICT strategy and plan, or information business plan for responding to a crisis or for engagement in a failed state intervention. Furthermore, there is little attention given to the role that information and the consideration of ICT play as essential services, as critical infrastructure, and as enablers of cross-section reconstruction. How to work with and leverage the private sector is also a deficiency in current USG civil-military thinking—it is not part of the current U.S. civilian and military government culture. There is an urgent need for the USG to change the way it does business in the information age. Some changes are starting to happen as a result of policy and doctrine changes, such as DoDD 3000.05 and DODI 8220.02, but changing culture takes time to affect TTPs and mindsets.

The assessment phase of an information and communications business plan should begin before the intervention. It must include analyses of both the information requirements and the available information technology as well as ICT business practices and government regulations and laws. Humanitarian assistance and disaster relief responses may not afford the opportunity to do a detailed assessment in advance, but even so, there is a need to do either some assessment in advance of a possible disaster, which can be used for crisis response planning, or to do a quick assessment that draws upon readily available information. Understanding what ICT capabilities might be available and whether the affected nation is a signature of the Tampere Convention,[8] is important in order to determine if and what type of ICT can legally be brought into the country and used. For more complex response operations, such as a failed-state intervention, there is generally a buildup period so there is time to prepare. An assessment should consider the pre-intervention state of information technology, infrastructure and services (voice, data, and Internet access), and the ICT business culture and information usage in the affected nation. It is important to recognize that baselines will differ in different affected nations and as a result of hostile actions.

Additionally, key elements of an information assessment will include evaluation of the affected nation's telecommunications laws and regulations, telecoms and IT services, and communication infrastructures—land line telephone system, cell phone capacity, Internet availability, cable, microwave and fiber networks, and satellite systems. It should also address usage patterns, language and literacy issues, technical and business training of locals, and financial resources.

Once an assessment has been undertaken, goals will need to be set for operationalizing the information business plan. Generally, it will be useful to time-phase the goals into an initial deployment phase, a middle phase (getting-things-going phase), and a long-term phase (exit-by-interveners). A critical point throughout is that the interveners' information business plan goals need to support the overall goals of the affected nation, and the affected nation will need to generate those goals as promptly as possible — the interveners can certainly help with developing affected nation goals.

The initial deployment phase will require the interveners to consider what deployable capabilities will be useful to help establish an affected-nation recovery. There are both structural information capabilities; such as deployable cell phone capacities, like "cell on wheels"; and the use of transportable satellites, like VSATs; and functional capabilities, like "health care in a box," shelters, renewable power, water purification, sanitization, lighting, and other capabilities that all need to be considered.

The virtue of preplanning is that key interveners can rationalize their capacities in the early, usually chaotic, days of an intervention by considering which capabilities each intervener might focus on. Equally important is to undertake such a discussion remembering that, first, numerous entities will already be in country with some capacities that can be utilized and, second, affected countries will likely have some capacity, and potentially significant capacity. Over the entirety of the intervention, the implementation of the information business plan will likely mean that the lead on different aspects of the plan will change. Broadly, one might expect a a progressive transition from military interveners to civilian interveners to the affected nation, although the reality is likely to be more complicated and complex because such a progression will not likely be an easily identifiable or set sequence of actions. The transitions will occur over time, so there will be overlaps that need to be carefully managed. If it is understood from the beginning that there will be complex transitions in the way the plan is implemented, it will make for a more realistic and effective approach to be made part of the strategy and plan.

The middle phase of an information business plan for the affected country will focus on five key elements. The first element is to *align the affected country so that it is connected to the collaborative mechanisms used by the interveners in some fashion*. While the key interveners likely can use high-tech means, it may be that the affected country will not be able to do so. An important task of an information business plan will be to allow for low-tech to high-tech connectivity. For example, in Afghanistan, the literacy rate is so low that Internet use is necessarily limited and cell phone connectivity may be much more important. In fact, in Afghanistan, the cell phone is the lifeline communications capability. These points can be more broadly generalized: if the information business plan is to succeed, it must take account of the affected nation's information culture and the related information technology culture and the skill sets of the managers, technical personnel, and the population in general.

The second element is to *help establish working government agencies*. Depending on the overall strategy, these could be a mix of central ministries to start with and then local/district/provincial offices. Information communications technology can be used to improve ministry effectiveness through facilitating collaboration and information sharing and extending government services from capital to urban areas to provincial and district centers to local officials. ICT and e-governance also allows for an analytic approach through budgeting and transparency of expenditures. These are crucial functions for the establishment of legitimate governance, and information technology can help each.

The creation of a viable telecom and IT business environment is key to setting the initial conditions needed to use ICT as an enabler of cross-sector reconstruction. The affected nation or host nation government needs to take important actions at the outset of the rebuilding process. A competent Minister of Communications with the intellectual and business expertise needs to be appointed to set in motion the nation's vision, strategy, and plans to grow and modernize its telecoms and IT infrastructure and services so as to become a part of the global information society. Telecom and IT laws need to be created and passed early on. A viable regulatory authority needs to be created and empowered and mechanisms need to be put in place to enforce the laws. Public sector telecoms and IT run services may be necessary to jump-start support to governance and civil security and to provide limited services to a broader population—contributing to the establishment of legitimacy, transparency, and to reduce corruption. However, it will also be necessary to consider early on the need to privatize state run enterprises as soon as it makes sense to do so to reduce corruption and provide a level playing field for private investments. Good public-private sector partnerships are important to enable the private sector to invest in growing the infrastructure and offering affordable service with a state of the industry level quality of performance. Two recent real world events illustrate the benefits of initially taking the right steps, and the resulting challenges, from not doing so. For example, Afghanistan ICT is one of the major success stories emerging after years of conflict and open warfare. On the other hand, Iraq has progressed somewhat more slowly due to the continuing security situation, but things are beginning to improve and telecoms reconstruction may emerge as one of Iraq's success stories as well.

A real world example of an ICT business model that worked is Afghanistan. Significant progress has been made in the telecommunications and IT sector in Afghanistan, and it is truly a "success story" emerging out of the recovery of a country left dysfunctional from 23 years of war. Progress towards bridging the digital divide and moving Afghanistan into the 21st century information age has not been accidental but is largely due to having the right people at the right place with the right vision, energy, and expertise to make reasonable decisions and to take action to make things happen. Donor intervention to provide resources to support ICT reconstruction was a key factor as well. Afghanistan ICT success was and continues to be enabled by a number of factors:

- A Government of the Islamic Republic of Aghanistan (GIRoA) understanding of the importance of ICT as an engine of economic development and its role as an enabler of cross-sector reconstruction.
- Early GIRoA establishment of ICT policies, regulations, laws, and a regulatory authority.
- Knowledgeable and experienced Minister of Communication (MoC).

- An agreed MoC vision, strategy, and plan for moving Afghanistan ICT into the 21st century information age supported at the highest level of government, by President Hamid Karzai:
  - Five-year MoC development plan states that GIRoA should:
    a. Use the private sector and appropriate regulations to help jump-start economic recovery through enabling private-sector investments in the rapid expansion of mobile voice services and introduction of Internet service.
    b. Use the government to develop the public ICT for governance and make affordable ICT services accessible to the broader population.
    c. Consideration the early of privatization of government owned telecom and IT.
  - Early International and Regional communications access:
    a. Satellite, fiber optic and digital microwave access.
    b. Private sector international and regional gateways.
  - Robust terrestrial backbone network such as the fiber optic ring and digital microwave.
  - Early emphasis on ICT capacity building, including the establishment of related educational institutions, training facilities, and capabilities.
- Proactive MoC provision of an ICT Strategy for the Afghan National Development Strategy that sets ambitious goals for extension of telecom and IT services to the population in general and to improve governance, national and civil security, drive economic development, and improve quality of life.

- Establishment of a good public-private partnership that enables private ICT investments and rapid growth of their networks.
- International and U.S. Government community support.
  - Placed early emphasis on ICT capacity building, including the establishment of related educational institutions, training facilities, and capabilities.
  - Willingness to invest in and support Afghan MoC creation of a national telecommunications and IT network with early international access.

Differences between Afghanistan and Iraq relate largely to host country government ICT institutions, leadership, strategies, and plans for modernizing the national ICT network. There are also differences in the state of integration of affected nation ICT infrastructure and capabilities. For example, in Afghanistan the MoC is an experienced ICT professional who has a vision, strategy, and a nationally agreed plan for modernizing Afghanistan ICT, and his proactive leadership is making things happen. Additionally, he has been in place since the 2002-03 timeframe and has the support of the Afghan President and other senior government representatives. Telecom and IT laws were enacted by the Afghan parliament early on, and an independent and transparent Afghan telecom regulatory authority was established early as well. Although an MoC state-owned telecom company, Afghan Telecom, was established initially to support government communications at provincial and district levels, and to initially provide local voice and Internet access services (telekiosks) down to district level, it has already been corporatized and is in the process of being privatized. With the move to privatize Afghan Telcom, the MoC has changed its name to Ministry of Communications and Information Technology (MCIT) and re-refocused its efforts on the use of ICT to improve Government and social services and initiatives including extension to the rural areas so the country can benefit further from ICT by becoming part of the global information society.

The ICT infrastructure of Afghan Telecom and private cellular providers is interconnected and calls can be made between the networks. The MCIT has invested in the construction of a national fiber optic ring around the country linking urban areas and providing regional cross-border and international gateway access. Cable is being implemented in urban areas and digital microwave links are being implemented throughout the country that will also have some access links to regional countries bordering Afghanistan. The private cellular providers are also building digital microwave backbone networks that include access links to regional countries. Satellite access is also used to provide connectivity and international gateway access. Finally, a good public-private partnership was created that enables the private sector to invest while discouraging unnecessary state interference.

In Iraq, the situation seems to be more problematic. The Iraqi MoC has had three different ministers in the last couple of years, and the most recent minister before the current minister was "acting," all of which negatively impacted the early leadership and decisionmaking process. A new minister has been appointed but is not a telecoms and IT experienced business person. There does not appear to be an agreed overall Iraq ICT strategy and plan, but one may emerge in the near future. On the other hand, the Kurdish region MoC has a strategy and plan, and progress is being made in their area to modernize ICT and improve services including regional and international access. Planning for the initial network included an assumption that demand would be 90 percent voice and 10 percent data, but in reality the demand is just the opposite and the networks have not yet been adapted to meet reality. Furthermore, the networks that have emerged are independent and not interconnected, and roaming is not allowed. Calls from one network to the other must go through an international gateway. The Communications and Media Commission (CMC), the Iraq telecom and IT regulatory authority, has been without strong leadership for some time, and there are concerns about its ability to function and enforce regulations. There are also concerns about its openness and transparency. The telecom law set forth in CPA 65 remains in use since the Iraqis have not yet been able to get their own law enacted by parliament. Privatization of the state own telecom and IT providers, ITPC and SCIS, has been discussed, but no real actions have yet been taken to start the process. It has been suggested that the existence of state-owned enterprises has created perceptions and concerns on the part of the private sector about possible unfair competition. Additionally, the ITPC span of control appears to be limited, with regional elements apparently operating autonomously. In contrast, in Afghanistan, Afghan Telecom has network-wide and regional control of plans, implementation, and operations of the government owned public network.

A good public-private sector partnership does not appear to have yet been created in Iraq, and this makes outside investors nervous as well. It has been noted by some private sector investors that they are more concerned about the Iraqi government than they are about the insurgents and, as such, this is not a situation that lends itself to promoting outside investment in Iraq. Although corruption is a common thread in both countries, it seems to be more of a concern in the Iraq ICT sector than in Afghanistan. Concerns have also been expressed regarding enough availability of Iraqi ICT trained expertise to support sustaining the operation of U.S. civil and military networks which will be turned over to the Iraqi government. The availability of ICT trained technical and management personnel is a shortfall in both Iraq and Afghanistan. Finally, in Iraq and Afghanistan the stove-piped operational performance and cost of service of the public-private sector ICT networks and services suffer from the lack of roaming among service providers and in Iraq, there is a lack of interconnection and adequate regional and international access and cost-effective service.

Use of embedded subject matter experts (SMEs) in the MCIT/MoC and regulatory authorities are also the common threads, but SMEs seemed to have been less successful in Iraq where they were used for only a short while and none, or few, are apparently being used at this time. The insurgent threat to SME safety has been a concern that is also a contributor to the unwillingness to provide SMEs to Ministries in the red zone. In Afghanistan, the SMEs have been embedded since 2002 in the MoC/MCIT providing trusted advice, continuity of support, and corporate memory. SMEs have also been used with success in other ministries and government organizations such as Afghan Telecom. Physical security threats have not been a major concern in the Afghan capital, but

SMEs are provided with contractor personal security details and they live in guarded safe houses in Kabul. Outside of Kabul it is a different story, and SMEs are not embedded in provincial or district ICT organizations. In both Iraq and Afghanistan, the attacks on ICT infrastructure have occurred, but in many cases seem to be more driven by criminal acts and extortion demands than terrorist actions. There have been incidents where towers have been blown up, switch sites attacked, and maintenance and installation staff kidnapped or even killed. Physical security is something that needs to be planned for and implemented in high threat environments and needs to be part of a national critical infrastructure protection plan. It is not clear if such plans exist in either Afghanistan or Iraq.

The third element for many stability operations will be to *increase connectivity and information flow between the central government and provincial/local governments.* Information communications technology can enhance this connectivity and information flow through, for example, the two-way flow of data and finances. It can also serve to extend government services and establish legitimacy of the government at all levels. Often, the cause of the crisis will have been differences between the central government and a region of the country, and working to bring warring elements together will be important. An information business plan can be an effective part of an overall effort.

In Afghanistan, the World Bank and USAID became engaged in ICT sector reconstruction and granted money to the Afghanistan MCIT to create a national telecommunications system to connect the central government with the country's 34 provinces and create public access centers for Internet and telephone communications at the district level. The World Bank invested $16.8 million to develop the government communications network (GCN) and another $3.7 million to rehabilitate the International Satellite Gateway in Kabul. The GCN is a 24 node VSAT-based network that provides international voice and Internet access and communications services to support governance to the provincial capital level—governor and key administration elements, including in some cases police chiefs. USAID invested $14.2 million to develop the 365 node VSAT-based district communications network (DCN) to extend voice and Internet access to the district level for use by local government officials and the local population. GCN and DCN serve to enable good governance at the provincial and district levels by helping remote communities and government offices throughout Afghanistan communicate effectively with each other and the world. Subsequently, China, India, and Iran expressed investment interest, but outside of investments by the U.S. Government, the UN, and the World Bank there was little interest from other Western nations or international organizations. A similar government ICT infrastructure arrangement does not exist in Iraq. In this case, commercial cellular and IT services are relied upon as well as ICT networks built especially for Ministries.

Some other common threads between Afghanistan and Iraq include the need for ICT-related capacity building within ministries. This includes the establishment of effective ministry CIOs and government IT business practices including the use of IT and e-Governance capabilities, and the limited ability to effectively exploit the advantages of the ICT sector to enable governance, expand economic opportunities, and improve education and healthcare services though implementation of an effective nationwide backbone

ICT infrastructure and leveraging e-Governance, e-Commerce, e-Education, e-Healthcare, and other e-Solutions. Additionally, there is a need for developing a cyber strategy and plan and for establishing a national cyber organization and capability to protect against and respond to cyber attacks. On the Afghan private sector side, with MCIT/ATRA support GSM providers, such as Roshan, have been more progressive, with funding support from USAID and others, to offer e-Solutions using SMS for financial transactions (the M-PAISA system) and commodities pricing (the TradeNet system) for farmers. Roshan also has a call center in Kabul where, for a fee for service, subscribers can get medical advice, weather reports, and other call-in services.

In both Afghanistan and Iraq, there is no coordinated strategy for implementing Ministry IT architectures, capabilities, training, management, or governance. ICT projects at different Ministries are likely redundant, not integrated, and possibly not compatible. Some Ministries have effective enterprise networks, while others do not. Best practices may already exist, but they are not shared due to lack of visibility and limited to no cross-Ministry coordination. National CIO Councils have been set up in both Afghanistan and Iraq to implement ICT measures supporting the government's agenda for anti-corruption, transparency in governance, and cost-effective investment in ICT capabilities, but they have had only limited success and it has been hard to maintain momentum. In Afghanistan, the National CIO Council is run by the Minister of Communications and IT, and in Iraq it has in the past been run by the Minister of Science and Technology and both report to the Prime Minister's Office.

In Iraq, a shared DoS and DoD initiative to train Iraqi CIOs was initiated. In August 2008, an NDU IRMC CIO training team conducted an intensive 10-day CIO training program in Erbil for Iraqi Ministry CIOs. In early 2009, several Iraqi CIOs were brought to the United States for additional training at NDU and to provide them the opportunity to visit with U.S. CIO counterparts (both government and industry) to gain a firsthand insight into their day-to-day operations. The notion of training Afghan Ministry CIOs has been proposed several times to the Minister of Communications and IT, but no real action has been taken to make this happen. There is some concern that Ministry CIOs may not yet be ready for such training.

The fourth element will often be to *provide certain important greater functionalities in government services to the populace.* While an information business plan may not be able to improve all functionalities significantly, health and education are two arenas of consequence in which such a plan can make an important difference. In the health arena, information technology can be used to build up and interconnect local centers of health care, such as hospitals and rural health care centers; support training of health care workers; and provide valuable functionalities, such as health surveillance systems and reach back to health care subject matter experts and medical library services. In the education arena, information technology can support the development of curriculum and the provision of instruction, as well as the training of teachers. For example, in Afghanistan, ICT is used in some limited instances to connect hospitals with medical schools and with health care centers, universities such as Kabul and Khost have Computer Science programs, universities such as Kabul have partnership programs and alliances with universities outside of Afghanistan, CISCO academies have been set up to train young girls and boys how to use computers and the Internet, and the MoC set up ICT technician training centers. There are other computer training centers emerging in the private sector as well.

The Afghanistan Ministry of Communications and IT recently initiated a Digital Inclusion Program that will enable the government of Afghanistan to adopt the modern culture of offering services to the public. The re-enabled administrative and governance system will bring transparency, efficiency, and reduce bureaucracy, but this will take some time to implement. The program will install and implement infrastructure, projects, and policies for the introduction of e-government in Afghanistan, which will empower the public to access information, communicate with government, take part in government decisionsmaking, and benefit from the economical opportunities brought by the new culture. The MCIT has also been exploring the use of the DCN as a means to provide voice and data services for health care and educational services in rural areas, as well as general public access to voice services. The wireless local loop contracts have a provision that encourages providers to also make Internet service available to schools in the areas they serve. The MCIT is also looking to use the Afghan Telecom Development Fund (based on a 2.5 percent tax on private sector cell phone calls) to extend access to ICT services to the rural areas. Similar initiatives do not appear to yet exist in Iraq, especially in rural areas. Both Afghanistan and Iraq ICT services for health care and education, and the extension of access to ICT services in rural areas, remain key challenges requiring more active host government attention.

The fifth element is to *provide for the private-sector development of information capabilities*. Two of the most important issues are informed regulatory mechanisms and useful seed financing. An overly constrained regulatory environment will make it difficult for private enterprise to operate at a profit. A properly structured set of incentives can help create an environment in which profit-making companies can contribute importantly to economic reconstruction. Seed money may be very important, especially in the early days of a stability operation, particularly to get local involvement in the development of the information business plan.

The middle phase of the plan often may be the equivalent of the medical "golden hour" for establishing a framework for effective use of ICT for the affected nation. While the information flow may be limited, meeting the expectations of the affected government and its population during this middle phase will be very important for long-term success. This lends itself to the need for a good strategic communications plan to tell the ICT story and help set and manage expectations, both ours and theirs.

The middle phase will naturally flow over into the long-term phase for the affected nation and the exit strategy for the interveners. That part of the information business plan strategy should have at least three key elements. First, as noted above, the private sector should become a key element. Early establishment of a good public-private sector partnership is essential for success. In this regard, creating an environment in which there are commercial opportunities for information communications technology solutions will encourage private sector telecom and IT firms to help seed economic revitalization. Second, the affected nation will need to consider what role it will play in the development of a national information technology infrastructure. Models range from full privatization to early phase ownership to ongoing involvement. If state owned telecom and IT institutions are employed at the outset, it is important to have a clear agreement to privatize and plan for doing this in a timely manner — the earlier the better. Third, as part of their in-country effort, interveners will have to establish IT capabilities to satisfy their needs, but at the same time, these capabilities can also serve to jump-start the affected nation's capabilities and in turn to enable it to start the recovery process. Hence, such facilities and datasets should not be automatically dismantled as the interveners leave. Rather, they should be built with the intent to be used as leave-behinds for local partners, both governmental and nongovernmental, whether commercial or nonprofit. Part of the leave-behind is the need for capacity building plans to ensure that the needed affected-country ICT and management skills are available to sustain operations.

An ICT strategy includes people, content, and technology. In complex operations, the information needs — the content of what must be provided in addition to the connectivity — of the affected nation require consideration. Broadly speaking, those information content needs will fall into the categories of security, humanitarian, economic, governance/rule of law, and social.

In analyzing how such information needs should be fulfilled, an ICT strategy will recognize that the information element will support functional strategies for each of these arenas — all of which will have significant subparts. For example, the establishment of prosecutorial, court, and prison functions will have security and rule of law/governance aspects. Significant programs will be under way to help create each of these elements as part of a stability operation. Responding to the information needs of those programs has to be an affiliated strategic effort or, to use the terms of the international community, needs to be aligned with the overall aims of the functional programs.

The specific needs may be provided with the use of information from one or more of the interveners. In a variety of ways, information technology can be utilized to provide expert assistance. A simple example is maintaining an online list of experts. More sophisticated efforts can be established, such as a call-in center for the provision of various kinds of information. Research arrangements can be set up online, as can connectivity with key national and international organizations, both governmental and nongovernmental, that are willing and able to provide assistance.

As is true for the technology itself, information needs change over time. In fact, the ability to provide information may become more important as the affected nation develops its own capacities. The capacity to access such information may be developed in two parallel fashions. First, in a traditional approach there could be an office to help facilitate access to expert management. More recently, a distributed approach, such as wikis and blogs, may be able to make a great deal of expert information available without a specific data manager, if the right information tools are provided. Issues of trust and reliability will arise, but the community approach to providing information via the Internet and Web 2.0 tools has been very powerful in other arenas, and its use in complex operations should be encouraged.[9]

The discussion of the management of information needs raises the important question of how to manage the ICT strategy in the course of the stability and reconstruction operation and how to mange the overlaps and transition from military to civilian lead. Adoption of a strategic approach and even operational activities will be greatly facilitated by the establishment of a forward field organization. Ideally, this would be a joint DoS-DoD function with the task of carrying out the information and ICT strategies and plan in country. In complex operations, the organization likely would initially be collocated with the military command activity and at some point transitioned to DoS/Embassy. Ad hoc arrangements such as the Afghan Reconstruction Group and the Iraq Reconstruction Management Office/Iraq Transition Assistance Office, along with their respective senior telecom advisor positions, are models worth reviewing for future operations. Additionally, the role and effectiveness of the I-Team and the reach back support to the Afghanistan ICT and the Iraq ICCE are other models to review. There is certainly a need to institutionalize the USG ICT support process for future operations and to revisit the creation of a senior telecoms advisor position to focus USG support on the affected nation ICT reconstruction and its use as a cross-sector enabler. There is also a need to develop an agreed approach to establishing a civil-military collaborative information environment to support complex operations collaboration and information sharing and shared reconstruction-oriented situation awareness with ICT as a key element to be tracked. Also, there is a need to include a strategic communications program to tell the ICT success stories and to make information available to stakeholders using open source technology such as portals and Web 2.0 and beyond capabilities. [10]

The role of the organization would include carrying out the USG aspects of the ICT strategy and plan. In addition, the organization would collaborate with the organizations with which preplanning took place, including key countries, the UN, the World Bank, and major NGOs. As promptly as possible, the organization would want to begin to work with the affected nation, though precisely what that means will depend on the unique circumstances of the operation. As a forward community of interest is being set up, the organization will want to create mechanisms that add additional entities to the effort that have not been part of the preplanning. The DoD is encouraging the development of an open-source, collaborative arena, tentatively called "the hub," that would use blogging, file-sharing, and Wikipedia-type and Web 2.0 approaches to create an open space for collaborative sharing.[11] This hub type approach may be very valuable, as may more structured relationships. In addition, the organization will want to work with the public affairs office (PAO) to facilitate interaction with the media and, most importantly, information for the public at large. For example, U.S. commanders in Afghanistan recently launched their "social networking strategy" for Afghanistan using the hugely popular website Twitter to release information about some of their operations,[12] a Facebook page,[13] and the popular YouTube video sharing site[14] to post videos about their work and the daily lives of U.S. troops. The decision to use the latest Internet fad was meant to "engage non-traditional audiences directly with news, videos, pictures, and other information from Operation Enduring Freedom," the U.S. military said, and to "preempt extremist propaganda."[15]

OBSERVATIONS

ICT can be important components for success in complex operations. To achieve successful results requires that a purposeful strategy be adopted to use these capabilities to achieve the desired end of facilitating recovery and building up the affected nation and to develop operational activities that effectively implement the strategy. A strategic approach causes coalition participants to undertake five key activities:
1. Conduct pre-event activities with partners,
2. Implement improved collaboration,
3. Ensure improved data usability,
4. Develop an information toolbox, and
5. Create a forward field information office.

Also, creating an overall focus to generate an effective affected nation information business plan consists of four actionable items:
1. Assess the affected nation information capacity and culture and business processes,
2. Build an affected nation information goal,
3. Create immediate, medium, and long-term in formation capacities, and
4. Analyze information needs and develop methods to fulfill those needs.

Civil-Military collaboration and information sharing activities can have decisive impacts in complex operations. To more effectively address shortfalls in responder activities, they need to be treated as a core part of the nation's overall strategy and, as noted earlier, not just as "nice to have" adjuncts to the kinetic phases of warfare. U.S. military and civilian government agencies need to start to "think" information and ICT. Key points to consider for future operations include:

- "Think" Information and Information Communications Technology (ICT)
  - Collaboration and information sharing
  - Enabler of cross-sector reconstruction
  - Influence operations
  - Enabler of "unity of effort" across the civil-military boundaries;
- Think and do "whole of government"
  - Diplomacy, defense, and development
  - Enable the "affected nation" do not do it for them;
- View ICT as an "essential service" and as "critical infrastructure";
- Engage and leverage the "new media" such as Web 2.0 and beyond;
- Metrics for ICT need to measure "outcomes" not just outputs;
- Employ information and ICT capabilities as a means to inform, influence, and build trust.

Furthering this argument, in complex operations the United States cannot achieve the social, political, and economic goals for which its military forces are committed unless the overall U.S. Government can engage effectively with local governments, businesses, and members of civil society.[16] Additionally, improvements in information sharing will need to proactively address changes that reflect:

- Culture: "The Will to Share";
- Policy: "The Rules for Sharing";
- Governance: "The Environment to Influence Sharing";
- Economics and Resources: "The Value of Sharing";

- Technology and Infrastructure: "The Capability to Enable Sharing.

As noted, Information and ICT can significantly increase the likelihood of success in complex operations—if they are engaged as part of an overall strategy that coordinates the actions of the whole of U.S. Government (interagency) and, as appropriate, outside IO, IGO, NGO, international business, and other civil-military stakeholders. The focus also needs to be on generating effective results for the host or affected nation—enable the host or affected nations to be successful. Properly utilized, ICT can help create effective initiatives and knowledgeable interventions, organize complex activities, and integrate complex operations with the host or affected nation, making the latter more effective.

Key to these results is a U.S. Government strategy that requires that: (1) the U.S. Government must give high priority to such a whole of government approach and ensure that the effort is a joint civilian-military activity; (2) the military and other U.S. Government elements need to "think" information and ICT and treat ICT as an "essential service" and make it a part of policy and doctrine for and the planning and execution of complex operation; (3) preplanning and the establishment of ICT partnerships is undertaken with key regular participants in complex operations, such as NATO, the United Nations (UN), the World Bank and others such as regional nations in affected nation area; (4) the focus of initiatives and complex interventions, including the use of ICT, is on supporting and enabling the host or affected nation governmental, security, societal, and economic development; and (5) key information technology capabilities are harnessed to support the strategy. Implementing the strategy will include: (1) development of an information business plan for host and affected nations so that ICT is effectively used to support security cooperation, capacity building, and stabilization and reconstruction; (2) agreements among complex operations stakeholders on data-sharing and collaboration, including data-sharing on a differentiated basis; and (3) use of commercial IT tools and data provided on an unclassified basis as appropriate.[17]

Enhancing the influence of U.S. Government responses to HA/DR and interventions into stability and reconstruction operations will require a multifaceted strategic communications strategy that differentiates the circumstances of the messages, key places of delivery, and sophistication with which messages are created and delivered, with particular focus on channels and messengers. To improve in these areas, the U.S. Government must focus on actions that include discerning the nature of the audiences, societies, and cultures into which messages will be delivered; increasing the number of experts in geographic and cultural arenas, particularly in languages; augmenting resources for overall strategic communications and ICT influence efforts; encouraging long-term communications and ICT influence efforts along with short-term responses; and understanding that successful strategic communications and ICT influence operations cannot be achieved by the U.S. Government acting on its own; allies and partners are needed both to shape our messages and to support theirs.[18]

ENDNOTES - CHAPTER 5

1. Frank Kramer, Stuart Starr, and Larry Wentz, *Cyberpower and National Security*, Washington, DC: Center for Technology and National Security Policy, National Defense University (NDU) Press, 2009.

2. Larry Wentz, *An ICT Primer: ICT for Civil-Military Coordination in Disaster Relief and Stabilization and Reconstruction*, Defense and Technology Paper 31, Washington, DC: Center for Technology and National Security Policy, National Defense University, July 2006.

3. See UN OCHA website for details on use the of foreign military assets in disaster relief, available from *ochaonline.un.org/AboutOCHA/Organigramme/EmergencyServicesBranchESB/CivilMilitaryCoordinationSection/PolicyGuidanceandPublications/tabid/1403/language/en-US/Default.aspx*.

4. Jock Covey, Michael Dziedzic, and Leonard Hawley, eds., *The Quest for Viable Peace: International Intervention and Strategies for Conflict Transformation*, Washington, DC: U.S. Institute for Peace Press, May 2005.

5. Wentz.

6. Website address is *www.star-tides.net*.

7. Frank Kramer, Stuart Starr, and Larry Wentz, "I-Power: Using the Information Revolution for Success in Stability Operations," *Defense Horizons*, No. 55, January 2007, pp. 1-8.

8. For nations that have ratified the Tampere Convention, regulatory barriers are waved for telecommunications to be used in disasters, available from *www.itu.int/ITU-D/emergencytelecoms/tampere.html*.

9. Mark Drapeau and Linton Wells II, *Social Software and National Security: An Initial Net Assessment*, Defense and Technology Paper 61, Washington, DC: Center for Technology and National Security Policy National Defense University, April 2009.

10. Kramer, Starr, and Wentz, *Cyberpower and National Security*.

11. Drapeau and Wells, *Social Software and National Security*.

12. Available from *twitter.com/usfora*.

13. Available from *tiny.cc/MJtsf*.

14. Available from *www.youtube.com/usfora*.

15. Paul Tait and Jerry Norton, "U.S. Military Turns to Twitter for Afghan Hard News," Reuters, June 2, 2009, available from *Reuters.com/article/idussp477109*.

16. Hans Binnendijk and Patrick M. Cronin, *Civilian Surge: Key to Complex Operations*, Washington, DC: Center for Technology and National Security Policy, National Defense University, December 2008.

17. Kramer, Starr, and Wentz, *I-Power*.

18. Franklin D. Kramer and Larry Wentz, "Cyber Influence and International Security," *Defense Horizons*, No. 61, January 2008, pp. 1-11.

PART II:

SOCIAL AND LEGAL ASPECTS

CHAPTER 6

THE INFORMATION POLITY: SOCIAL AND LEGAL FRAMEWORKS FOR CRITICAL CYBER INFRASTRUCTURE PROTECTION

Michael M. Losavio
J. Eagle Shutt
Deborah Wilson Keeling

INTRODUCTION

This chapter examines how public policy may evolve to adequately address cybercrime. Traditional legal protections against criminal activity were developed in a world wherein any criminal violation was coupled with physical proximity. Global information networks have created criminal opportunities in which criminal violation and physical proximity are decoupled.

We argue that cyberspace public policy has not adequately incentivized and supported protective behaviors in the cyber community. We examine the roles that user-level/consumer-level conduct, social engagement, and administrative policy play in protecting information infrastructure. We suggest proactive work with laws and administrative/citizen-level engagement to reform the cyberspace community. To that end, we examine applicable legal and transnational regimes that impact such a strategy and options for expanding administrative and citizen engagement in the cyber security enterprise.

The cyber infrastructures of the United States and Europe offer inviting targets for attack, whether for profit, malice, or state objectives. The enmeshing natures of computer networks have changed the calculus for both delineating and protecting critical cyber infrastructure. The boundaries between such infrastructure and external systems using the infrastructure have become so intertwined that it may be impossible to separate them. Those external systems may become threat vectors themselves.

This enmeshing has blurred the identity between physical and "logical" frontiers for purposes of state boundaries, jurisdiction, and sovereignty. Cyber security issues move quickly past the national level to that of provinces, states, localities, businesses, and citizens.

Carolyn Pumphrey discussed in detail how local law enforcement strategies might effectively be blended with military/homeland security efforts to protect cyber systems. She noted that transnational threats, including those of cyber security, straddle "domestic and foreign spheres" that present "profound constitutional and security challenges" for the United States.[1]

Public security is a function of several factors, including law and effective law enforcement, social norms, and technical protections. Effective security in cyberspace requires a similar configuration. A neighborhood where neighbors watch out for each other and discourage criminality; timely response by police and the courts; and where residents lock their windows and doors will be much more secure. Together, the community's norms, habits, and formal institutions serve protective functions.

The conceit we call cyberspace can equally benefit from an equivalent set of protective elements. Yet efforts to incentivize such protective elements have not been sufficiently developed. Of particular concern are the capabilities of local law enforcement, business, and individuals to play their part in cyber security as a necessary component of protection of all cyber infrastructures.

Law, norms, and technology impact these capabilities. At the same time, they may raise issues relating to the preservation of rights and liberties of liberal Western countries seeking to respond to external threats.

Review of laws and administrative systems can avoid misunderstandings as to proper conduct in investigating the misuse of computers and networks. It can also aid in protecting researchers from legal problems in their work, especially for research done outside of government.

The significance of the threat is seen in the March 29, 2009, GhostNet cyber espionage study and analysis report of the Information Warfare Monitor on distributed malware attacks originating out of China.[2] These attacks use a combination of Trojan malware-Gh0st RAT (Remote Access Tool) and social engineering via e-mail to infect vulnerable machines. The key findings were:

- Compromise of at least 1,295 computers in 103 countries, of which nearly 30 percent might be high-value targets,
- GhostNet penetration of sensitive computer systems of the Dalai Lama and other Tibetan targets, and
- GhostNet is a covert, difficult-to-detect system capable of taking full control of affected systems.[3]

Compromised systems included government offices of Iran, Bangladesh, Latvia, Indonesia, Philippines, Brunei, Barbados, Bhutan, and embassies of India, South Korea, Indonesia, Romania, Cyprus, Malta,

Thailand, Taiwan, Portugal, Germany, and Pakistan.

This report comes on the heels of U.S. Government reports that computing systems at power utility companies where compromised by overseas attacks.[4]

The GhostNet report further suggests that cyber security outside of classified government operations is woefully inadequate, whether in commercial or civic organizations.

We suggest a proactive strategy that blends law enforcement, military, and citizen engagement for the protection of the cyber infrastructure and enhancement of cyber security. To that end, we examine applicable legal and transnational regimes that impact such a strategy and options for expanding administrative and citizen engagement in the cyber security enterprise. These options may offer a vital complementary element to the cyber security of the United States as well as other countries.

JURISDICTION AMONG DISTRIBUTED SOVEREIGNS

The exclusive power and jurisdiction to regulate is a jealously guarded prerogative of sovereign nations. Jurisdiction may refer to a particular entity asserting a right to regulate conduct, such as a nation or a province, and in addition to the right of that entity to regulate conduct, but also to punish conduct. The right to regulate is usually bounded by a grant of rights itself limited by physical boundaries, such as the boundaries of a nation, state, province, or locality. It encompasses regulation through substantive criminal law that defines wrongful conduct, procedural criminal law that defines how the law is enforced, and laws for resolving problems between jurisdictions, e.g., extradition and transfer of an offender found in one jurisdiction to another jurisdiction for offenses committed in that latter state.

A state may also assert the right to act against conduct outside of its boundaries that has an impact inside those boundaries. It may assert jurisdiction over acts of its citizens that occur abroad. It may assert jurisdiction based on treaties, maritime law, or international law.

In the distributed, transnational environment of cyberspace, the assertion of a right to regulate must still address the practical problems of enforcement in foreign jurisdictions. If the domestic cyber infrastructure is attacked by someone operating in another jurisdiction, cooperation by the authorities in that foreign jurisdiction may be needed. If investigative data on an attack are to be found in a foreign jurisdiction, even if the attacker is in yet another jurisdiction, speedy local cooperation is needed. Obtaining this cooperation may be difficult.

For example, in the Gorshkov/Ivanov cases, the defendants broke into various U.S. corporate computer systems from their home base in Russia; they then offered their computer security expertise for hire.[5] To simplify the jurisdictional problems, the U.S. Federal Bureau of Investigation (FBI) convinced them to demonstrate these skills in a meeting in the United States that was videotaped and keylogged. After logging in to his home machine to download his toolkit, Ivanov was arrested. The agents then took the keylogger data, logged into Ivanov's home machine in Russia, and downloaded files evidencing his illegal access to machines in the United States. Both were convicted and sentenced to prison. However, Russian authorities were not happy with the actions of the U.S. authorities and initiated criminal proceedings against the two FBI agents involved in the remote (but unauthorized) access to Ivanov's machine in Russia.

The complexity of transnational actions increases with other issues of data and computing regulation in each country. The most effective tool to remedy this is cooperation, which may be manifested in treaty law promoting mutual benefit. This may not be possible with any country that expressly or implicitly condones cyber attacks against foreign targets. But it can still be effective in rallying countries to work together and set a foundation for diplomatic solutions. First, we provide a general discussion of local law in this area and then proceed to the use of treaty law to create a more effective transnational regime.

LOCAL SUBSTANTIVE CRIMINAL LAW AND THE EXERCISE OF SOVEREIGNTY

Criminal and delictual law adapt to injuries and misconduct with new technologies, particularly where those technologies threaten rights in new and unforeseen ways. The legal regime for computer misuse addresses the core function of these machines; their ability to store, manipulate, and transmit information.

A traditional crime may be committed with a new computer tool, such as murder by entering false information in a medical database.[6] Crimes previously the province of technical specialists, such as criminal copyright infringement, may now easily be committed by laypersons. Some crimes require new, *sui generis* statutes to control misconduct unseen before the rise of computing technologies.

Review of computer misuse must consider several issues:

- Misuse may fit traditional criminal law elements. For example, a computer can be used to store or transmit information on terrorist activity or other criminal dealings, like a notebook.
- Computer misuse may only partially correspond to traditional criminal law elements, requiring legal revisions to correspond to technical facts of computers and networks. For example, a computer may be used to copy and transmit information in violation of intellectual rights and for industrial espionage, violations that in the past required significant time and resources.
- Or that misuse may not fit within the elements of standard crimes, requiring use of new criminal statutes to address the danger. For example, a computer can be used to transmit information that, while harmful, does not fit the elements of traditional crimes requiring proximity of the offender to the target or financial motive. The Filipino computer student who wrote the "I Love You" computer virus was not prosecuted because the Philippines had no law at the time criminalizing such conduct.[7]

The intersection of the old and the new with cybercrime make for an evolving area of practice. Review of incidents of computer misuse will require a combination of both traditional and innovative case analysis in law enforcement, especially where the computer crime itself shares elements of old and new types of offenses, as seen in Figure 6.1.

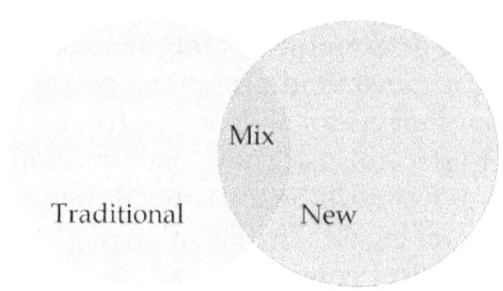

Figure 6.1. Evolving Law Enforcement Practice.

Examples of Local Substantive Criminal Laws.

The issue of jurisdiction and sovereignty plays a major role in the promulgation of laws as each sovereign may choose to create its own set of criminal laws relating to computer misconduct. They may do so with little regard for what any other jurisdictions may choose to regulate.

The general categories of regulation in this area are exemplified by the Council of Europe's Convention on Cybercrime, discussed further below. Those categories are:

- Unauthorized access to computer, (this includes exceeding authorized access to a computer),
- Unauthorized interception of data,
- Unauthorized interference with data,
- Unauthorized interference with a system,
- Misuse of devices.

Different jurisdictions may adopt criminal laws in each of these areas or only some of them; the particular provisions may vary from one jurisdiction to another.

Some primary U.S. federal criminal statutes related to computer intrusions that reflect these categories are:

- 18 U.S.C. § 1029. Fraud and Related Activity in Connection with Access Devices
- 18 U.S.C. § 1030. Fraud and Related Activity in Connection with Computers
- 18 U.S.C. § 1362. Communication Lines, Stations, or Systems
- 18 U.S.C. § 2510 et seq. Wire and Electronic Communications Interception and Interception of Oral Communications
- 18 U.S.C. § 2701 et seq. Stored Wire and Electronic Communications and Transactional Records Access
- 18 U.S.C. § 3121 et seq. Recording of Dialing, Routing, Addressing, and Signaling Information.

Each of the American states has its own computer crime laws that may reflect some or all of these issues. For example, Kentucky statutes focus on unlawful access to a computer:

- KRS 434.845 Unlawful access to a computer in the first degree (fraud).
- KRS 434.850 Unlawful access to a computer in the second degree (damage).
- KRS 434.851 Unlawful access in the third degree (damage).
- KRS 434.852 Unlawful access in the fourth degree (access).
- KRS 434.855 Misuse of computer information.
- KRS 150.363 Computer-assisted remote hunting unlawful — Citizens with disabilities.

While its primary focus is on unlawful access, Kentucky's prohibition on computer-assisted remote hunting is a good example of how special local concerns may lead to unique laws on computing.

Similarly, other countries have laws designed to regulate various types of misconduct with computing devices, such as:

- Canada
  - Unauthorized use of computer interception of communications
- United Kingdom
  - Computer Misuse Act 1990, as amended
  - Data Protection Act 1998
- India
  - Information Technology Act 2000
- Germany
  - Unauthorized acquisition of data
  - Unauthorized circumvetion of system security

This structure for substantive criminal laws that define prohibited conduct is also matched by systems of procedural laws by which the substantive law is enforced. These laws may vary between jurisdictions.

Procedural Criminal Laws.

Enforcement of substantive criminal law is guided by rules of procedure that seek to assure reliability and fairness in the administration of justice. They may also reflect national interests in the protection of certain rights of citizens. As with substantive criminal law, criminal procedure may vary between jurisdictions.

One area of procedure deals with the proper use of evidence. Electronic evidence alone or matched with other evidence may indicate a crime and additional evidence of that crime. That additional evidence, once obtained, can correlate the electronic record with other actions. This correlation and development role is particularly important for remote data collected over networks; correlation to other evidence is a key function of electronic evidence in prosecuting a digital crime.

Another area addresses the protection of privacy rights of citizens from government intrusion. For example, absent special circumstances, the search or seizure of a person or his effects without consent is illegal in the United States unless an application under oath is made before a neutral magistrate that sets out facts to establish "probable cause" to believe a crime has been committed and evidence of that crime will be found in the place searched and things seized. Probable cause itself means a fair probability under a commonsense analysis that evidence is to be found at the place to be searched. This and other rules define procedural law for law enforcement and prosecution in the United States.

For example, Figure 6.2 shows a diagram of the process by which computational forensic data may be used within the criminal justice process in the United States.

Meeting the procedural requirements of each jurisdiction may slow computer crime investigation across multiple jurisdictions. It may, in fact, render an investigation impossible. To counter investigative obstacles, a transnational legal regime is developing through bilateral and multilateral treaties to harmonize substantive and procedural criminal law between countries and to create a system for mutual assistance and cooperation in cybercrime investigation and prosecution. That developing regime is seen in cooperation between nations as outlined by the Convention on Cybercrime of the Council of Europe.

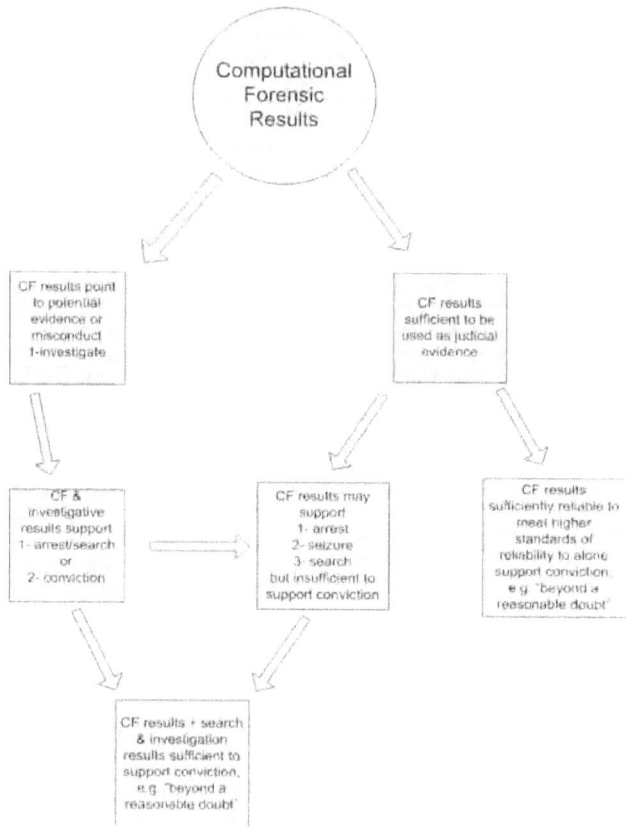

Figure 6.2. The Use Path for Computational Forensic (CF) Results.[8]

A TRANSNATIONAL LEGAL REGIME AND COOPERATION ACROSS FRONTIERS—THE CONVENTION ON CYBERCRIME

Miles Townes and others argue that an international regime to protect our interconnected information infrastructure is needed.[9] Nicholas Seitz, Townes, and Lorenzo Valeri all support the premise that an international regime of information assurance is essential; Valeri calls for "specific international 'clusters of rules or conventions,' the content of which cannot be just independently devised by states or international businesses."[10]

The Council of Europe's Convention on Cybercrime[11] is a primary component of such an evolving regime. This treaty emerged after lengthy negotiations between members of the Council of Europe and nonmember states; Canada, Costa Rica, Dominican Republic, Japan, Mexico, Philippines, South Africa, and the United States.

The Convention is structured to address the issues of substantive criminal law, procedural criminal law, and interjurisdiction relations. By harmonizing these three areas, the Convention promotes greater uniformity between national laws and facilitates cooperation between states, vital for the preservation of time-sensitive, evanescent electronic evidence. It does this by requiring each country joining the Convention to:

- adopt criminal laws that define crimes in five fundamental areas of computer and network misuse, creating a common base of substantive criminal law;
- adopt and implement procedures for investigation, evidence collection, evidence preservation, and prosecution of digital crime and use of electronic evidence, building a common base of procedural criminal law across countries; and,
- Building on the common foundation in both substantive and procedural criminal law, states must then adopt measures to assure international cooperation and mutual assistance in

investigations involving multiple jurisdictions, addressing particularly difficult problems of the preservation and disclosure of data and the extradition of citizens to foreign jurisdictions.

The five key areas for substantive crimes where each state must adopt criminal laws are:
1. Unauthorized access to computer, (this includes exceeding authorized access to a computer),
2. Unauthorized interception of data,
3. Unauthorized interference with data,
4. Unauthorized interference with a system, and
5. Misuse of devices.

The Convention looks at intentional conduct "without right."

The Convention permits variations between nations. In our earlier list of U.S. laws, these five areas are addressed by those statutes; 18 U.S.C. § 1030. "Fraud and Related Activity in Connection with Computers," in particular, addresses unauthorized access and interference with data and systems.

The common procedural criminal law for law enforcement investigative and prosecutorial activities include the preservation, acquisition, and use of electronic evidence. The most sensitive of the three areas relates to requirements for international cooperation and mutual legal assistance. Cross-jurisdictional law enforcement efforts entail risks that range from different procedures to different communications protocols to challenges to national sovereignty. The Convention seeks to minimize these problems by first harmonizing criminal laws and then having states adopt procedures and practices for cooperation and mutual assistance between countries on cybercrime matters.

These procedures should address assistance and co-operation in data preservation and disclosure and the extradition of suspects.

The Convention creates a foundation for cooperation between countries in investigating cybercrime between countries, including activities impacting criminal cyber infrastructure. But this foundation must be supplemented by other human participant elements within the cyber community. The enmeshed nature of our cyber-information world has made the home front the frontier of cyber conflict. Local matters of law enforcement and public security are intertwined with those of national cyber security.

We discuss possible ways to incentivize protective behaviors in the following section.

SOCIAL NORMS AND CRIMINOLOGICAL THEORY

Law enforcement is not the sole factor in assuring public security. The values and actions of a community contribute to its security. As Stanley Cohen argues, the strength of social control depends on formal and informal social control.[12] Laws and law enforcement represent formal social control, whereas the attitudes and actions of individuals represent informal social control. Both spheres can impede unlawful activities, but states with strong overall levels of social control will have high degrees of both formal and informal social control.

The opportunity theory perspective provides a useful way of conceptualizing the potential effect of informal social control on cyber security. Routine activities theory (RAT) is made up of three distinctive elements:

1. A suitable target is available,
2. There is a lack of a suitable guardian, and
3. There is a motivated offender.[13]

Where all of these elements are present, the risk of criminal conduct increases. Conversely, the absence of one of these elements reduces the risk of misconduct.

In the context of cyber security, there is an abundance of suitable targets and a lack of suitable guardians. However, changes in attitudes, present in the informal sphere of social control, can increase rates of suitable guardianship.

Attitudes have been used to explain a wide range of behaviors, including racism, prejudice, voting, and attraction. There is no universal definition of attitude, and the concept itself has been measured in hundreds of ways. As M. Fishbein and I. Azjen write, "[A] definition of attitude appears to be a minimal prerequisite for the development of valid measurement procedures."[14] J. M. Olson and M. P. Zanna define an attitude as favorable or unfavorable evaluative reactions toward an object which may be manifested through beliefs, feelings, or inclinations toward action.[15]

Social psychological research in value diffusion[16] and norms[17] suggest that attitudes can be manipulated via intervention. Boyd and Richerson argue that values can differentially spread in a population based on biasing factors. When an individual is exposed to different values, an individual's decision to adopt one of the values and not the other may be biased from randomness by properties of the social context which render the selected value more appealing. Preferential value diffusion has been borne out in economics and diffusion of innovations research.[18]

A norm favoring a particular value may cause that value to become ubiquitous in a population. There is no universally agreed upon definition of "norm": the Merriam-Webster Dictionary defines a norm as "a principle of right action binding upon the members of a group and serving to guide, control, or regulate proper and acceptable behavior." A norm has two primary subtypes, social and legal. A social norm, unlike a legal norm, is informal and appears to arise and be enforced[19] without deliberate planning, writing, or enforcement.[20]

In the externality model of norm development, norms emerge when the actions of individuals produce either costs or benefits to others.[21] When individual X does an act that individual Y does not like or perceives as harmful, Y may respond negatively, often reasoning that "you shouldn't do that." An individual's being harmed is not enough to generate a norm; however, if enough similarly situated individuals perceive the same harm, this response will become a norm and have a constraining effect on behavior. As long as the benefit/harm is easily identified (such as death, theft, or pollution), the externality model accounts for why certain deviant behaviors are punished (they are viewed as harmful rather than harmless) and punished to varying degrees (certain behaviors are viewed as extremely harmful or intolerable); in many cases, however, the benefit/harm is often culturally defined and subject to debate.

Using the externality model puts an onus on information because an externality is socially constructed: Individuals need to decide what is harmful, and definitions thereof may vary depending on social and contextual factors. For example, the linking of complex issues such as cyber security and individual autonomy may be hotly debated. For example, some individuals may argue that individuals are responsible for others but bear no responsibility for others' cyber security (referred to hereinafter as isolationist norm). By contrast, others may argue that such an orientation is too myopic and is subject to the freeloader fallacy. While such an approach would be effective for a security-minded individual if everyone else was like-minded, such an approach is suboptimal if others fail to consider cyber security. In that case, the community's cyber security vulnerabilities will create widespread opportunities for network-based attacks, which ultimately may compromise the isolationist individual's cyber security.

Based on this externality model, we argue for cyber security policy changes to foster information that supports an integrationist norm, wherein individuals recognize that their failure to be proactive in pursuing cyber security is morally irresponsible and exposes them and others to harm. Successful informational campaigns have changed public norms. For example, public awareness of harms created by littering and second-hand smoking have largely emerged over the last 40 years as a result of commercials, scientific studies, and laws. National awareness of littering was heightened by commercials featuring a weeping Native American surveying a litter-strewn American landscape. Such commercials transformed littering from a local problem to a collective problem. The act of littering acquired a moral dimension and was re-conceptualized as harmful and disrespectful to others. Littering itself may be punished informally by others via informal sanctions, such as rude responses. Current informal norms disfavor littering in many contexts, and many children are taught not to litter from early ages.

In cyber security contexts, information campaigns could foster integrationist norms by presenting cyber security as a moral obligation of personal responsibility, wherein the failures of the few may lead to great harm for others. Recent cyber attacks have utilized cyber security flaws on un-updated computers to create drones of attack computers. Educating the public about operating such computers would harden targets by presenting such actions as not only foolish and shortsighted but leading to the harm to others.

Ultimately, optimal public policy changes social values relating to personal responsibility. Information campaigns could be reconceptualized as moral imperatives. In so doing, motivated individuals will harden cyber targets by proactively pursuing cyber security.

ADMINISTRATIVE ENGAGEMENT – MARSHALLING AND ENABLING EXISTING LAW ENFORCEMENT

Enabling local law enforcement to address cyber-crime matters can increase the presence of "suitable guardians" and reduce the motivations of some offenders. U.S. law enforcement at the local level expects growth in the use of electronic evidence as proof of system misuse. Lawyers and judges have also expressed the desire for better training in this area. This reflects the vast expansion of consumer computing devices in society.

It also reflects a dangerous skills gap in law enforcement relating to consumer computing and telecommunications devices. For example, in 2006 cellular telephones were recovered in investigations in a majority of violent crimes and in over 80 percent of drug crimes.[22] See Figure 6.3.

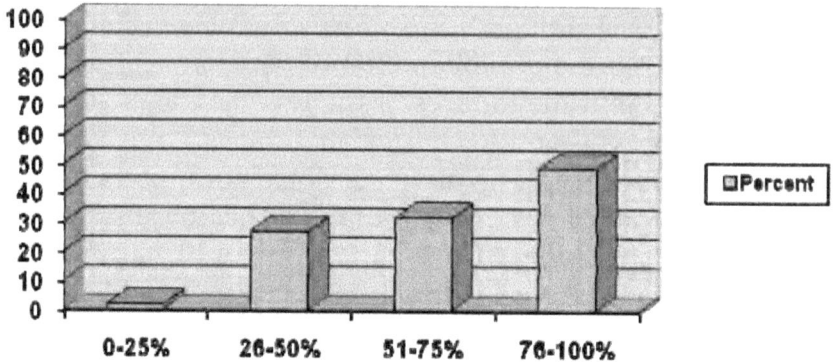

Figure 6.3. Involvement of Cell Phones In Violent Crimes.[23]

Yet a majority of police executive officers also reported an inability to use evidence from those systems due to lack of training or access to forensic specialists. See Figure 6.4.

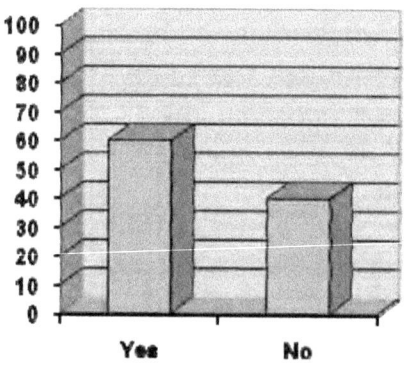

Figure 6.4. Inability to Search for Cell Phone Evidence Due to Timely Access to Forensic Examiners and Lack of Forensic Skills.[24]

Similar surveys relating to general electronic evidence and systems produced indications of expectations of increased use and desire for training in this area among judges, attorneys, and even corrections officers.[25]

If the resources to address cybercrime at all levels are to be marshaled at all levels, we must enable local law enforcement to address these threats.

Expanded Law Enforcement Engagement.

Expanded law enforcement engagement may be achieved through cross-disciplinary training for necessary skills and for the support of their use via local capacity-building. This engages law enforcement, public defenders, prosecutors, corrections, and the judiciary in the training and support services.

Training would focus on:

- Law enforcement training. Computer forensic examination training on how and where to manually locate data on digital media storage devices, use of automated computer forensic tools locate, identify, and report information of evidentiary value, including specific information in formats such as hexadecimal or binary within data sets, carve information from the data set in a forensically sound manner, and articulate the findings.
- Law enforcement training. Digital evidence collection training to provide a measurable proficiency in digital evidence recognition, seizure, packaging, transportation, and storage.[26]
- Law enforcement administrative officer training. Training for administrative officers on managing and supervising their people on the

use and analysis, collection and preservation of digital evidence, particularly from cell phones and other portable electronic devices.

- Defender training. Support for training public defenders in the effective assistance of counsel in cases involving digital evidence.
- Prosecutorial training. The prosecutorial use of computer forensic data in the courtroom.
- Judicial training. Judicial practice relating to the use of computer forensic data in the courtroom.

Support services should include statewide networks of resources, such as self-service digital forensic workbenches available to local law enforcement that may not be able to afford their own forensic systems but continue to collect digital evidence repositories. Where evidentiary issues may require higher-level analysis, this workbench system would support chain-of-custody valid transmittal to regional computer forensic laboratories and other forensic analysts capable of such high-level analysis.

This distributed local investigative capacity would expand the protective capabilities needed to protect systems from cyber attack. Feeding local investigative results into the system of transnational cooperation envisioned by the Convention on Cybercrime would speed response while effectively leveraging all resources in what is already an asymmetric risk environment.

Given the cross-jurisdictional issues noted earlier, such a system could use national and state-level organizations to mobilize collaboration. Law enforcement, prosecutors, and judges all have national organizations to help implementation at the state level. Similarly, these groups have statewide organizations that can carry implementation to local jurisdictions.

Many states have resources within the computer science, computer engineering, and computer information systems departments of state universities to further support this effort with their expertise. The expertise and experience developed within these departments is a significant resource that will decrease the cost of training development and delivery, and resource development.

Sustainability and expansion will depend on the selection of state and local law enforcement, prosecutors, and judicial professionals who themselves will serve as resources and future trainers to maintain and further the skills relating to computer forensics, cell phone forensics, and digital evidence.

CITIZEN ENGAGEMENT

The home front is the frontier in this conflict. The citizen computer user must be engaged in this process. Risk can evolve when home/business systems "... are being increasingly subverted by malicious actors to attack critical systems."[27] Community awareness and training on basic cyber security are needed for home and small business users; the threat mandates such action.[28] The strategy emphasizes the role of public-private engagement.[29]

This framework encompasses all who use computer systems. The National Institute of Standards and Technology (NIST) has outlined standards on technical security and security training and awareness for nontechnical users of computer systems.[30] NIST's Computer Security Resource Center (CSRC), the Small Business Administration (SBA), and the

National Infrastructure Protection Center (Infragard) have together advocated computer security trainings for small businesses.[31] Educause, the association for IT in education, advocates starting cyber security education in kindergarten.[32] The Awareness and Outreach Task Force of the National Cyber Security Partnership, an industry association, recommends the development and distribution of cyber security guidebooks and toolkits for small business and home computer users.[33]

Collaboration between government, business, schools, and consumers improves security by mitigating the exploitation of home and small business systems for computer security attacks. It prevents the use of compromised home computers to help storm the security bastions of any other computer on the Internet in a coordinated, multitiered, and destructive attack. It limits risks of compromise to critical systems, such as medical and mechanical systems, that are real, mortal threats.

Direct Engagement — A Training Response.

There must be direct engagement of school, home, and small businesses in securing computers and broadband connections from attack and compromise. This engagement requires the training of users for their own protection and the protection of others.

Three barriers hinder that engagement. As a matter of cost, home and small business users may not be able to hire expertise for computer security. As a matter of training, the generally low-level of computing literacy makes it difficult for home and small business users to implement secure practices themselves. As a matter of culture, school, home, and small business users may defer to others in reference to their systems' operations.

These are overcome by basic computer security training for consumers and by ongoing efforts of business and government to provide security tools for the home and small business computer user. A cost-effective model of such training was proposed by the University of Louisville student chapter of the Association for Computing Machinery (ACM). [34]

First, training identifies the threats to home and small business systems. Often, even with news coverage of virus and worm outbreaks, consumers are unaware of the level of threat associated with Internet and broadband usage. Second, training looks to "best practices" with the use of; (a) protective technology, and (b) safe user practices. System maintenance practices, though inconvenient, offer better security for systems. Safe personal computer use practices secure the users themselves, especially children.[35]

The Benefits of Engagement.

Citizen engagement has the dual benefit of hardening the vast distributed set of available targets and developing new guardians in the form of the computer users themselves. Securing home and small business computers can only happen with the engagement of citizens in the security enterprise. By the very nature of the Internet, individuals must be active participants in the security of their own systems. Civil engagement highlights the need for all Americans, in their homes and businesses, schools and churches, to be part of the security solution. Personal responsibility in this effort is essential for success.

This requires the computer security community to educate the public about personal security efforts.

Information technology is not a profession and is not bound by proactive professional ethical mandates,[36] even though proactive attention to safety and security may be expected.[37]

This training solution promotes safety, security, and social responsibility by advancing the understanding of computing in the critical area of security.[38]

CONCLUSION

Cyber infrastructure needs security that can only happen via collaboration between citizens/system users, businesses, law enforcement agencies, and civil institutions that provide the knowledge and improved technologies needed for secure computing. Should such collaboration fail to develop, computing in our country, and its benefits, will suffer.

As a collaborative effort, cyber security requires personal responsibility from citizens and institutions. Protective factors in cyber security are minimized when participants blindly delegate all responsibility to others and continue to deploy and use networked systems.

Optimally, public policy will foster both law enforcement and citizen engagement in information security. Failure to engage these resources will continue to leave gaps in protection and create opportunities for harm to our people and our country.

ENDNOTES - CHAPTER 6

1. Carolyn Pumphrey, "Introduction," in Carolyn Pumphrey, ed., *Transnational Threats: Blending Law Enforcement and Military Strategies*, Carlisle, PA: Strategic Studies Institute, U.S. Army War College, 2000, pp. 1-17, available from *www.strategicstudiesinstitute.army.mil/pubs/display.cfm?pubid=224*.

2. Ron Deibert and Rafal Rohozinski, "Tracking GhostNet: Investigating a Cyber Espionage Network," *Information Warfare Monitor*, March 29, 2009, available from *www.infowar-monitor.net/ghostnet*.

3. *Ibid.*, p. 6.

4. Justin Blum, "Hackers Target U.S. Power Grid: Government Quietly Warns Utilities To Beef Up Their Computer Security," *Washington Post*, March 11, 2005, p. E01.

5. Art Jahnke, "Alexey Ivanov, and Vasiliy Gorshkov: Russian Hacker Roulette," CSO Online, January 1, 2005, available from *www.csoonline.com/article/219964/Alexey_Ivanov_and_Vasiliy_Gorshkov_Russian_Hacker_Roulette*.

6. Susan Brenner, "Cybercrime Metrics: Old Wine, New Bottles?" *Virginia Journal of Law and Technology*, Vol. 9, No. 13, Fall 2004.

7. Wayne Arnold, "TECHNOLOGY; Philippines to Drop Charges on E-Mail Virus," *New York Times*, August 22, 2000, available from *www.nytimes.com/2000/08/22/business/technology-philippines-to-drop-charges-on-e-mail-virus.html*.

8. C-T Li, *Handbook of Research on Computational Forensics, Digital Crime and Investigation: Methods and Solutions*, Hershey, PA: IGI Global, 2010.

9. Miles Townes, "International Regimes and Information Infrastructure," *Stanford Journal of International Relations*, Vol. 1, No. 2, Spring 1999.

10. *Ibid.*; Nicholas Sietz, "Transborder Search: A New Perspective on Law Enforcement?" *International Journal of Common Law and Policy*, Vol. 9, No. 2, Fall 2004; Lorenzo Valeri, "Securing Internet Society: Toward an International Regime for Information Assurance," *Studies in Conflict & Terrorism*, Vol. 23, Iss. 2, January 2000, pp. 129-146, particularly p. 141.

11. Council of Europe CETS No. 185 Convention on Cybercrime, opened for signature November 23, 2001, available from *conventions.coe.int/Treaty/en/Treaties/Html/185.htm*, signed and ratified by 27 states.

12. Stanley Cohen, *Visions of Social Control: Crime, Punishment, and Classification*, Cambridge, UK: Polity Press, 1985.

13. M. Ouimet, "Internet Crime and Trends," in F. Schmallager and M. Pittaro, eds., *Crimes of the Internet*, Upper Saddle River, NJ: Pearson Education Inc., 2009, pp. 408-416.

14. M. Fishbein and I. Azjen, *Belief, Attitude, Intention and Behavior: An Introduction to Theory and Research*, Reading, MA: Addison-Wesley, 1975.

15. J. M. Olson and M. P. Zanna, "Attitudes and Attitude Change," *Annual Review of Psychology*, Vol. 86, 1993, pp. 852-875.

16. Robert Boyd and Peter J. Richerson, *The Origin and Evolution of Cultures*, Oxford, UK: Oxford University Press, 2005.

17. Christine Horne, "Sociological Perspectives," in Michael Hechter and Karl-Dieter Opp, eds., *Social Norms*, New York: Russell Sage, 2001, pp. 3-34.

18. Everett Rogers, *The Diffusion of Innovations*, New York: Free Press, 1983.

19. Robert C. Ellickson, "The Evolution of Social Norms: A Perspective from the Legal Academy," in Michael Hechter and Karl-Dieter Opp, eds., *Social Norms*, New York: Russell Sage, 2001, pp. 35-75.

20. Michael Hechter and Karl-Dieter Opp, "Introduction," in Michael Hechter and Karl-Dieter Opp eds., *Social Norms*, New York: Russell Sage, pp. xi-xx.

21. Harold Demsetz, "Toward a Theory of Property Rights," *American Economic Review*, Vol. 57, No. 2, 1967, pp. 347-359.

22. Michael Losavio, Deborah Wilson, and Adel Elmaghraby, "Prevalence, Use and Evidentiary Issues of Digital Evidence of Cellular Telephone Consumer and Small Scale Digital Devices," *Journal of Digital Forensic Practice*, Vol. 1, December 2006, pp. 291-296.

23. *Ibid.*

24. *Ibid.*

25. Michael Losavio, Julia Adams, Marc Rogers, "Gap Analysis: Judicial Experience and Perception of Electronic Evidence," *Journal of Digital Forensic Practice*, Vol. 1, March 2006, pp. 13-18; Michael Losavio, Deborah Wilson, Adel Elmaghraby, "Implications of Attorney Experiences with Digital Forensics and Electronic Evidence in the United States," Third International Workshop on Systematic Approaches to Digital Forensic Engineering, Institute of Electrical and Electronic Engineers (IEEE), May 22, 2008, Berkeley, CA; Survey of digital forensics session attendees of the Kentucky Council on Crime and Delinquency, September 2008 (unpublished); Survey of attendees at federal defender training, New Orleans, LA, February 2008 (unpublished).

26. See Technical Working Group for Electronic Crime Scene Investigation, *Electronic Crime Scene Investigation: A Guide for First Responders*, Washington, DC: National Institute of Justice, July 2001.

27. Michael Losavio *et al.*, *The Key Asset Protection Partnership: Computer Security, Homeland Security and Community Engagement*, The American Community Preparedness Conference, Louisville, KY, May 12, 2004, p. 38.

28. Federal Information Processing Standards (FIPS) Publication 199, *Standards for Security Categorization of Federal Information*

and Information Systems, Gaithersburg, MD: National Institute of Standards and Technology, February 2004, as applied to the collateral impact of home system compromise on infrastructure.

29. *Ibid.,* p. ix.

30. M. Wilson, and J. Hash, *NIST Special Publication 800-50, Building An Information Technology Security Awareness and Training Program,* Gaithersburg, MD: National Institute of Standards and Technology, October 2003.

31. Available from *csrc.nist.gov/securebiz/index.html;* presentation of Dr. Alicia Clay of NIST to the Department of Computer Engineering and Computer Science, Speed School of Engineering, University of Louisville, March 2004.

32. R. Peterson, *Protecting Our Nation's Cyber Space: Educational Awareness for the Cyber Citizen,* Testimony before the Subcommittee on Technology, Information Policy, Intergovernmental Relations and the Census, Committee on Government Reform, United States House of Representatives, 2004, available from *www.educause.edu/ir/library/pdf/SEC0407.pdf.* In his remarks, Peterson notes that training is not sufficient; secure technology must be an objective of all software development.

33. Awareness and Outreach Task Force of the National Cyber Security Partnership, *2004 Task Force Report,* 2004, available from *www.educause.edu/ir/library/pdf/SEC0403.pdf.*

34. *CyberBlockWatch,* available from *www.speedacm.org/dhs.*

35. Available from *www.staysafeonline.info/.*

36. J. L. Linderman and W. T. Schiano, "Information Ethics in a Responsibility Vacuum," *The DATA BASE for Advances in Information Systems,* Vol. 32, No. 1, 2001, pp. 70-74.

37. P. J. Denning, "Who Are We?" *Communications of the ACM,* Vol. 44, No. 2, 2001, pp. 15-19.

38. M. Losavio, "Cybersecurity and Homeland Security," *Kentucky Bench and Bar,* Vol. 67, No. 6, 2003, pp. 36-38.

CHAPTER 7

THE ATTACK DYNAMICS OF POLITICAL AND RELIGIOUSLY MOTIVATED HACKERS

Thomas J. Holt

INTRODUCTION

There is a significant body of research focused on mitigating cyber attacks through technical solutions. Though these studies are critical to decrease the impact of various vulnerabilities and hacks, researchers still pay generally little attention to the affect that motivations play in the frequency, type, and severity of hacker activity. Economic gain and social status have been identified as critical drivers of computer hacker behavior in the past, but few have considered how nationalism and religious beliefs influence the activities of some hacker communities. Such attacks are, however, gaining prominence and pose a risk to critical infrastructure and web based resources. For example, a number of Turkish hackers engaged in high profile web defacements against Danish websites featuring a cartoon of the prophet Muhammad in 2005. In order to expand our understanding of religious and nationalist cyber attacks, this chapter will explore the active and emerging hacker community in the Muslim majority nation of Turkey. Using multiple qualitative data sets, including interviews with active hackers and posts from multiple web forums, the findings explore the nature of attacks, target selection, the role of peers in facilitating attacks, and justifications through the lens of religious and national pride. The results can benefit information security professionals, law enforcement, and the intelligence community by providing unique insights on the social dynamics driving hacker activity.

The growth and penetration of computer technology has dramatically shifted the ways that individuals communicate and do business around the world. The beneficial changes that have come from these technologies have also led to a host of threats posed by computer criminals generally, and hackers specifically. In fact, the number of computer security incidents reported to the U.S. Computer Emergency Response Team (CERT) has grown in tandem with the number of individuals connected to the Internet.[1] Data from CERTs around the world suggest that the number of computer attacks have increased significantly since 2001.[2] Computer attacks are also costly, as unauthorized access of computer systems cost U.S. businesses $20 million dollars in 2006 alone.[3]

Research from the social sciences has explored computer attackers and malware writers in an attempt to understand their reasons for engaging in malicious activity. Criminological examinations of hacker subculture found that computer hackers value profound and deep connections to technology, and judge others based on their capacity to utilize computers in unique and innovative ways.[4] Similar research on virus writers suggests they may share hackers' interests in technology, though they are driven by more malicious interests.[5]

A small body of research has also considered the motives that drive the hacker community.[6] The Honeynet Project argues that there are six key motivations in the hacker community: money, entertainment, ego, cause, entrance to a social group, and status. A number of studies have identified the significant financial gain that can be made by hacking databases to steal credit cards and financial information.[7] Additionally, a burgeoning market has developed around the sale of malicious software and stolen data, particularly in Eastern Europe and Russia.[8] Additionally, research on the enculturation process of hacker subculture has found that peer recognition is vital to gain status and recognition.[9]

Research on cause-based hacking has, however, increased in recent years as more countries become connected to the Internet. Mainstream and alternative political and social movements have grown to depend on the Internet to broadcast their ideologies across the world. Groups have employed a range of tactics depending on the severity of the perceived injustice or wrong that has been performed.[10] For example, the native peoples, called Zapatistas, in Chiapas, Mexico, used the Internet to post information and mobilize supporters to their cause against governmental repression.[11] Chinese hackers frequently engage in cyber attacks against government resources in the United States and other nations to obtain sensitive information and map network structures.[12] Finally, a massive online conflict developed between Russian and Estonian factions in April 2006 when the Estonian government removed a Russian war monument from a memorial garden.[13] This conflict became so large in scope that hackers were able to shut down critical components of Estonia's financial and government networks, causing significant economic harm to citizens and industry alike.[14]

Though there is a growing body of research considering hacking as a means to a political or patriotic end, few have considered the ways that religion affects hacker behavior. This is a particularly salient issue when considering the growing number of Muslim nations connecting to the Internet. The penetration of high speed Internet connectivity and computer technology in Muslim-majority nations is changing the landscape of the Internet, enabling political and religious expression and global exposure to various perspectives.

These benefits are, however, offset by the growth of hacker communities that are motivated by religious beliefs. For example, a Danish newspaper published a cartoon featuring the prophet Muhammad with a bomb in his turban in 2005.[15] This image was deemed offensive by the Muslim community, and the newspaper's website was defaced repeatedly, along with any other site that featured the cartoon.[16] Thousands of websites were hacked or defaced by Turkish hackers, who in turn received a great deal of attention by the press for their efforts.[17] As a consequence, Turkish hacker groups have become active participants in a range of attacks against various targets across the globe.[18]

In light of the potential threats and the under-examined nature of this problem, this chapter explores the ways that the specific motives of religion and nationalism affect hacker attitudes and activities. Using multiple qualitative data sets collected from active Turkish hackers, the findings consider how political and religious ideologies shape perceptions and justifications of hackers within this community.

DATA AND METHOD

The data for this chapter consists of two unique resources: a series of 10 in-depth interviews conducted via e-mail or instant messaging with prominent hackers in the Turkish community, and explorations of six websites operated by and for Turkish hackers.

The first data set consists of interviews that probe individuals' experiences and impressions of the Turkish hacker community on and offline. They were asked to describe their experiences with hacking, interactions with others in on and offline environments, and their direct opinions on the presence of a hacker subculture in Turkey.

Interviewees were identified and contacted through the use of two fieldworkers with significant status among Turkish hackers. Individuals who responded to the solicitation were sent a copy of the survey protocol, allowing the respondent to complete the instrument at their leisure. In addition, individuals were given the option to complete the instrument in either Turkish or English. Interviews completed in Turkish were transcribed from Turkish to English by a certified translator to ensure accurate and reliable data.

To gain more insight into the Turkish hacker community, ethnographic observations were conducted in six Turkish hacker web forums where the interviewees claimed to visit or post content on a regular basis. Participants in these forums interact with one another by posting on "threads" within the forum. Threads are textual conversations that are organized chronologically within the forum.[19] These posts are cultural artifacts that are amenable to analysis as they resemble a running conversation between participants.[20] These sites were also publicly accessible, in that anyone could access the forum content without the need to register with the site. This sort of publicly accessible web forum is common in online ethnographic research, as individuals who are unfamiliar with a certain form of behavior may be most likely to access a public forum first.[21] Specific web addresses and names of these sites are not provided to protect the anonymity of the users. The content of these sites were translated using machine translation programs to ensure accurate translation.

Both data sets were printed and analyzed by hand using the three-stage inductive analysis methodology derived from grounded theory.[22] This coding and analysis scheme is particularly useful as it permits the researcher to develop a thorough, well-integrated examination of any social phenomena. Any concepts found within the data must be identified multiple times through comparisons to identify any similarities.[23] In this way, findings are validated by their repeated appearances or absences in the data, ensuring they are derived and grounded in the data.

For this analysis, the techniques of hacking and significance of religion and national values were inductively derived from the repeated appearance of specific actions, rules, or ideas in the data. The value of these concepts is generated from positive or negative comments of the respondents. In turn, theoretical links between these concepts are derived from the data to highlight the value of nationalism, Islam, or other interests that structures the behavior of hackers. The findings are discussed using direct quotes from both data sets where appropriate.

FINDINGS

Knowledge Among Turkish Hackers.

To understand the Turkish hacker community, it is necessary to first consider how individuals relate to computer technology, and their peers. To that end, Turkish hackers suggested that their ability to target and engage in attacks depended on their knowledge of computers and networked systems. Those with a deeper understanding were able to engage in more successful and novel attacks than others.[24] Hackers across the data sets gained knowledge on computer systems in two ways: personal experience and through peer mentoring. The interviewees argued that learning through practice and trial and error are essential to increase knowledge of computer systems, in keeping with research on hacker communities around the globe.[25] For example, "Agd_Scorp" stated that he learned computer systems and hacking through "trial and error, and some documents on the Internet. But trial and error is the best method."[26] Similarly, "The Bekir" described gaining access to information online, but needed to expand his knowledge through firsthand experience: "In the beginning I looked at illustrated explanations on the web and acted accordingly, but they were not sufficient for me. I wanted to learn how this was done, how these were provided and I fiddled about with them a lot until they broke down."[27]

Several of the individuals interviewed also stated that they gained practical knowledge through direct and indirect assistance from others in the hacker community. Individuals could gain indirect assistance from their peers by accessing videos or documents posted in a number of outlets online. These materials provide detailed information on system processes, as well as step-by-step instructions on methods of hacking. For example, "Iscorpitx" made video tutorials on web defacements in order to help the community. He succinctly explained his reasons, stating: "In general, I like sharing the things I do after a while. A lot of videos I recorded while defacing online were very useful for a lot of people who are on the security side of this business. Of course, you can't be skilled and informed in every subject. Everybody needs help."[28] Similarly, "Axe" stated that his hacking activities began in earnest when he felt "it was the time to apply what I saw in the videos I watched."[29]

Forums are also an important resource for information since they act as repositories for information on computers and hacking. All of the forums in this sample had sections devoted to computer security, networking, and hacking, with distinct subsections centered on specific operating systems, programming languages, and tools. Thus, visiting a forum enabled an individual to learn on his own by reading the various materials posted. Forums also provide individuals with indirect assistance through tutorials written by skilled hackers that provide direct information on the process of engaging in attacks. For example, two of the forums in this sample had how-to guides on structured query language (SQL) injection and the process of defacing websites. Three others had detailed tutorials on how to perform cross-site scripting attacks against a variety of sites. These resources are written so as to inform other hackers, and provide clear advice to the larger population of hackers. Thus, myriad resources are available to facilitate indirect social learning in the Turkish community.

Direct interactions with others online are also important to the development of Turkish hackers. Only three interviewees suggested that they were directly taught how to hack by their peers, suggesting this is an infrequent practice among Turkish hackers. For example, "Blue Crown" described his introduction to hacking through a unique interaction:

I had some interest in hacking but I wasn't planning to get involved in this business. One day, an interview with a hacking group on television caught my attention. . . I turned on my computer and immediately started to browse. I met a hacker with a code name SheKkoLik in Ayyildiz Tim. I owe him/her a lot. . . I thought I couldn't do anything but s/he helped me and taught me a few things. I learned quickly thanks to the interest I had.[30]

Online discussions with other hackers were, however, very common and critical to provide useful information on technology and hacking. In fact, the majority of respondents suggested that they visited either forums or chatted with others using Microsoft (MSN) Instant Messaging. Forums enable individuals to connect with and ask questions of other hackers. When an individual asked a question, forum users would give web links that would help answer the question. These links provided specific information about an issue or topic discussed in the string without repetition or wasted time for the other posters. This would also encourage self-discovery as the user would have to actively open the link and read to find their answer. Some users would also provide brief instructions that would help to address the issue, though this could often encourage debate over the accuracy of the answer. In fact, "The Bekir" espoused the value of forums, stating: "There was a web forum, which was created by a very close friend of mine. I was in that forum for 2-3 years and it was quite nice . . . I learned a lot of things at that site and helped them to learn a lot of things as well."[31] This suggests knowledge is vital to facilitate attacks and develop skills within the Turkish hacker community.

Knowledge and Attack Methods.

The process of acquiring knowledge of computers and hacking has a critical impact on the types of attacks individuals perform. Those with greater skill could complete more sophisticated attacks. "Iscorpitx" succinctly described this issue, stating:

> If a hacker wants to harm a site where s/he has an obsession, s/he will. If s/he can't, s/he can get help. If s/he can't do anything, s/he can stop the publication of the website using a DDoS attack. But if s/he wants, s/he can cause harm. The ones who have enough knowledge and information can manage this; otherwise it is very difficult. The ones who don't have enough knowledge can't get help as well.[32]

This statement emphasizes the range of attacks that hackers can engage in. In fact, "Amon" was a very skilled hacker who indicated he could complete hacks related to "ASP, SQL union, update, Linux root, etc. It is easy to use if you know what you are doing. Of course, I generally use my own tools."[33]

The types of tools used also depend on the target and end goal of the hack. For example, "Crazy King" suggested that he and his colleagues:

> use a key logger and trojan in personal and special/private attacks. We use bots to overstrain the server and put it out of operation in transcendent systems ... They are the sources that we develop ourselves and belong to us.[34]

"Blue Crown" made a similar point, suggesting:

> When I'm going to perform a personal hack, I need an undetected keylogger or trojan. Some trojans

are subject to payment and some of them are free of charge. The only difference between these two trojan types is that trojans subject to payment are undetectable (they can't be caught). I can make a free of charge trojan "undetectable" by using some Crypt programs. Friends who develop the Crypter work for this. They usually use well-known and existing weak points/holes. If Turkish hackers find a hole/weak point, they share this after exploiting it.[35]

The notion that Turkish hackers use existing flaws and weaknesses is an important point due to the fact that the forums also provided access to a variety of resources and attack tools. Individuals could quickly and efficiently download a variety of malware, such as Turkojan. This tool is an efficient Turkish made trojan that is designed to "steal passwords, act as a remote viewing tool, and efficiently alter system processes."[36] Multiple versions of this tool were available, as were a variety of other programs, such as password sniffers, rats, virus code, and rootkits made by hackers in other countries. Thus, access to web forums coupled with a strong knowledge of computer technology enable Turkish hackers to engage in a variety of attacks against global targets.

Religion, Politics, and Hacking.

Turkish hackers across the data sets placed significant emphasis on using their knowledge to support "the mission." In this case, the mission referred to attacks against a variety of targets based on religious and national beliefs. The importance of a mission was evident across interviewees, and reflected these beliefs. For example, "Amon" suggested that "everything is for the mission. . . . Which other nation is as patriotic as Turks."[37] "Ghost 61" also described how the mission makes Turkish hackers unique relative to other communities: "everyone does this [hacking] for money and financial benefits, but Turkish hackers do it for the flag, for the homeland."[38] "Iscorpitx" also reflected on the range of interests and missions evident in the Turkish hacker community:

> Among Turkish hacker groups, we can count Islamic groups, revolutionist groups, groups with ideas supporting Ataturk, nationalist groups, etc. There are very talented and skilled young people. . . But these talents are very rare. They have much respect for their national and moral values.[39]

The forums also supported the notion of a military-style mission, as individuals regularly evoked nationalistic and religious symbols as part of their avatar, or personal image. Forum users across the sites used images of the Turkish flag as part of their avatar background, or featured pictures of the national soccer team players because of their pride in the team. Others' avatars used military images, such as soldiers carrying rifles, bombs, or missiles. Some used pictures of masked militants holding rifles or making threatening gestures with swords or knives.

The mission within the Turkish hacker community affects the nations targeted in their attacks. Several of the individuals interviewed argued that they target resources in countries that are perceived as threats to or enemies of Muslim nations. For example, "Ghost 61" stated "I determine it [targets] according to the agenda; usually they are countries like the USA, Israel, Russia, in other words, enemies of Muslims."[40] "Agd_Scorp" echoed this sentiment stating that he targeted those countries that "deliberately attacks Muslims . . . America is the country which killed the most Muslims in the world. And United Nations also killed many Muslims and innocent people."[41] In fact, "Blue Crown" noted that Danish websites were a particularly large target due to their portrayal of the prophet Mohammed in a disparaging cartoon. He indicated that "nearly HALF of the sites with the .dk extension were hacked by Turkish hackers in order to protest the disgusting and dreadful cartoons by Denmark."[42]

The types of sites Turkish hackers targeted were also impacted by the mission. Individuals actively attacked websites and resources that are perceived as either against Islamic religious precepts or actively harmed Turkish interests. For instance, "The Bekir" wrote that: "I determine my targets in terms of hits. I was working on hacking websites that were involved in terrorism; if the hacked website is big then it makes a greater splash, I'm usually working on hacking terrorism sites, etc."[43] "Blue Crown" suggested that he and his peers "hack PKK and pornographic sites."[44]

One of the most important and common forms of attacks used to support the mission are web defacements. This involves using an exploit or vulnerability to replace or remove a web page with a new image of the hackers' choosing.[45] Defacements enable hackers to post messages and images that indicate their perspectives and beliefs, as well as gain status by listing their name and group affiliation. To that end, the interviewee "Iscorpitx" held a world record for mass defacements and used this type of attack as a means to support his religious agenda. He actively selected sites that act in opposition to Islamic tenets, particularly "gambling sites, child pornography and disgusting pornography were always my targets. . . I think there's no other defacer who harmed sites in these sectors as much."[46]

The forums also had teams that operate in support of web defacements. One such forum had an "operations" section dedicated to discussions and listings of all the sites that the group's members have defaced. The titles of threads within this subforum clearly indicate the diverse range of targets defaced by Turkish hackers, and to a lesser extent, their connection to Islam:

- Threat to French Site
- Korean Yahoo Sites – "I have defaced a famous Korean site."
- The group has defaced 1,000 sites!
- Join our site and help deface
- Our martyrs have defaced many sites
- Deface Announcements
- We will eliminate the world (world wide web)
- Web sites hacked
- 20 web site templates hacked
- Adina Hotel hacked
- 20 Video Sites Hacked
- English Receiving Site Hacked
- USA Enterprises Hacked
- Buddhism and Satanism Sites Hacked.[47]

The importance of "the mission" also affects social organization practices among Turkish hackers. Though many individuals stated they hacked by themselves, they would work with others depending on the size and scope of the target. "Amon" emphasized this point, writing:

> They [Turkish hackers] form groups. It doesn't take long, it is done quickly. They do not team-up for a single website. Then somebody comes up and announces that he broke into a site...You check it and it is really broken... But then it becomes a team job, although a single person discovers it usually.[48]

"Crazy King" also elaborated on this point, writing:

> If popular events (like war) are the case, they come together as a team in order to harm the systems with country extensions. Individually they target large systems and work individually in order to leave protesting messages. They do this by telling their common actions to each other or with the documents they write in the forums or videos or texts. If there is a very important event involving the world and people, they can immediately come together.[49]

The forums also provided some important insights into organizational hierarchies. For example, one site established its leadership and attack command structure based on individual performance in a hacking challenge set up through their website. Individuals must progress through 13 missions, and their performance establishes how they will participate in the larger group. The missions include the following activities:

1. HTML code
2. SQL Injection
3. RC4 Encryption
4. Zip Crack
5. Page Redirect
6. PWL Crack
7. Secret Question
8. VB Script Encode
9. JS Password
10. Serv-U FTP
11. ICQ Dat Crack
12. Front Page
13. Carefully

All of the forums also provide a detailed command structure for their forums, composed of administrators who supervise and control the sites that house the forums, co-administrators who handle certain aspects of the site and forums, super-moderators who manage the entire web forum, and forum moderators who deal with content-specific subforums. This structure ensures easy operation and management, and establishes clear levels of respect and status that must be afforded to the management structure. One site even provided a flow chart to specify forum operations and dictate how complaints and suggestions move through the chain of command. Thus, religion and national pride clearly affect the actions, targets, and practices of Turkish hackers.

DISCUSSION AND CONCLUSION

This chapter sought to explore the impact of religious and political motives on the activities of the Turkish hacker community. The findings indicate that they place significant value on understanding computer technology because their level of knowledge impacts their ability to hack. Hackers could increase their understanding of computer systems by working with various technologies on their own, or by reading tutorials and watching videos posted online. Interacting with other hackers in forums is also important as these relationships can foster an individual's development as a hacker. In this way, the Turkish hacker community reflects the critical role of technology in structuring hacker and virus writer behavior across the globe.[50]

The interviewees and forum users also indicated that they were heavily influenced by their religious and national affiliations. In fact, the importance of Islam for the Turkish community cannot be understated as it provided a "mission" that must be completed. The types of attacks that Turkish hackers engaged in also appeared to encompass the entire spectrum of the global hacker community. Individuals used malware, SQL injection attacks, and web defacements in order to attack various resources. The scope of their attacks were, however, heavily focused on websites and resources in countries that are perceived to either slight the Muslim community, or Turkey specifically.

As a result, it may be that cause-driven hackers are apt to attack high value or visibility targets, rather than large populations of computer users and general resources. This is quite different from the practices of financially motivated hackers, such as in Russia and Romania.[51] As such, further comparative research is needed with a sample of hackers from a variety of Muslim-majority nations to understand the significance of political and religious ideology on hacker activity.

In addition, there may be some distinctive attack signatures that can be developed based on cause-driven attacks. The consistent recognition of "the mission" across the data sets, and the organizational hierarchies present in the forums and interviewee experiences suggest that the tactics employed by religious or politically motivated hackers may differ from those driven by other agendas. Thus, there may be value in developing baseline predictive models of attacker behavior using log files from actual incidents. Future research analyzing multiple real world attacks may be useful in developing technical solutions to mitigate attacks against critical infrastructure and computer resources. Yet there is a strong likelihood that the form and shape of hacker activity varies across countries and political ideologies. Thus, it is essential that researchers begin to focus on computer attackers in a global context to better understand the individuals that attempt to compromise computer systems.

ENDNOTES - CHAPTER 7

1. T. A. Longstaff, J. T. Ellis, S. V. Hernan, H. F. Lipson, R. D. McMillian, L. Hutz Pesante *et al.*, "Security of the Internet," in M. Dekker, ed., *The Froehlich/Kent Encyclopedia of Telecommunications,* Vol. 15, 1997, pp. 231-255.

2. T. J. Holt, "Examining a transnational problem: An analysis of computer crime victimization in eight countries from 1999 to 2001," *International Journal of Comparative and Applied Criminal Justice,* Vol. 27, 2003, pp. 199-220.

3. Computer Security Institute, "Computer Crime and Security Survey," 2007, available from *www.cybercrime.gov/FBI2007.pdf.*

4. T. J. Holt, "Subcultural evolution? Examining the influence of on- and off-line experiences on deviant subcultures," *Deviant Behavior,* Vol. 28, pp. 171-198, 2007; T. Jordan and P. Taylor, "A Sociology of Hackers," *The Sociological Review,* Vol. 40, pp. 757-80, 1998; P. A. Taylor, *Hackers: Crime in the Digital Sublime,* New York: Routledge, 1999; D. Thomas, *Hacker Culture,* Minneapolis: University of Minnesota Press, 2002.

5. A. Bissett and G. Shipton, "Some human dimensions of computer virus creation and infection," *International Journal of Human – Computer Studies,* Vol. 52, 2000, pp. 899-913; S. Gordon, "Virus Writers: The End of the Innocence?" 2000, available from *www.research.ibm.com/antivirus/SciPapers/VB2000SG.pdf;* S. Gordon and Q. Ma, *Convergence of Virus Writers and Hackers: Fact or Fantasy?* Cupertine, CA: Symantec, 2003.

6. A. Bissett and G. Shipton, "Some human dimensions of computer virus creation and infection"; Gordon, "Virus Writers"; The Honeynet Project, *Know Your Enemy: Learning About Security Threats,* 2nd Ed., Boston, MA: Addison-Wesley, 2004.

7. S. Furnell, *Cybercrime: Vandalizing the Information Society*, Boston, MA: Addison-Wesley, 2002; G. Newman and R. Clarke, *Superhighway robbery: Preventing e-commerce crime.* Cullompton, UK: Willan Press, 2003; L. James, *Phishing Exposed*, Rockland, MA: Syngress, 2005.

8. James, *Phishing Exposed*; Honeynet Research Alliance, "Profile: Automated Credit Card Fraud," *Know Your Enemy Paper* series, 2003; R. Thomas and J. Martin, "The underground economy: Priceless"; *login,* Vol. 31, pp. 7-16, 2006; T. J. Holt and E. Lampke, "Exploring stolen data markets online: Products and market forces," Criminal Justice Studies, Forthcoming.

9. Holt, "Subcultural evolution"; Jordan and Taylor, "A Sociology of Hackers"; Taylor, *Hackers;* Thomas, "Hacker Culture."

10. D. E. Denning, "Activism, hacktivism, and cyberterrorism: The Internet as a tool for influencing foreign policy," in J. Arquilla and D. Ronfeldt, eds., *Networks and Netwars: The Future of Terror, Crime, and Militancy,* Santa Monica, CA: RAND, 2001, pp. 239-288; T. Jordan and P. Taylor, *Hacktivism and Cyberwars: Rebels With a Cause,* New York: Routledge, 2004.

11. Denning, "Activism, hacktivism, and cyberterrorism"; R. Cere, "Digital counter-cultures and the nature of electronic social and political movements," Y. Jewkes, in *Dot.cons: Crime, deviance and identity on the Internet,* Portland, OR: Willan Publishing, 2003, pp. 147-163.

12. Denning, "Activism, hacktivism, and cyberterrorism"; S. W. Brenner, *Cyberthreats: The Emerging Fault Lines of the Nation State,* New York: Oxford University Press, 2008.

13. Brenner, *Cyberthreats;* G. Jaffe, "Gates Urges NATO Ministers To Defend Against Cyber Attacks," *The Wall Street Journal On-line,* June 15, 2006, available from *online.wsj.com/article/SB118190166163536578.html?mod=googlenews_wsj;* M. Landler and J. Markoff, "Digital Fears Emerge After Data Siege in Estonia," *The New York Times,* May 24, 2007, available from *www.nytimes.com/2007/05/29/technology/29estonia.html.*

14. Brenner, *Cyberthreats;* Landler and Markoff "Digital Fears Emerge After Data Siege in Estonia."

15. M. Ward, "Anti-cartoon protests go online," *BBC News,* February 8, 2006, available from *news.bbc.co.uk/2/hi/technology/4692518.stm.*

16. *Ibid.*

17. *Ibid;* D. Danchev, "Hundreds of Dutch web sites hacked by Islamic hackers," *ZDNet,* available from *blogs.zdnet.com/security/?p=1788.*

18. Danchev, "Hundreds of Dutch web sites hacked by Islamic hackers."

19. D. Mann and M. Sutton, "Netcrime: More Change in the Organization of Thieving," *British Journal of Criminology,* Vol. 38, pp. 201-29, 1998.

20. *Ibid.*; Holt, "Subcultural evolution."

21. Holt, "Subcultural evolution."

22. J. Corbin and A. Strauss, "Grounded Theory Research: Procedures, Canons, and Evaluative Criteria," *Qualitative Sociology,* Vol. 13, 1990, pp. 3-21.

23. *Ibid.*

24. Holt, "Subcultural evolution"; Jordan and Taylor, "A Sociology of Hackers"; Taylor, *Hackers: Crime in the Digital Sublime;* Thomas, *Hacker Culture.*

25. *Ibid.*

26. Agd-Scorp, Interview, personal email, August 8, 2008.

27. The Bekir, Interview, personal email, July 29, 2008.

28. Iscorpitx, Interview, personal email, July 30, 2008.

29. Axe, Interview, personal email, August 1, 2008.

30. Blue Crown, Interview, personal email, July 30, 2008.

31. The Bekir, Interview.

32. Iscorpitx, Interview.

33. Amon, Interview, personal email, August 10, 2008.

34. Crazy King, Interview, personal email, August 10, 2008.

35. Blue Crown, Interview.

36. Forum, address withheld.

37. Amon, Interview.

38. Ghost GI, Interview, personal emails, August 9, 2008.

39. Iscorpitx, Interview.

40. Ghost GI, Interview.

41. Agd-Scorp, Interview.

42. Blue Crown, Interview.

43. The Bekir, Interview.

44. Blue Crown, Interview.

45. James, *Phishing Exposed*; Brenner, *Cyberthreats*.

46. Iscorpitx, Interview.

47. Forum, address withheld.

48. Amon, Interview.

49 . Crazy King, Interview.

50. Holt, "Subcultural evolution"; Jordan and Taylor, "A Sociology of Hackers"; Taylor, *Hackers: Crime in the Digital Sublime;* Thomas, *Hacker Culture;* Gordon, "Virus Writers"; Gordon and Ma, *Convergence of Virus Writers and Hackers.*

51. James, *Phishing Exposed;* Honeynet, "Profile"; Thomas and Martin, "The underground economy"; Brenner, *Cyberthreats.*

PART III:

TECHNICAL ASPECTS

CHAPTER 8

RESILIENCE OF DATA CENTERS

Yehia H. Khalil*
Adel S. Elmaghraby*

INTRODUCTION

Data centers (DC) are the core of the national cyber infrastructure. With the incredible growth of critical data volumes in financial institutions, government organizations, and global companies, data centers are becoming larger and more distributed posing more challenges for operational continuity in the presence of experienced cyber attackers and occasional natural disasters. The need for resilience assessment emerged due to the gap in existing reliability, availability, and serviceability (RAS) measures. Resilience as an evaluation metric leads to better proactive perspective in system design and management. An illustration of the need for resilience evaluation and a survey of relevant research are presented.

Many organizations now depend on their ability to access their data for their daily operations. Despite the increased power of personal computers and departmental workstations, we notice an increased dependency on centralized data centers due to the needs for data integration, data consistency, and data quality. With the enormous growth of critical data volumes

* This work was partially funded by a grant from the U.S. Department of Treasury through a subcontract from the University of Kentucky. The opinions and conclusion in this paper are the sole responsibility of the authors.

for financial, global, institute, and governmental organizations, data centers have evolved to become the key nerve center of the operations of these organizations. A data center is a facility used for housing a large number of servers/workstations, data storages devices, communications equipment, and monitoring devices as shown in Figure 8.1. The complex architecture of a data center and the variety of data types hosted or processed in a data center complicates their design, planning, and management.[1]

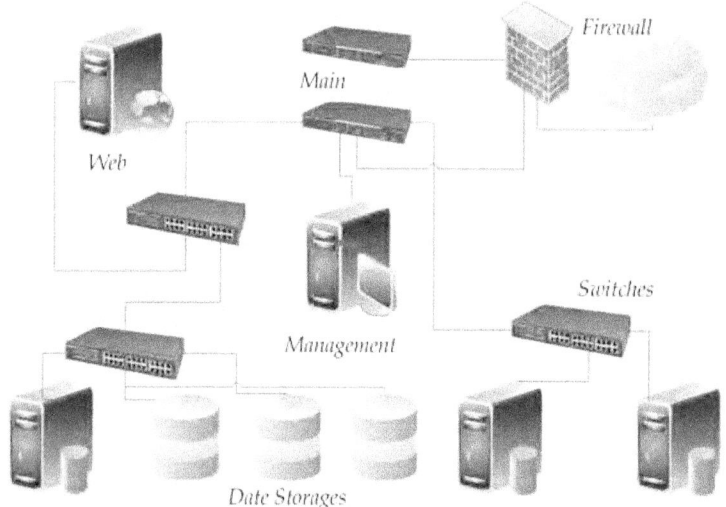

Figure 8.1. A Typical Data Center.

The fundamental purpose of any data center is to furnish application data access requirements; data center design must include operational requirements such as:
- Physically secure and safe location.
- Afford reliable and dependable power supply.
- Healthy environment to run these devices safely.

- Afford communications within the data center and with the outside world.

A well designed data center will have the following properties:
- Flexibility: The ability of a DC to support new applications, services, and hardware substitution without major technology compatibility problems.
- Availability: There is no room for risk with critical applications so a DC should be in a good running condition all the time and maintain a high service level without any unplanned shutdowns related to hardware failures.
- Scalability: Variations in the data volume should not affect the DC's quality of service.
- Security: It maintains different factors; physical, operational, communication network, data storage, and application security.
- Manageability: Simplicity makes it easier for technical support, administration staff, and for troubleshooting errors.[2]

In many scenarios, the data center is used as a standalone facility which is not always the case; data centers can play different roles for cyber legacy infrastructure. Data center sites can be classified as having one of three main roles:

1. Active Site: The main data center which processes all client requests and maintains local data backups.

2. Stand-by Site: This data center is ready to process client requests at any point of time if any request was redirected to it for load balancing. It is connected to the active site thought fiber optics to perform synchronous data replication and it is located within a small distance from the active site.

3. Disaster Recovery Site: It is located geographically far away from the active site for security reasons; it is not ready to process user clients while the active site is up; and it is connected to the active site to perform asynchronous data replication.[3]

In some scenarios, those roles can be combined based on system requirements and the need to implement designer goals and objectives as shown in Figure 8.2.

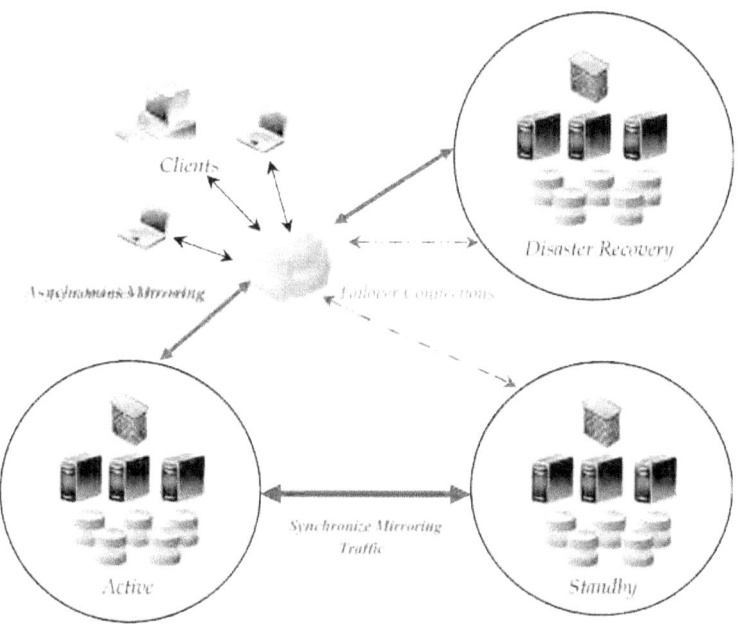

Figure 8.2 . Data Center Roles Summary.

To ensure the operational continuity of critical applications it is mandatory for the data center to provide satisfactory levels of data availability, integrity, and consistency. Yet the growing challenges that data centers face necessitate new methodologies and approaches to ensure data center operational continuity, and threats like natural and man-made disasters and industrial spying elevate the necessuty for extremely resilient data centers. Elements of rational data centers include computer networks, data storage, security, and data mirroring as shown on Figure 8.3.

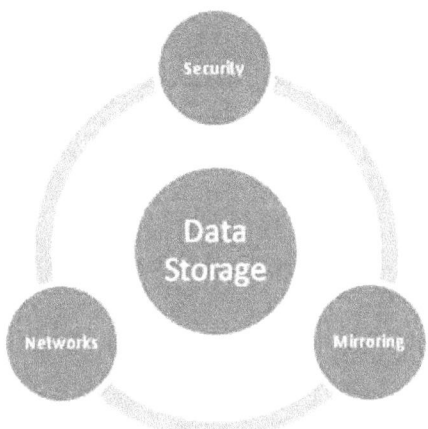

Figure 8.3. Data Center Rational Elements.

Cyber system infrastructure evaluation is a significant process toward systems enhancement and management. Conventional computer system evaluators intend to examine levels of RAS for their systems where:

- A reliable system does not deliver results that include uncorrected corrupted data, and it works to correct the corruption if applicable or shuts the system down.
- Availability is the uptime of device operating as the percentage of total time.
- Serviceability measures the ease to maintain, diagnose, and repair the system.

With new and emerging technologies, system complexity, data volumes, and new threats confirm the need for novel methodologies and approaches to assess of the resilience of data centers.

Resilience is the ability of a system to resist illegitimate activity and its ability to effect a speedy recovery as shown in Figure 8.4.[4] The main aspect is to show how the system will be affected by the variation of the operational environment circumstances. However, it is used quite differently in different fields, for example, computer network resilience is the ability of the network to provide and maintain an acceptable level of service under different fault or an abnormal conditions caused by cyber threats or any other threats. While in business, resilience is the ability of a company, resource, or structure to sustain the impact of a business interruption, recover, and resume its operations to continue to provide minimum services.

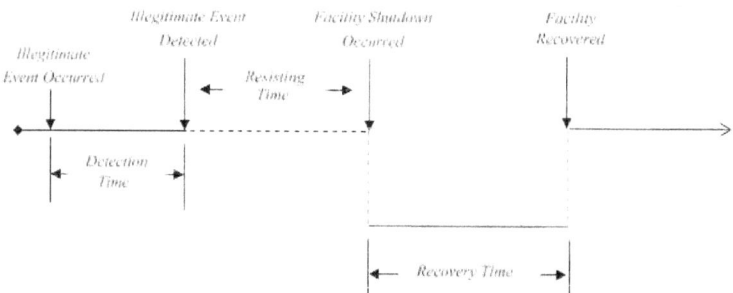

Figure 8.4. DC Facility Failure Process Summary.

The current data center metrics cover many of the concerns of data center designers and mangers, however there is still another set of concerns that lacks answers. All of the current metrics evaluate systems while they are operating or after a failure has occurred. A proactive metric is needed to evaluate a system during all of its stages: launched attacks, resisting/adaptation to attacks, failure and recovery time, and patterns.

STATE OF THE ART

Storage Research and Technologies.

Data storage is an integral part of the architecture of a data centers, over the years several storage solutions have been developed to satisfy applications requirements and demands.[5] Storage Area Networks (SAN) and Network Area Storage (NAS) are dominating data center storage alternatives.

NAS are data storage devices that are connected-directly to the network with their own IP addresses, while SANs are storage devices which are connected to each other and connected to a server or a group of servers which act as access points for clients.[6] Table 8.1 presents preliminary guidelines for a storage solution selecting process.

Criteria	SAN	NAS
Cost	Expensive	Inexpensive
Setup	Complicated	Straightforward
Management	Easy	Complicated for large environment
Environment size	Better for large	Better for small
Disk system compatibility	Any	Device orientated
Impact on network	None	Can swamp a network

Table 8.1. SAN vs. NAS Summary.

SAN setup costs are getting cheaper and with less complicated management, so the future of SAN is more promising for data centers which make it the focus of this work. Rationally, SAN solutions have two components: *storage servers and storage clients*. The physical elements of SANs are as shown in Figure 8.5:

1. *Disks* can be connected as point-to-point without an interconnection device or they can be a part of server-storage model. SANs are independent from disk types; disks, tapes, RAIDs, and file servers can be used.

2. *Servers* are fundamental elements of a SAN, which can be a mix of platforms and OS.

3. *Communications* are implemented by a fiber channel, where data loss rate is zero, and there is a high throughput rate.

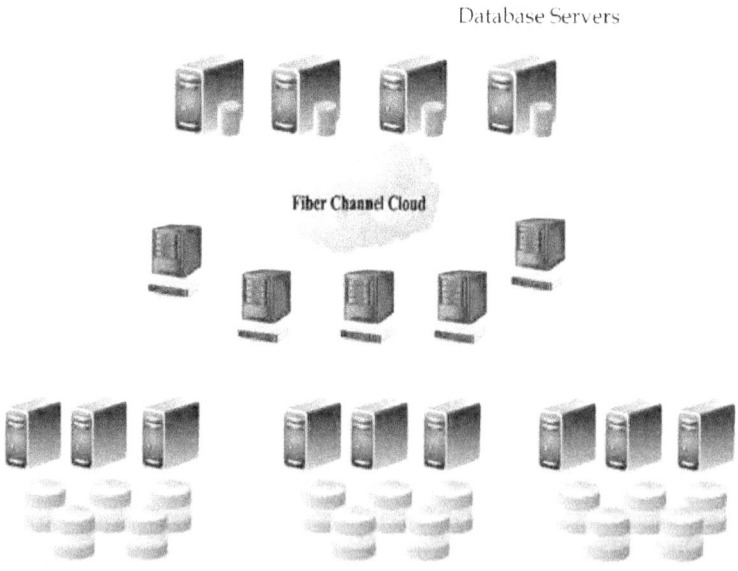

Figure 8.5. Elements of Storage Area Networks.

Regardless of which type of storage technology is used within data center, storage devices are required to: support data *Access; Protect; Store; Move; and Recover* with minimum cost (management and setup). Traditionally researchers and engineers utilized *Latency* as a performance metric, which naturally characterizes hard drive access time. Input/Output (I/O) issues are a critical aspect of any storage solution, the gap between the server processing rate and the I/O rate is large. SAN producers aim to overcome this limitation by improving Cache memory size and Caching algorithms. Yet, on the other hand, latency did not show how storage solutions protect & recover data, hence resilience metrics are required.

It is highly recommended designating between two categories of the data hosted in a data center:

1. *In use data:* which are accessed, modified and updated.

2. *In rest data:* which are not used at the moment and only stored to be used later or for recovery purposes.

Normally, "Data In Rest" is easier to protect and recover while "Data In Use" requires more effort. Data storage solution resilience evaluation results in the following concerns:

1. Availability of alternative routing paths within the fabric cloud.

2. Routing protocols' capability to utilize an alternative path with minimum cost (converging time and routing table size).

3. Optimum number of local disk images, backups to ensure fast recovery.

4. Data backup/ mirroring process frequency.

5. Mirroring approach impact on response time.

6. Protection techniques strength and overhead.

A resilient storage solution will not only provide the optimum answer for the concerns highlighted above, but will also tune them up jointly, to achieve the maximum resilience level.

Data Mirroring Techniques and Methodologies.

Data mirroring, data replication, and data backup are popular terms used in the context of data availability, consistency, and recovery. It is vital to differentiate their usage, limitation, and challenges to utilize them for a resilient data center.[7] By definition, *Data Backup* is the process of copying data (files/databases) into other data storage to be retrieved when needed in case of device failure. It is considered a regular process of system management and usually done overnight, which means a full working day's data may be lost in case of a device failure. For critical applications, this amount of lost data is unacceptable.[8]

Data Replication is the act of increasing the number of database servers which are available for clients, mainly for load balancing. Data replication can be done within or off the facility. For speedy recovery and critical data application, *Data Mirroring* is mandatory. Data mirroring is the copying of data from one location to a storage device or different location in real time. It is always a good idea to have the mirroring site a safe distance from the main site.[9]

For resilient data centers, in addition to data replication, data mirroring is mandatory. Data mirroring can be implemented as synchronous or asynchronous. In the case of synchronous mirroring, each transaction is sent to the mirror site and the clients do not get a response until the main site gets acknowledgment from the mirror site as shown in Figure 8.6. This approach affects the system performance and increases service response time.

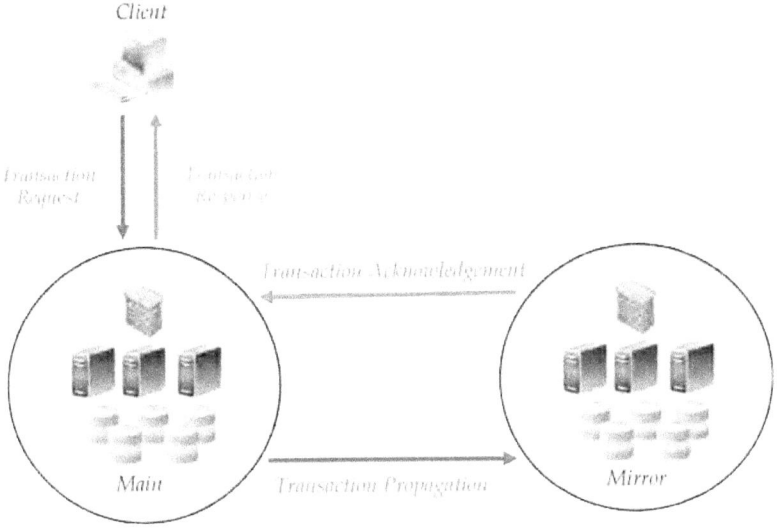

Figure 8.6. Synchronous Data Mirroring Process.

Also, data mirroring can be implemented as asynchronous where the main site receives the client's request, processes it, responds to the client, and then sends updates to the mirror site as shown in Figure 8.7. In this case, the mirror site will be a few transactions behind; but the system performance will not be affected.

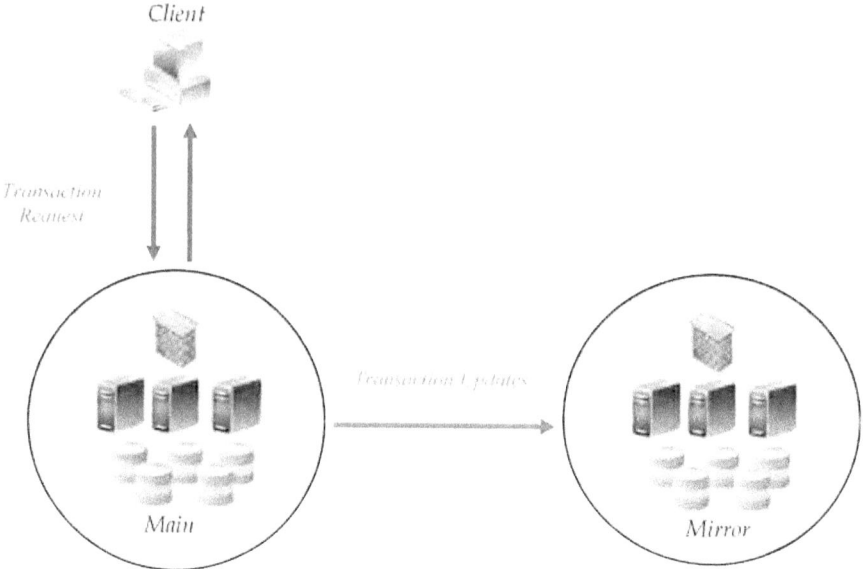

Figure 8.7. Asynchronous Data Mirroring Process.

Many database mirroring technologies are available on the market which require detailed investigation for the following aspects to simplify selection processes:

1. Supported Platforms: Multiple platforms provide more flexibility for data centers.

2. Change Check Capability: Current tools focus on only the net data change after the last mirroring process occurrence.

3. Computability Issues: Most of the current tools work as "plug-in" with no change required for database scheme and support several network topologies (server-server, hub-and-spokes).

4. Public Networks: New challenges for mirroring tools are raised when data are transmitted over public networks. These include: data security, TCP/IP vulnerability, and firewalls.

5. Scalability: Adding/removing sites is always needed regardless of how easy the reconfiguration process is.

For resilient data center systems, remote sites are mandatory which infuses the need for powerful mirroring tools over public networks/Internet where a "hand-shaking" process requires more effort. Also sequential data block transmission is not appropriate because of the public network/Internet nature. IBM Global Mirroring employs flash copy technology which permits data blocks to be partitioned into smaller portions by sending them to the mirror site, reassembling it, and writing it to the database.

Mirroring time is the time required to mirror data to the remote site while pause time is where the mirroring tool is inactive. For many mirroring tools, those parameters can be controlled either by direct or indirect ways. Figure 8.8 illustrates two scenarios that show how critical the tuning of those parameters can be in combination with the detection time of malicious activities for system resilience.

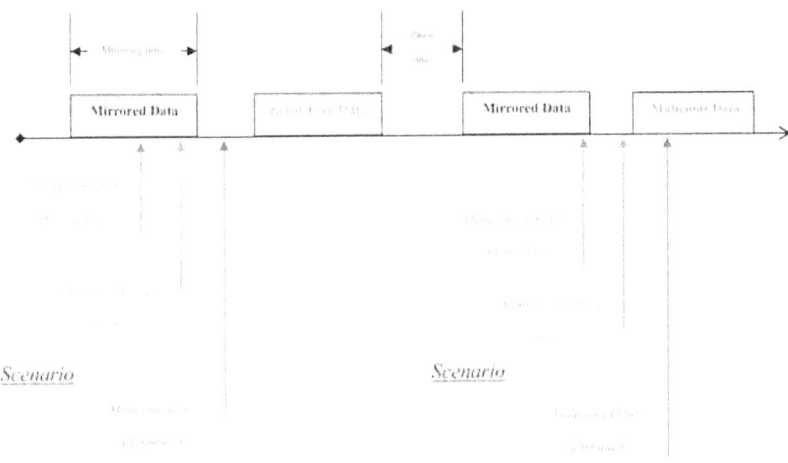

Figure 8.8. Data Mirroring Parameters and Attack Scenarios.

In scenario A, data mirroring parameters worked together with malicious activities detection time to ensure that the data sent to the mirror site were error free, while in scenario B the parameters were not correctly tuned, which resulted in sending malicious data to the mirror site. Mirroring corrupted data to the recovery site ruins the objectives of the recovery site and system resilience.

Network Connectivity Alternatives.

Network connectivity represents a significant portion of data center architecture, for Interconnection, Data Storage, Mirroring, and Public Access as shown in Figure 8.9. Also, computer network subelements (topologies, links, connecting devices, routing protocols and load balancing) are very critical aspects of computer network performance and resilience level.[10]

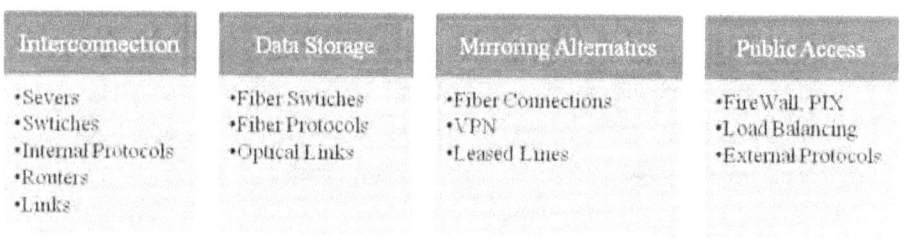

Figure 8.9. Data Center Network Roles Summary.

Resilience, Redundancy, and *Fault Tolerance* are widely used terms within computer network assessment and design context. For decades network designers and analysts used redundancy to improve network availability and reliability. It is essential to define each term. *Redundancy* is the process of installing extra equipment to overcome any node failure.

It requires having a plan and tools to direct traffic through the replacement node, thus redundancy cannot enhance network resilience by itself. The main idea of *Fault Tolerance* is to recognize how a node or device can fail and therefore take the necessary steps to prevent the failure. The definition of *Resilience* is the ability of a system to maintain any disturbance with minimum change on performance efficiency, and to effect a speedy recovery from any disturbance.

For critical applications and legacy systems, connectivity failure is an extremely hazardous situation because it revokes system integrity and operational continuity. In addition, the nature of connectivity failures is different than other computer system failures in the following aspects:

1. *Detection*: In some cases it is a complicated process. For instance, chronic failure detection is harder than sudden (crash) failure detection.

2. *Cascading Nature:* A simple failure can affect a large number of services or clients. In addition, this simple failure can overload other parts of the network, causing the system to crash resulting in more harm.

3. *Origin*: The same failure can be originated by many factors, for example, a node failure can be caused by power outage, software failure, or malicious activities.

Network resilience assessment comprises two main aspects:

1. Alternatives: It is very critical to have alternatives for network elements which are not limited only to redundant equipment but also include alternative traffic routing paths. The alternative paths must be reserved only for major failures and ensure *approximately* the same cost of original route in terms of laten-

cy and response time without causing other network parts failures.

2. Recovery Tools: Redundancy is mandatory for resilience, in addition to tools to employ those devices in timely manner; routing protocols (RP) and load balancing algorithms (LBA) are fundamental tools to ensure network resilience. The ability of RP to utilize alternative routing paths with minimum converging time is essential for a resilient network. The ability of LBA to detect failed/recovered servers in a minimum amount of time is a critical issue for network resilience.

Consider the following scenario; a system that is using LBA with less than optimal parameter tuning as shown in Figure 8.10. In the first case traffic is sent to the server while it is down, in the second case no traffic is sent to server after recovery. In both cases it offers poor resilience level for server failure and recovery.[11]

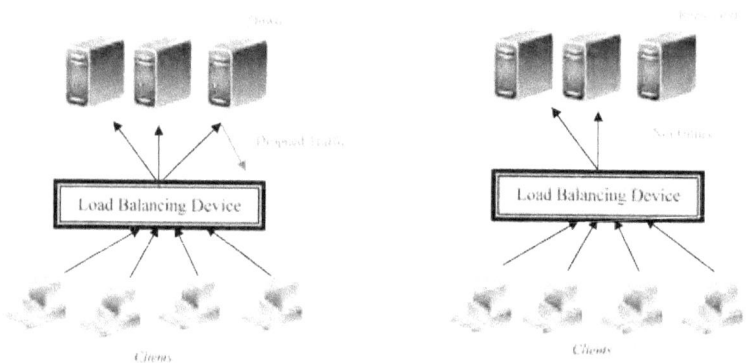

Case 1: Down Server undetected.   Case 2: Recovered Server undetected.

Figure 8.10. Load Balancing with a Poor Parameters Tuning Scenario.

One of the vital parameter routing protocols challenged by multiple failures of network parts, is the route cost. Consider traffic sent from point A to point B; assuming that main route R1=(x1, x2, x7) and the alternatives routes are R2=(x4, x5, x6) and R3=(x4, x3, x7) as shown in Figure 8.11. It is clear that x4 is common for both alternative routes which is not conventional particularly in the case of an x4 failure. Also alternative routing costs might lead to an overload of certain parts of the network causing even more failures.

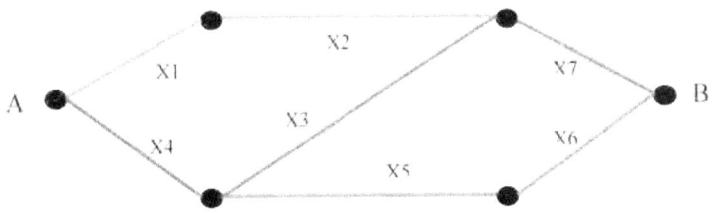

Figure 8.11. Routing Protocols Concerns Summary.

Security Challenges and Opportunities.

The fact that the data center is the core of any legacy system and it hosts large critical data volumes make it a target for all type of attacks, physical or cyber. Surveillance cam, high-tech doors, and other technologies improve the data center's physical security. However, on the other hand, data center cyber security is a much more challenging process.[12]

Potential network *Vulnerabilities, Threats, and Attacks* must be identified to minimize security concerns. System *Vulnerabilities* refer to weaknesses in the system that can be attacked, while *Threats* are the potential to cause damage to data center resources. *Attacks* are the actual use of system *Vulnerability* to put *Threats* into action. System hacking is a continuous process where hackers continue to discover system vulnerabilities to develop attacks as depicted in Figure 8.12.

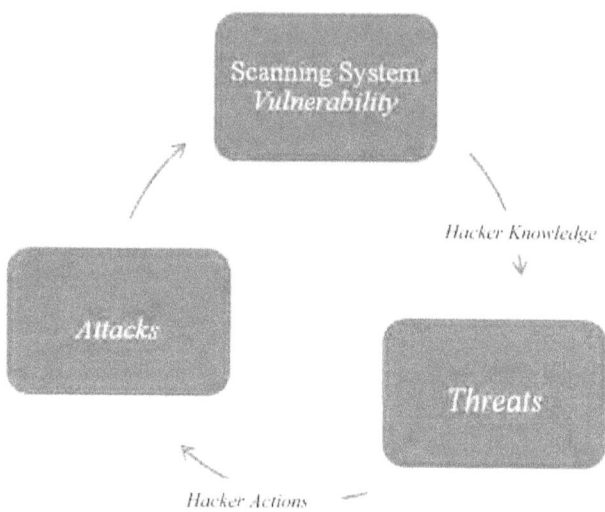

Figure 8.12. Developing Attacks Process.

Enumerating all possible data center vulnerabilities, threats, and attacks in an exact list is not feasible, yet they can be categorized as Table 8.2 shows.

Vulnerabilities	Threats	Attacks
Designing	Intrusion	Denial of Service (DoS) and Distributed DoS (DDoS)
Technologies	Spam	Un-authorized Access
Applications	Worm	Information Tampering
Database	Virus	Cross-site Scripting
Networks	Malware	IP Spoofing
Monitoring tools	Spyware	Insider Malicious Activities

Table 8.2. Vulnerabilities, Threats, and Attacks Categories Summary.

Even as the hacker is working hard to elude data center security, data center designers, venders, and security teams are working just as hard to ensure data center safety and security. Their efforts have produced many technologies such as firewalls, intrusion detection and prevention tools, DoS and DDoS detection and mitigation, access lists, and access restriction.

Data center security has three layers: (1) networks, (2) applications, and (3) databases. Figure 8.13 demonstrates the security mechanisms that are currently available.

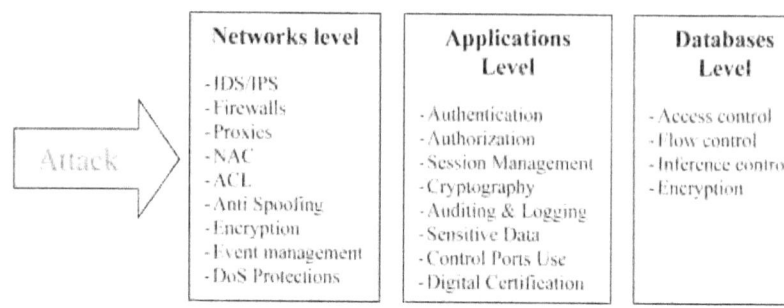

Networks level	Applications Level	Databases Level
- IDS/IPS - Firewalls - Proxies - NAC - ACL - Anti Spoofing - Encryption - Event management - DoS Protections	- Authentication - Authorization - Session Management - Cryptography - Auditing & Logging - Sensitive Data - Control Ports Use - Digital Certification	- Access control - Flow control - Inference control - Encryption

IDS: Intrusion Detection Systems
IPS: Intrusion Prevention Systems
NAC: Network Admission Control
ACL: Access Common List.

Figure 8.13. Security Layers Summary.

Security evaluation is done for different purposes:
1. Products, organization, application accreditation.
2. For the development and enhancement of security policies, methodologies, and technologies.

Researchers and system developers focus on the second perspective: Legacy system security assessment is a very complex process for many reasons:
- *Data Characteristics*: Each data type is targeted by certain hackers and attacks, as in the case of financial, military, and industrial data.
- *Data Status*: Data that is in an *Operation* mode is harder to protect, while data in a *Rest* mode requires less effort.
- *System Design*: Used for utilities, manufacturing companies. These systems will have two networks: business and control. This type of design increases system vulnerabilities and requires special arrangements to ensure network isolation.

For a resilient data center, security technologies and methodologies are expected to guarantee system functionality, information assurance, events management, and correlations. Consequently, security policies must ensure a speedy detection process and the ability to utilize system resources to mitigate attack effects.

CONCLUSION

The assessment process of cyber infrastructure security requires a number of metrics including performance, availability, and reliability. The rapid growth of data volumes, increased complexity of cyber infrastructure, and the heightened levels of threat highlight the gap in existing evaluation metrics. Increased awareness for a proactive approach addressing resilience in various systems including data centers demands a new evaluation approach. Resilience measurement of alternative data center designs assesses their ability to face man-made and natural disasters. Data center subsystems must be considered for a comprehensive resilience evaluation in addition to recovery plans and policies. The proposed resilience metric is proactive and assesses system behavior before, during, and after an attack.

ENDNOTES - CHAPTER 8

1. Mauricio Arregoces and Maurizio Portolani, *Data Center Fundamentals*, Cisco Press, 2004, available from *www.cisco.com/web/about/ac123/ac220/about_cisco_cisco_press_book_series.html*.

2. *Ibid.*

3. Kehia H. Khalil, Anup Kumar, and Adel Elmaghraby, "Design Considerations for Resilient Distributed Data Centers," ISCA 20th International Conference on Parallel and Distributed Computing Systems (PDCS), 2007, pp. 51-55.

4. The definition of resilience is available from *www.merriam-webster.com/*.

5. Richard L. Villars, "IBM Total Storage Software: Building Storage Solutions in Alignment with Current and Future Business Requirement," White paper sponsored by IBM, 2004.

6. Gary Orenstein, *IP Storage Networking: Straight to the Core*, Addison-Wesley, 2003, available from *www.pearsoned.co.uk/imprints/addison-wesley/*.

7. Jim´Enez-Peris, R. Pati, M. ~No-Mart´Inez, G. Alonso, and B. Kemme, *How to Select a Replication Protocol According to Scalability, Availability, and Communication Overhead*, The International Symposium on Reliable Distributed Systems (SRDS), New Orleans, LA: IEEE Computer Society Press, 2001, pp. 24–33.

8. Wang Changxu and Xu Rongsheng, "Analysis and Research of Data Backup System in Corporation," *Computer Applications and Software*, Vol. 25, No. 10, 2008, pp. 121–123.

9. M. Wiesmann, F. Pedone, A. Schiper, B. Kemme, and G. Alonso, "Understanding Replication in Databases and Distributed Systems," the 20th International Conference on Distributed Computing Systems, 2000, pp. 464-486.

10. Alberto Leon-Garcia, and Indra Widjaja, *Communication Networks: Fundamental Concepts and Key Architectures,* New York: McGraw-Hill Professional, 2004.

11. Yehia H. Khalil and Adel Elmaghraby, "Evaluating Server Load Balancing Algorithms For Data Center's Resilience Enhancement," New Orleans, LA: ISCA 21st International Conference on Parallel and Distributed Computing and Communication Systems, September 2008, pp. 111-116.

12. Merrill Warkentin and Rayford Vaughn, "Enterprise Information Systems Assurance and System Security: Managerial and Technical Issues," Idea Group Pub., 2006, available from *www.igi-global.com/.*

13. Shoukat Ali, Anthony A. Maciejewski, Howard Jay Siegel, and Jong-Kook Kim, "Measuring the Robustness of a Resource Allocation," *Transactions on Parallel And Distributed Systems*, 2004, Vol. 15, No. 7, New York: IEEE, pp. 630-641.

14. R. Jain, *The Art of Computer Systems Performance Analysis,* New York: John Wiley & Sons, 1991.

15. Denis Trček, *Managing Information Systems Security and Privacy*, Basel, Switzerland: Birkhäuser, 2006.

16. M. Castro, P. Druschel, A.-M. Kermarrec, and A. Rowstron, "A Large-scale and Decentralized Application-level Multicast Infrastructure," *Journal on Selected Areas in Communication* (JSAC), 2002, New York: IEEE, pp. 20-27.

17. Albert Greenberg, Parantap Lahiri, David A. Maltz, Parveen Patel, and Sudipta Sengupta, "Towards a Next Generation Data Center Architecture: Scalability and Commoditization," ACM workshop on programmable routers for extensible services of tomorrow, Seattle, WA, 2008, pp. 57-62.

CHAPTER 9

DEVELOPING HIGH FIDELITY SENSORS FOR INTRUSION ACTIVITY ON ENTERPRISE NETWORKS

Edward Wagner and Anup K. Ghosh

INTRODUCTION

Future success in cyber will require flexible security, which can respond to the dynamic nature of current and future threats. Much of our current defenses are based upon fixed defenses that attempt to protect internal assets against external threats. Appliances like firewalls and proxies positioned at network segment perimeters similar to the Maginot Line attempt to prevent outsiders from breaking in. There are other mechanisms such as Public Key Infrastructure and antivirus software, which also provide security. This added layer is referred to as a "Defense in Depth" methodology. However, in each component of our security architecture vulnerabilities are revealed over time. These defenses lack any agility. Our defenses must become agile and responsive.

In large-scale enterprise network defense, intrusions are detected by monitoring network flows from untrusted sources. Primarily, network intrusion detection systems examine traffic at Internet gateways, and then again at individual enterprise units or at enclave routers. Intrusions detected at lower organizational structures are detected then reported to higher reporting entities. The current approach to detecting intrusions suffers from two main problems: (1) intrusion sensors are placed in locations that do not allow high fidelity examination of intrusion behavior; and (2) intrusions are detected by comparing network traffic to known malicious intrusion patterns. In this chapter, we propose a supplemental method to correct for these two deficiencies. We propose high fidelity sensors in the form of virtualized applications on each user's machine to complement network-based sensors. In addition, we equip each user such that even as they are reporting intrusions, their machine and data is protected from the intrusions they are reporting. Our approach will protect users from broad classes of malicious code attacks, while being able to detect and report both known and unknown attack code.

One of the core strengths of our approach is that most attacks are realized at the endpoint. Attack code is often embedded and obfuscated in network traffic that often flies by network sensors unnoticed. When reaching a vulnerable host, the code is executed. Our contention is that the endpoint (host) is the best place to detect most attack codes because it is at this point that the behavior of the attack codes can be observed. Of course, once the attack code runs, it poses a high potential risk to the host and network, so we virtualize networked applications to protect the host from the attack code.

The user operating environment can remain on the existing infrastructure, but operate in a virtual workspace. Bringing virtual computing to the host will allow compartmentalization of the environment, wherein untrusted applications or applications that run untrusted content are partitioned from the trusted host itself. If the untrusted application environment is compromised, the underlying host will remain uncompromised. We also leverage sensor technology in the virtualized environment to detect illicit changes and then report these to a database. The environment is then "refreshed" removing any persistent presence of a threat. The environment can be configured and updated frequently, then copied and distributed en mass. Since the provisioning of the virtual environment is done centrally, changes to the environment can be easily identified and captured.

This new environment becomes agile and dynamic. It regains the initiative that the threat has taken and retained for over a decade. Malware can be stamped and collected as it appears. Malicious or compromised websites can be identified and blocked if desired, or monitored for intelligence purposes.

CURRENT ISSUES

According to the Center for Strategic and International Studies report on Cybersecurity prepared for President Barack Obama, potential adversaries have compromised and penetrated computer networks in the United States. These perpetrators have accessed and retrieved large quantities of information. In 2007, the compromises included the unclassified e-mail account of the Secretary of Defense and the exfiltration of terabytes of data from the Department of State. The report says that the loss of government data and intellectual property threatens our economic and national security.[1]

Given this threat environment, there are significant efforts to monitor networks. The current array of Intrusion Detection Systems (IDS) and Intrusion Prevention Systems (IPS) are dependant on the continual development of signatures to find threats operating within the network. IDS are devices that monitor network segments with a set of signatures to match ne-farious activity. An alert is created when a match is found. Analysts monitoring these systems must make a subjective decision whether or not to investigate the alert. Even if the information is correlated with other security devices such as firewall alerts in an Enterprise Security Management tool, the assessment of risk is imprecise. The IPS is different because it will drop the packets of the related session when the signatures match. The dropping of packets is the equivalent of disrupting the attack. This prevents the attack from being successful. While there has been continuous in-novation to improve the ability to identify threat activ-ity, this capability is limited by the signature's ability to know the method of attack.

The use of antivirus suffers from the same inherent limitations of a signature-based system. The volume of malware is frequently described as an antivirus prob-lem but, in fact it affects the entire system. According to multiple reports released in the beginning of 2008, the number of unique malware files is increasing at an alarming rate. One study said it found almost 5.5 mil-lion unique files, up from approximately 973,000 in the previous year.[2] The development of signatures cannot keep pace in a timely manner, neither can the ability to distribute, store, and analyze files on client hosts from these large databases. Thus, signature-based antivirus suffers from the temporal dynamics of rate of change of malware, the broad proliferation of malware, and the scalability of the distribution and storage of anti-virus signatures. Attacks will frequently elicit the as-sistance of users through an e-mail directing them to a website with malware. At other times, legitimate websites are unknowingly compromised. One study of 145,000 commonly visited Chinese websites found 2,149, or 1.49 percent, had malicious content."[3]

The development of signatures requires the investment of resources to analyze attacks to understand the
tactics, techniques, and procedures and then develop
corresponding signatures. The cycle typically begins
with actors identifying vulnerabilities, it next moves
to the development of exploit code where defenders
are continually seeking the formulation of mitigation
strategies to prevent attacks.

There are huge resources poured into the discovery of vulnerabilities. Those who seek information
on vulnerabilities are both network attackers and defenders alike. Sutton and Nagle describe the emerging
economic market of identifying vulnerabilities in their
paper to the Workshop on Economics of Information
Security, 2006 titled: "iDefense gains revenue by directly reselling the information, while TippingPoint
profits by offering exclusive protection against the
vulnerabilities they purchase via their intrusion detection system (IDS) product."[4] Frequently, observers
focus on the price paid as a result of cyber attacks, but
few recognize the transactions occurring to develop
signatures and other network defense measures versus the effort to exploit them.

Large organizations spend considerable resources
to maintain their IDS/IPS infrastructure and the corresponding signature base. Smaller organizations frequently outsource some of the effort through signature
subscription services. In order to support the development of signatures, there is a heavy dependence on
analytical work to find anomalies, collect malware,
reverse engineer them, and finally develop signatures.

Companies that provide this service do so in two
ways. Some companies provide a fee for service. They
rely on their own collection infrastructure to collect
malware traversing the Internet. They may use a network of "honeypots" to collect the malware. Once

collected they analyze the malware and develop a signature. These signatures and the associated threat warnings are then provided to their customers.

Other companies provide analytical support directly to organizations and rely on the collection infrastructure of the supported organization. Many organizations object to completely outsourcing their security services due to information disclosure concerns. The Department of Defense follows this example. The collection of information and resulting analysis is complex and laborious. Colonel Barry Hensley, Director of the Army Global Network Operations Security Center, described the growing demand for forensic analysis at the Army LandWarNet conference in 2008. He said, "People don't realize the forensics handling process involved with identifying malicious code. . . . It can take weeks or months."[5]

Consumers of signature support and services finds it difficult to measure the effectiveness of their purchase. There are many key questions for example: How many attacks were never detected because a signature was never developed? Were any of the signatures ignored by a poorly trained IDS analyst?

Victor Oppleman, Oliver Friedrichs, and Brett Watson further describe the breadth and width of the problem with IDS/IPS in *Extreme Exploits: Advanced Defenses Against Hardcore Hacks*. They identify three significant reasons for the problem: (1) "The granularity of the signature syntax," (2) "Whether the signature detects a specific exploitation of a vulnerability or the core vulnerability itself," and (3) "The author of the signature and the protocol knowledge he possesses."[6]

Some signatures are more effective than others. Some signatures will alert to real threats as well as other traffic, which is not actually an attack. Frequently this is referred to as a false positive rate. A more granular signature can frequently address this problem. Some signatures are written based on known exploit code, but there may be other exploit codes that attack the same vulnerability, but do not alert the same signature. Finally, the effectiveness of a signature can be a reflection of the skill and knowledge of its author.

The problems with IDS/IPS do not simply stem from the development and deployment of effective signatures. Potential attackers are constantly looking for ways to avoid detection. In "Insertion, Evasion, and Denial of Service: Eluding Network Intrusion Detection," Ptacek and Newsham provide three examples of how threats will attempt to elude IDS at the network (IP) and transport (TCP) layer. The three examples are "IP Checksum, IP TTL, and IP Fragmentation."[7]

In the IP Checksum example, the method data is verified when it travels across the Internet and can be manipulated to confuse an IDS/IPS. If the IDS/IPS does not conduct a checksum validation, it will accept data in an invalid packet, which would normally be dropped. This may result in fake data being used to throw off packet inspection.

The second method is when an IDS/IPS accepts a packet with an invalid Time-To-Live (TTL) value in the IP header. Normally the endpoint would drop the packets with an invalid value; however, the IDS/IPS placed at various points in the architecture may accept packets with an invalid value. The result is the complication of the data inspection process.

The third example of obfuscation is IP Fragmentation. Threats can cause an IDS/IPS to accept inserted or crafted fragmentation packets for inspection that would normally be discarded by the endpoint. In each of these examples, the threat is adding packets for inspection that are used to confuse the inspection of other packets used in an attack.

These examples are just three ways that threats can avoid detection by signature-based IDS/IPSs. There are many more, and the number of attack techniques are only limited by the imagination of the attacker. The limitations of signature-based IDS/IPSs described thus far do not consider the evolutionary nature of the attack themselves. The shift from targeting hosts with exploit codes to targeting users with phishing e-mails highlights the difficulty in detecting attacks.[8] The attacker may target individual users or large groups of users with malware attached to an e-mail message. The malware can compromise the host and initiate a communication request to an external host controlled by the attacker. This reverses the attack sequence that IDS/IPSs look for when an external host attacks an internal host.

If an attacker establishes an encrypted connection between his jump off point and the compromised friendly host, the traffic is never assessed. IDS and IPSs are not able to decrypt such traffic, no signature will cause an alert and the analyst is never able to assess the connection.

THE VIRTUAL ENVIRONMENT

Using the innovation of the Internet Cleanroom, developed previously at GMU,[9] the user can operate in a virtualized environment. This provides the first level of protection by isolating the user from the underlying host. Tools to monitor and collect information about threats operate in the separate host operating system (OS), which provides integrity to the collection of threat information. In signature based monitoring efforts, the volume of data is enormous and unmanageable. Since the virtual environment presents a known good, changes from that state can easily be identified and logged. This reduces the volume of monitoring data.

Figure 9.1 displays the architecture of the Internet Cleanroom. It shows the separation of OSs, which is the basis for the reliability of collected data. It also shows the ability to compartmentalize the user's environment.

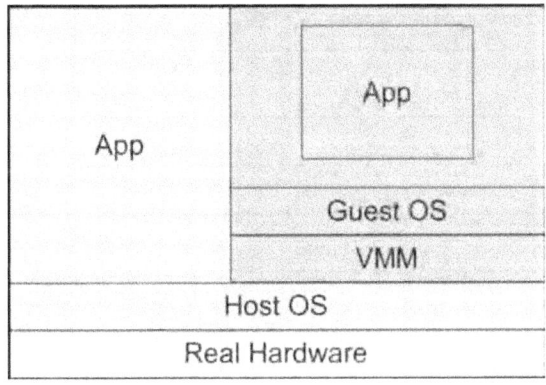

Figure 9.1. Internet Cleanroom Architecture.[10]

The collection architecture that is possible in this environment is displayed in Figure 9.2. Segmentation of the collection mechanism and user environments is achieved through the use of virtualization. Another benefit to collecting compromised URLs at the host is the easy identification of the host involved in the incident. Currently, the collection of data occurs at the network perimeter. The Domain Name Service (DNS) architecture begins below the collection point and the volume of name resolution prevents logging, therefore many hosts visiting known compromised websites cannot be identified. Even if the URL is identified and blocked a host possessing malware may operate on the network indefinitely without remediation.

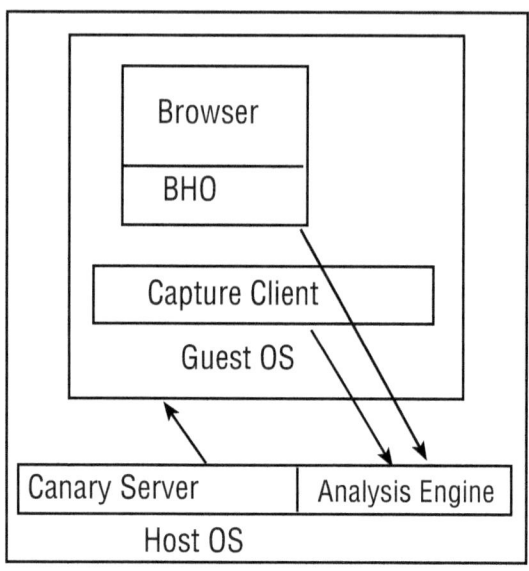

Figure 9.2. Collection Architecture.

The Internet Cleanroom is best deployed to coincide with an existing security architecture as shown in Figure 9.3. To maximize protection, monitoring at the enclave access points should continue. As noted before, the use of traditional IDS/IPS tools remain limited in their ability to detect new and sophisticated threats. Alternatives like extensive review of router logs and netflow can be very helpful. The integration of the Internet Cleanroom into the Security Information Manager architecture allows the correlation of host data from the Internet Cleanroom with network alerts from IDS/IPS. The combination of these two technologies brings more accurate alerts to the SIM analyst. In the past, information security professionals have desired to have access to full packet capture and host logs in near real time. However, the data storage requirements outweighed the usefulness of the data. Additionally, it overwhelms the analyst with too much data to review. The Internet Cleanroom's ability to gather specific information about threats as it is integrated into a SIM enables greater responsiveness for network defense.

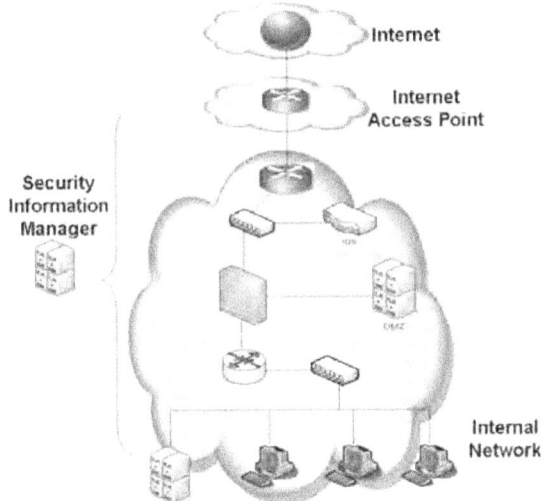

Figure 9.3. Security Architecture.

Making Granular Data Capture Meaningful.

The Internet Cleanroom addresses the capture problem by logging change data. Since the host is provisioned in a VM Client, changes can be easily logged and sent to a SIM via a syslog. Though the number of host remains large, smart data capture makes this type of collection feasible.

Figure 9.4 shows the analyst's view of summary information for hosts including infections that were downloaded and infected websites. The infected websites information provides actionable information in a more timely manner. This information can be provided immediately to any program to block access to those websites.

Figure 9.4. Analyst's Report View.

While the bad URLs remain of interest, the MD5 Hash of any malware downloaded by the host is of great interest to the defenders of the network. To gather this information typically requires a forensic collection on an individual host. This is a manual and time intensive process. However, much of this collection can now be automated in the Internet Cleanroom.

As noted in Figure 9.5, the Internet Cleanroom is able to automate the collection of MD5 Hash of malware and that information is immediately available to the analyst. Instead of the lengthy analysis of forensic media to collect this information, it can be obtained as it happens. If shared with scanning tools, which search for malware by MD5 Hash, network defenders can be more responsive in their ability to identify infected hosts.

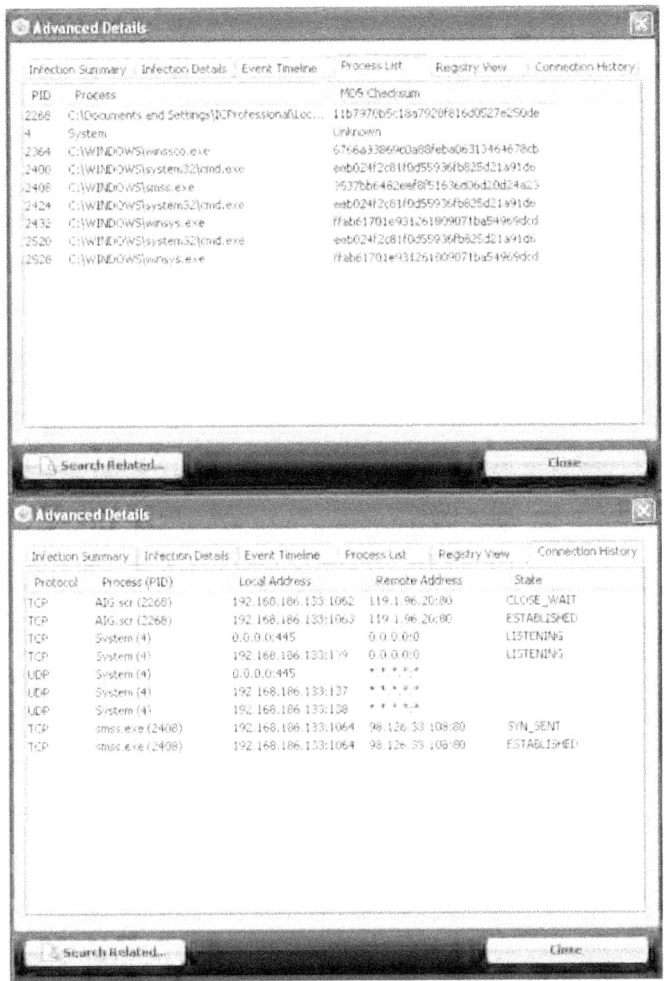

Figure 9.5. MD5 Hash of Malware.

The discovery of malware in near real time can assist in the recognition of new threat trends. Adjustments to perimeter defenses can be made before the loss of the initiative. This type of dynamic defense changes the static intransient defense that has been unable to respond in time to developing threats.

CONCLUSIONS

Current defenses largely rely on signature-based mechanisms in the network or on the host to detect attacks. These techniques have become largely ineffective as the proliferation of malicious software shows. The primary reason for their ineffectiveness is because malware changes its signatures faster than the mechanisms have been developed to capture malware, and then create and distribute those signatures. In addition, we argue that network-based sensors are not adequate for detecting threats against networks. To address these deficiencies, we propose that the enterprise computer network defense architecture should include a virtualized application solution that: (a) protects users from unknown future infections (signature-free defenses), and (b) provides detecting and reporting of unauthorized system changes to a collection database.

The most obvious example of our proposed approach is a virtualized browser that users employ just as they use their native browser. The proposed virtualized browser, Internet Cleanroom, protects the user from malicious web content, while also monitoring the virtual OS for any unauthorized changes that may occur as a result of browsing. The virtualized architecture effectively partitions untrusted applications and content from the underlying operating system and other applications. Any unauthorized changes are noted, then the virtual OS is discarded, and a pristine environment restored, all without any virtualization expertise required. The proposed approach provides high-fidelity detection of malicious code threats that can be later analyzed in forensic detail, while also protecting the user from currently unknown threats.

ENDNOTES - CHAPTER 9

1. Co-Chairs, Representative James R. Langevin, Representative Michael T. McCaul, Scott Charney, Lieutenant General (USAF, Ret.) Harry Raduege, and Project Director James A. Lewis, "Securing Cyberspace for the 44th Presidency," Washington, DC: Center for Strategic and International Studies, December 2008.

2. T. Wilson, "Malware Quietly Reaching Epidemic Levels: New Reports Say Malware Increased by a Factor of Five to 10 in 2007," *Dark Reading*, January 16, 2008, available from *www.darkreading. com/security/vulnerabilities/showArticle.jhtml?articleID=208803810.*

3. Jianwei Zhuge, Thorsten Holz, Chengyu Song, Jinpeng Guo, Xinhui Han, and Wei Zou, "Studying Malicious Websites and the Underground Economy on the Chinese Web," Workshop on the Economics of Information Security, WEIS, 2008, available from *weis2008.econinfosec.org/papers/Holz.pdf.*

4. Michael Sutton and Frank Nagle, "Emerging Economic Models for Vulnerability Research," Workshop on the Economics of Information Security, WEIS, 2006, available from *weis2006. econinfosec.org/docs/17.pdf.*

5. Wyatt Kash, "Army cyber ops faces forensic backlog," *Government Computer News (GCN)*, August 20, 2008, available from *www.gcn.com/online/vol1_no1/46946-1.html.*

6. Victor Oppleman, Oliver Friedrichs, and Brett Watson, "Chapter 7, Intrusion Detection and Prevention," *Extreme Exploits: Advanced Defenses Against Hardcore Hacks*, Emeryville, CA: McGraw-Hill/Osborne, 2005, available from *common.books24x7. com/book/id_11979/book.asp.*

7. Thomas H. Ptacek and Timothy N. Newsham, "Insertion, Evasion, and Denial of Service: Eluding Network Intrusion Detection," available from *insecure.org/stf/secnet_ids/secnet_ids.html.*

8. "Chapter XII, Deception in Cyber Attacks," in Lech J. Janczewski and Andrew M. Colarik, eds., *Cyber Warfare and Cyber Terrorism*, Hershey, PA: IGI Publishing, 2008, available from *common.books24x7.com/book/id_20791/book.asp.*

9. Wang Jiang, Anup K. Ghosh, and Huang Yih, "Internet Cleanroom: A System to Use On-Demand Virtualization to Enhance Client-Side Security," Washington, DC: Center for Secure Information Systems (CSIS), George Mason University, June 6, 2008.

10. Wang Jiang, Anup K. Ghosh, and Huang Yih, "Web Canaries: a Large-scale Distributed Sensor for Detecting Malicious Web Sites via a Virtualized Web Browser," Washington, DC: Center for Secure Information Systems (CSIS), George Mason University, November 2008, p. 6, available from *CollaborateCom.org/2008/program.php.*

CHAPTER 10

VOICE OVER IP:
RISKS, THREATS, AND VULNERABILITIES*

Angelos D. Keromytis

INTRODUCTION

Voice over Internet Protocol (VoIP) and Internet Multimedia Subsystem (IMS) technologies are rapidly being adopted by consumers, enterprises, governments, and militaries. These technologies offer higher flexibility and more features than the traditional public-switched telephone network (PSTN) infrastructure, as well as the potential for lower cost through equipment consolidation and, for the consumer market, new business models. However, VoIP/IMS systems also represent a higher complexity in terms of architecture, protocols, and implementation, with a corresponding increase in the potential for misuse. Here, we begin to examine the current state of affairs on VoIP/IMS security through a survey of known/disclosed security vulnerabilities in bug-tracking databases. This chapter should serve as a starting point for understanding the threats and risks in a rapidly evolving set of technologies that are more frequently being deployed and used. Our goal is to gain a better understanding of the security landscape, with respect to VOIP/IMS, to encourage future research toward this and other similar emerging technologies.

The rate at which new technologies are being introduced and adopted by society has been steadily

*This work was supported by the French National Research Agency (ANR) under Contract ANR-08-VERS-017.

accelerating throughout human history. The advent of pervasive computing and telecommunications has reinforced this trend. In this environment of constant innovation, individuals, governments, and organizations have been struggling to manage the tension between reaping the benefits of new technologies while understanding and managing their risks. In this struggle, cost reductions, convenience, and new features typically overcome security concerns. As a result, security experts (but also the government and courts of law) are often left with the task of playing "catch up" with those who exploit flaws to further their own goals. This is the situation we find ourselves in with respect to one popular class of technologies collectively referred to as VoIP. VoIP, sometimes also referred to as Internet Multimedia Subsystem (IMS), refers to a class of products that enable advanced communication services over data networks. While voice is a key aspect in such products, video and other capabilities (e.g., collaborative editing, whiteboard file sharing, and calendaring) are all supported. The key advantages of VoIP/IMS are flexibility and low cost. The former derives from the generally open architectures and software-based implementation, while the latter is due to new business models, equipment, network-link consolidation, and ubiquitous consumer-grade broadband connectivity. Due to these benefits, VoIP has experienced a rapid uptake in both the enterprise and consumer markets. An increasing number of enterprises are replacing their internal phone switches with VoIP-based systems, both to introduce new features and to eliminate redundant equipment. Consumers have embraced a host of technologies with different features and costs, including Peer to Peer (P2P) calling, Internet-to-phone network bridging, and wireless VoIP. These new technologies and business models are being promoted by a new generation of startup companies that are challenging the traditional status quo in telephony and personal telecommunications. As a result, a number of PSTN providers have already completed or are in the process of transitioning from circuit-switched networks to VoIP-friendly packet-switched backbones. Finally, as the commercial and consumer sectors go, so do governments and militaries due to cost reduction concerns and the general dependence on Commercial-off-the-Shelf (COTS) equipment for the majority of their computing needs. However, higher complexity is often the price we pay for more flexibility. In the case of VoIP/IMS technologies, a number of factors contribute to architectural, protocol, implementation, and operational complexity.

The number and complexity of the various features integrated in a product are perhaps the single largest source of complexity. For example, voice and video transmission typically allow for a variety of codecs which may be used in almost-arbitrary combinations. Since one of the biggest selling points for VoIP/IMS is feature-richness and the desire to unify personal communications under the same umbrella, this is a particularly pertinent concern.

Openness and modularity, generally considered desirable traits, allow for a number of independent implementations and products. Each of these comes with its own parameters and design choices. Interoperability concerns and customer feedback then lead to an ever-growing baseline of supported features for all products. A compounding factor to increasing complexity for much of the open VoIP is the "design-by-committee" syndrome, which typically leads to larger, more inclusive specifications than would otherwise be the case (e.g., in a closed, proprietary environment such as the wire line telephony network from 20 years ago).

Because VoIP systems are envisioned to operate in a variety of environments, business settings, and network conditions, they must offer considerable configurability, which in turn leads to high complexity. Of particular concern are unforeseen feature interactions and other emergent properties. Finally, VoIPs are generally meant to work over a public data network (e.g., the Internet), or an enterprise/operator network that uses the same underlying technology. As a result, there is a substantial amount of non-VoIP infrastructure that is critical for the correct operation of the system, including such protocols/services as Dynamic Host Configuration Protocol (DHCP),[1] Domain Name System (DNS),[2] Trivial File Transfer Protocol/Bootstrap Protocol (TFTP/BOOTP),[3] Network Address Translation ([NAT],[4] and NAT traversal protocols such as Simple Traversal of UDP through NATs [STUN]),[5] Network Time Protocol (NTP),[6] Simple Network Management Protocol (SNMP),[7] routing the web (HTTP,[8] LS/SSL,[9] etc.), and many others. As we shall see, even a "perfectly secure" VoIP system can be compromised by subverting elements of this infrastructure. Because of this complexity, which manifests itself both in terms of configuration options and size of the code base for VoIP implementations, VoIP systems represent a very large attack surface. Thus, one should expect to encounter, over time, security problems arising from design flaws (e.g., exploitable protocol weaknesses), undesirable feature interactions (e.g., combinations of components that make new attacks possible or existing/known attacks easier), unforeseen dependencies (e.g., compromise paths through seemingly unrelated protocols), weak configurations, and, not least, implementation flaws. In this chapter, we attempt a first effort at mapping out the space of VoIP threats and risks by conducting a survey of the "actually seen" vulnerabilities and attacks, as reported by the popular press and by bug-tracking databases. Our work is by necessity evolutionary in nature, and this chapter represents a current (and limited) snapshot of the complete space. Nonetheless, we believe that it will serve as a valuable starting point for understanding the bigger problem and as a basis for a more comprehensive analysis in the future.

Chapter Organization.

The remainder of this chapter is organized as follows. The second section contains a brief over view of two major VoIP technologies, Session Initiation Protocol (SIP) and Unlicensed Mobile Access (UMA). While we refer to other VoIP/IMS systems throughout the discussion, we focus on the specific two technologies as they are representative, widely used, and well-documented. We discuss VoIP threats in the third section, placing known attacks against VoIP systems within the taxonomy proposed by the VoIP Security Alliance. We analyze our findings in the fourth section. In the final section, we conclude with some preliminary thoughts on the current state of VoIP security, and on possible future directions for security research and practices.

VOIP TECHNOLOGIES OVERVIEW

In their simplest form, VoIP technologies enable two (or more) devices to transmit and receive real-time audio traffic that allows their respective users to communicate. In general, VoIP architectures are partitioned in two main components: signaling and media transfer. Signaling covers both abstract notions, such as endpoint naming and addressing, and concrete protocol functions such as parameter negotiation, access control, billing, proxying, and NAT traversal.

Depending on the architecture, quality of service (QoS) and device configuration/management may also be part of the signaling protocol (or protocol family). The media transfer aspect of VoIP systems generally includes a comparatively simpler protocol for encapsulating data, with support for multiple codecs and (often, but not always) content security. A commonly used media transfer protocol is Real-time Transport Protocol (RTP),[10] with a version supporting encryption and integrity, Secure Real-time Transport Protocol (SRTP),[11] defined but not yet widely used. The RTP protocol family also includes RTP Control Protocol (RTCP), which is used to control certain RTP parameters between communicating endpoints. However, a variety of other features are also generally desired by users and offered by providers as a means for differentiation by competing technologies and services, such as video, integration with calendaring, file sharing, and bridging to other networks (e.g., to the "regular" telephony network). Furthermore, a number of different decisions may be made when designing a VoIP system, reflecting different requirements and approaches to addressing, billing, mobility, security and access control, usability, and other issues. Consequently, there exists a variety of differ-ent VoIP/IP Multimedia Subsystem (IMS) protocols and architectures. For concreteness, we will focus our attention on a popular and widely deployed technol-ogy: the Session Initiation Protocol (SIP).[12] We will also discuss the UMA architecture,[13] as a different ap-proach to VoIP that is gaining traction among wireless telephony operators. In the rest of this section, we give a high-level overview of SIP and UMA, followed by a brief description of the salient points of a few other popular VoIP systems, such as H.323 and Skype. We will refer back to this overview in the third section of this chapter when we provide a discussion of the the threat and specific vulnerabilities.

Session Initiation Protocol (SIP).

SIP is a protocol standardized by the Internet Engi-neering Task Force (IETF) and is designed to support the setup of bidirectional communication sessions in-cluding, but not limited to, VoIP calls. It is similar in some ways to HTTP in that it is text-based, has a re-quest-response structure, and even uses a mechanism based on the HTTP Digest Authentication[14] for user authentication. However, it is an inherently stateful protocol that supports interaction with multiple net-work components (e.g., middle boxes such as PSTN bridges). While its finite state machine is seemingly simple, in practice it has become quite large and com-plicated, an observation supported by the fact that the main SIP Requests for Comments (RFC) [15] is one of the longest ever defined. SIP can operate over a number of transport protocols, including Tranmission Control Protocol (TCP),[16] User Datagram Protocol (UDP),[17] and Stream Control Transmission Protocol (SCTP).[18] UDP is generally the preferred method due to simplicity and performance, although TCP has the advantage of supporting Transport Layer Security (TLS) protection of call setup. However, recent work on Datagram TLS (DTLS)[19] may render this irrelevant. SCTP, on the other hand, offers several advantages over both TCP and UDP, including Denial of Service (DoS) resistance,[20] multi-homing and mobility support, and logical connection multiplexing over a single channel. In the SIP architecture, the main entities are endpoints (whether soft phones or physical devices), a proxy server, a registrar, a redirect server, and a location server. Figure 10.1 shows a high-level view of the SIP entity interactions.

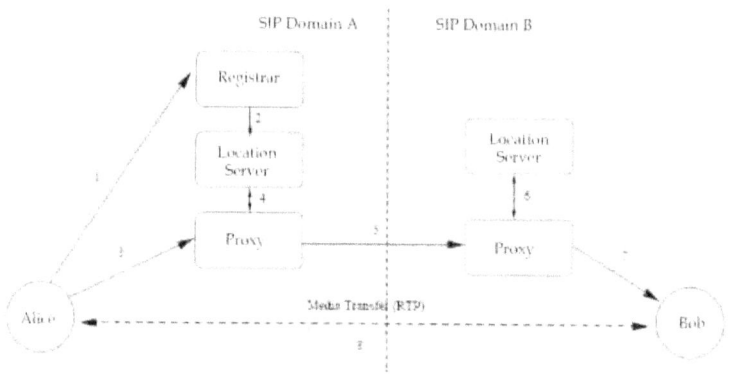

Figure 10.1. Session Initiation Protocol (SIP) Entity Interactions.

The User, Alice, registers with her domain's Registrar (1), which stores the information in the Location Server (2). When placing a call, Alice contacts her Local Proxy Server (3), which may consult the Location Server (4). A call may be forwarded to another Proxy

Server (5), which will consult its domain Location Server (6) before forwarding the call to the final recipient. After the SIP negotiation terminates, RTP is used directly between Alice and Bob to transfer media content. For simplicity, this diagram does not show the possible interaction between Alice and a Redirection Server (which would, in turn, interact with the Location Server). The registrar, proxy, and redirect servers may be combined, or they may be separate entities operated independently. Endpoints communicate with a registrar to indicate their presence. This information is stored in the location server. A user may be registered via multiple endpoints simultaneously. During call setup, the endpoint communicates with the proxy which uses the location server to determine where the call should be routed. This may be another endpoint in the same network (e.g., within the same enterprise), or another proxy server in another network. Alternatively, endpoints may use a redirect server to directly determine where a call should be directed and, redirect servers consult with the location server in the same way that proxy servers operate during call setup.

Once an end-to-end channel has been established (through one or more proxies) between the two endpoints, SIP negotiates the actual session parameters (such as the codecs, RTP ports, etc.) using the Session Description Protocol (SDP).[21] Figure 10.2 shows the message exchanges during a two-party call setup. Alice sends an INVITE message to the proxy server, optionally containing session parameter information encoded within SDP. The proxy forwards this message directly to Bob, if Alice and Bob are users of the same domain. If Bob is registered in a different domain, the message will be relayed to Bob's proxy, and from there to Bob. Note that the message may be forwarded to multiple endpoints if Bob is registered from multiple locations. While these are ringing (or otherwise indicating that a call setup is being requested), RINGING messages are sent back to Alice. Once the call has been accepted, an OK message is sent to Alice containing Bob's preferred parameters encoded within SDP. Alice responds with an ACK message. Alice's session parameter preferences may be encoded in the INVITE or the ACK message. (See Figure 10.2.)

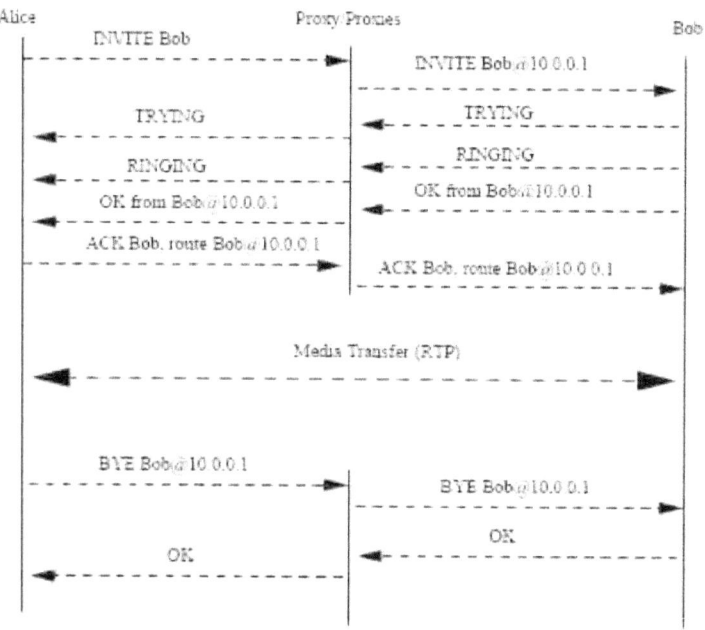

Figure 10.2. Message Exchanges During an SIP-Based Two-Party Call Setup.

Following this exchange, the two endpoints can begin transmitting voice, video, or other content (as negotiated) using the agreed-upon media transport protocol, typically RTP. While the signaling traffic may be relayed through a number of SIP proxies, the media traffic is exchanged directly between the two endpoints. When bridging different networks, e.g., PSTN and SIP, media gateways may disrupt the end-to-end nature of the media transfer. These entities translate content (e.g., audio) between the formats that are supported by the different networks.

Because signaling and media transfer operate independent of each other, the endpoints are responsible for indicating to the proxies that the call has been terminated, using a BYE message which is relayed through the proxies along the same path as the call setup messages. There are many other protocol interactions supported by SIP that cover many common (and uncommon) scenarios including call forwarding (manual or automatic), conference calling, voicemail, etc. Typically, this is done by semantically overloading SIP messages such that they can play various roles in different parts of the call. The third section contains examples of how this flexibility and protocol modularity can be used to attack the system. All SIP traffic is transmitted over port 5060 (UDP or TCP). The ports used for the media traffic, however, are dynamic and negotiated via Session Description Protocol (SDP) during call setup. This poses some problems when NAT or firewalls are traversed. Typically, these have to be stateful and understand the SIP exchanges so that they can open the appropriate RTP ports for the media transfer. In the case of NAT traversal, endpoints may use protocols like STUN to enable communication. Alternatively, the Universal Plug-and-Play (uPnP) protocol 2 may be used in some environments, such as residential broadband networks consisting of a single subnet behind a NAT gateway. Authentication between endpoints, the registrar, and the proxy typically uses HTTP Digest Authentication, as shown in Figure

10.3. This is a simple challenge-response protocol that uses a shared secret key along with a username, domain name, a nonce, and specific fields from the SIP message to compute a cryptographic hash. Using this mechanism, passwords are not transmitted in plaintext form over the network. It is worth noting that authentication may be requested at almost any point.

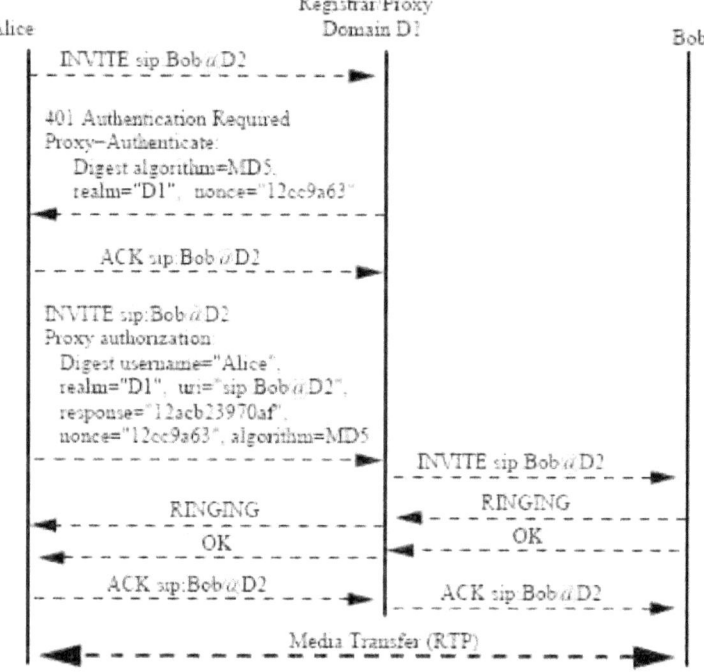

Figure 10.3. SIP Digest Authentication.

Later, we will see an example where this protocol can be abused by a malicious party to conduct toll fraud in some environments. For more complex authentication scenarios, SIP can use Secure/Multipurpose Internet Mail Extensions (S/MIME) encapsulation[22] to carry complex payloads, including public keys and certificates. When TCP is used as the transport protocol for SIP, TLS can be used to protect the SIP messages. TLS is required for communication among proxies, registrars, and redirect servers, but only recommended between endpoints and proxies or registrars. Alternatively, IPsec[23] may be used to protect all communications, regardless of the transport protocol. However, because few implementations integrate SIP, RTP, and IPsec, it is left to system administrators to figure out how to setup and manage such configurations.

Unlicensed Mobile Access.

UMA is a 3 Generation Partnership Project (3GPP) standard for enabling transparent access to mobile circuit-switched voice networks, packet-switch data networks, and IMS services using any IP-based substrate. Handsets supporting UMA can roam between the operator's wireless network (usually referred to as a Radio Access Network, or RAN) and the Internet without losing access. For example, a call that is initiated over the RAN can then be routed without being dropped and with no user intervention over the public Internet if conditions are more favorable (e.g., stronger WiFi signal in the user's premises, or in a hotel wireless hotspot while traveling abroad). For consumers, UMA offers better connectivity and the possibility of lower cost by enabling new business models and reducing roaming charges (under some scenarios). For operators, UMA reduces the need for additional spectrum; cell phone towers and related equipment. A variety of cell phones supporting UMA over WiFi currently exist, along with home gateways and USB-stick soft phones. More recently, some operators have introduced femto cells (ultra-low power RAN cells intended for consumer-directed deployment) that can act as UMA gateways, allowing any mobile handset to take advantage of UMA where such devices are deployed. The basic approach behind UMA is to encapsulate complete Global System for Mobile (GSM) and 3rd Generation (3G) radio frames (except for the over-the-air crypto) inside IP packets. These can then be transmitted over any IP network, including the Internet. This means that the mobile operator can continue to use the existing back-end equipment; all that is needed is a gateway that encapsulates the GSM/3G frames and injects them to the existing circuit-switched network (for voice calls), as can be seen in Figure 10.4. To protect both signaling and media traffic confidentiality and integrity while traversing un-trusted (and untrustworthy) networks, UMA uses Internet Protocol Security (IPSec). All traffic between the handset (or, more generally, UMA endpoint) and the provider's UMA Network Controller (or a firewall/Virtual Private Network [VPN] concentrator screening traffic) is encrypted and integrity-protected using Encapsulating Security Payload (ESP).[24]

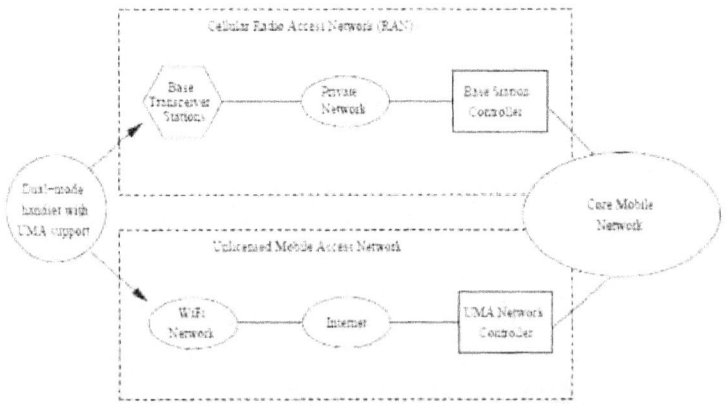

Figure 10.4. Unlicensed Mobile Access (UMA) Conceptual Architecture During a Call Setup.

The use of IPSec provides a high level of security for network traffic, once keys and other parameters have been negotiated. For that purpose, the Internet Key Exchange version 2 (IKEv2) key management protocol[25] is used. Authentication uses the Extensible Authentication Protocol method for GSM Subscriber Identity Module (EAP-SIM)[26] (for GSM handsets) and Extensible Authentication Protocol method for UMTS Authentication and Key Agreement (EAP-AKA)[27] (for UMTS handsets) profiles. Authentication is asymmetric: the provider authenticates to the handset using digital signatures and public key certificates, while the handset authenticates using a SIM-embedded secret key. It is worth pointing out that UMA provides stronger authentication guarantees than the baseline cell phone network in that the provider does not authenticate to the handset in a RAN. Furthermore, the cryptographic algorithms used in IPSec Advanced Encryption Standard and 3 Data Encryption Standard (AES and 3DES) are considered significantly stronger than the on-the-air algorithms used in GSM. Despite the use of strong cryptography and sound protocols, UMA introduces some new risks in the operator networks, since these now have to be connected to the public Internet in a much more intimate fashion. In particular, the security gateway must process IPSec traffic, including the relatively complex IKEv2 protocol, and a number of UMA-related discovery and configuration protocols. These significantly increase the attack surface and overall security exposure of the operators.

Other VoIP/IMS Systems.

H.323 is an ITU defined protocol family for VoIP (audio and video) over packet-switched data networks. The various sub protocols are encoded in Abstract Syntax Notation One (ASN.1) format. In the H.323 world, the main entities are terminals (software or physical phones), a gateway, a gatekeeper, and a back-end service. The gate keeper is responsible for address resolution, controlling bandwidth use, and other management functions while the gateway connects the H.323 network with other networks (e.g., PSTN, or a SIP network). The back-end service maintains data about the terminals, including configuration, access billing rights, etc. An optional multipoint control unit may also exist to enable multipoint communications, such as a teleconference. To setup an H.323 call, terminals first interact with the gatekeeper using the H.225 protocol over either TCP or UDP to receive authorization and to perform address resolution. Using the same protocol, they then establish the end-to-end connection to the remote terminal (possibly through one or more gateways). At that point, H.245 over TCP is used to negotiate the parameters for the actual media transfer, including ports, which uses RTP (as in the case of SIP). Authentication may be requested at several steps during call setup, and typically depends on symmetric keys but may also use digital signatures. Voice encryption is also supported through SRTP and MIKEY.[28] Unlike SIP, H.323 does not use a well-known port, making firewall traversal even more complicated. Skype3 is a P2P VoIP system that was originally available as a soft phone for desktop computers but has since been integrated into cell phones and other handheld devices, either as an add-on or as the exclusive communication mechanism. It offers voice, video, and text messaging to all other Skype users free of charge, and provides bridging (typically for a fee) to the PSTN both for outgoing and incoming calls and text messages (SMS). The underlying protocol is proprietary, and the software itself incorporates several anti-reverse engineering techniques. Nonetheless, some analysis[29] and reverse engineering[30] have taken place, indicating both the ubiquitous use of strong cryptography and the presence of some software bugs (at the time of the work). The system uses a centralized login server but is otherwise fully distributed with respect to intra-Skype communications. A number of chat (IM) networks, such as the AOL Instant Messenger, Microsoft's Live Messenger, Yahoo! Messenger, and Google Talk offer voice and video capabilities as well. Although each network uses its own (often proprietary) protocol, bridges exist between most of them, allowing inter-IM communication at the text level. In most of these networks, users can place outgoing voice calls to the PSTN. Some popular IM clients also integrate SIP support.

VOIP THREATS

In trying to understand the threat space against VoIP, our approach is to place known vulnerabilities within a structured framework. While a single taxonomy is not likely to be definitive, using several different viewpoints and mapping the vulnerability space along several axes may reveal trends and other areas that merit further analysis. As a starting point, we use the taxonomy provided by the Voice over IP Security Alliance (VOIPSA). VOIPSA is a vendor-neutral, not for profit organization composed of VoIP and security vendors, organizations, and individuals with an interest in securing VoIP protocols, products, and installations. In addition, we place the surveyed vulnerabilities within the traditional threat spa of confidentiality, integrity, and availability (CIA). Finally, we ascertain whether the vulnerabilities exploit bugs in the protocol, implementation, or system configuration. In future work, we hope to expand the number of views to the surveyed vulnerabilities and to provide more in-depth analysis. The VOIPSA security threat taxonomy[31] aims to define the security threats against VoIP deployments, services, and end users. The key elements of this taxonomy are:

1. Social threats are aimed directly against humans. For example, misconfigurations, bugs, or bad protocol interactions in VoIP systems may enable or facilitate attacks that misrepresent the identity of malicious parties to users. Such attacks may then act as stepping stones for further attacks such as phishing, theft of service, or unwanted contact (spam).

2. Eavesdropping, interception, and modification threats cover situations where an adversary can unlawfully and without authorization from the parties concerned listen in on the signaling (call setup) or the content of a VoIP session, and possibly modify aspects of that session while avoiding detection. Examples of such attacks include call re-routing and interception of unencrypted RTP sessions.

3. Denial of service (DoS) threats have the potential to deny users access to VoIP services. This may be particularly problematic in the case of emergencies, or when a DoS attack affects all of a user's or an organization's communication capabilities (i.e., when all VoIP and data communications are multiplexed over the same network which can be targeted through a DoS

attack). Such attacks may be VoIP-specific (exploiting flaws in the call setup or the implementation of services), or VoIP-agnostic (e.g., generic traffic flooding attacks). They may also involve attacks with physical components (e.g., physically disconnecting or severing a cable) or through computing or other infrastructures (e.g., disabling the DNS server, or shutting down power).

4. Service abuse threats covers the improper use of VoIP services, especially (but not exclusively) in those situations where such services are offered in a commercial setting. Examples of such threats include toll fraud and billing avoidance.[32]

5. Physical access threats refer to inappropriate/ unauthorized physical access to VoIP equipment, or to the physical layer of the network (following the ISO 7-layer network stack model).

6. Interruption of services threats refer to nonintentional problems that may nonetheless cause VoIP services to become unusable or inaccessible. Examples of such threats include loss of power due to inclement weather, resource exhaustion due to oversubscription, and performance issues that degrade call quality.

In our discussion of vulnerabilities (whether theoretical or demonstrated) that follows, we shall mark each item with a tuple (V, T, K), where: $V \in \{1, 2, 3, 4, 5, 6\}$, where each number refers to an element in the VOIPSA threat taxonomy from above; $T \in \{C1, I1, A1\}$, referring to confidentiality, integrity and availability, respectively; $K \in \{P2, I2, C2\}$, referring to protocol, implementation, and configuration respectively; and confidentiality via a configuration problem or bug. In some cases, the same underlying vulnerability may be used to perform different types of attacks. We will be discussing all such significant attack variants.

Disclosed Vulnerabilities.

Threats against VoIP system availability that exploit implementation weaknesses are fairly common. For example, some implementations were shown to be vulnerable to crashes or hanging (live clock) when given empty, malformed, or large volumes of[33] INVITE or other messages (3, A1, I2). It is worth noting that the same vulnerability may be present across similar protocols on the same platform and product[34] due to code sharing and internal software structure, or to systems that need to understand VoIP protocols but are not nominally part of a VoIP system.[35] The reason for the disproportionately large number of denial of service vulnerabilities is because of the ease with which such failure can be diagnosed, especially when the bug is discovered through automated testing tools (e.g., fuzzers). Many of these vulnerabilities may in fact be more serious than a simple denial of service due to a crash, and could possibly lead to remote code injection and execution. Unexpected interactions between different technologies used in VoIP systems can also lead to vulnerabilities. For example, in some cases cross-site scripting (XSS) attacks were demonstrated against the administrator- and customer-facing management interface (which was web-based) by injecting malicious Java script in selected SIP messages[36] (1, I1, I2), often through Structured Query Language (SQL) injection vulnerabilities.[37] The same vulnerability could also be used to commit toll fraud by targeting the underlying database (4, I1, I2). XSS attacks that are not web-oriented have also been demonstrated, with one of the oldest VoIP-related vulnerabilities[38] permitting shell command execution. Another web-oriented attack vector is Cross Site Request Forgery (CSRF), whereby users visiting a malicious page can be induced to automatically (without user intervention, and often without any observable indications) perform some action on the web servers (in this case, VoIP web-based management interface) that the browser is already authenticated to).[39] Other privilege-escalation vulnerabilities through the web interface also exist.[40] The complexity of the SIP finite state machine has sometimes led to poor implementations. For example, one vulnerability[41] allowed attackers to confuse a phone receiving a call into silently completing the call, which allowed the adversary to eavesdrop on the device's surroundings.

The same vulnerability could be used to deny call reception of the target, since the device was already marked as busy. In other cases, it is unclear to developers what use of a specific protocol field may be, in which case they may silently ignore it. Occasionally, such information is critical for the security of the protocol exchange, and omitting or not checking it allows adversaries to perform attacks such as man-in-the-middle, or traffic interception,[42] or bypass authentication checks.[43]

Since SIP devices are primarily software-driven, they are vulnerable to the same classes of vulnerabilities as other software. For example, buffer overflows are possible even against SIP "headphones," much less soft phones, allowing adversaries to gain complete control of the device.[44] Such vulnerabilities typically arise from a combination of poor (nondefensive) programming practices, insufficient testing, and the use of languages, such as C and C++ that support unsafe operations. Sometimes, these vulnerabilities appear in software that is not directly used in VoIP but must be

VoIP-aware, e.g., fire walls[45] or protocol analyzers.[46] It is also worth noting that these are not the only types of vulnerabilities that can lead to remote code execution.[47] Other input validation failures can allow attackers to download arbitrary files from a user's machine (1, C1, I2) or to place calls[48] (1, I1, I2) by supplying specially encoded URIs[49] or other parameters. A significant risk with VoIP devices is the ability of adversaries to misrepresent their identity (e.g., their calling number). Such vulnerabilities[50] sometimes arise due to the lack of cross-checking of information provided across several messages during call setup and throughout the session (1, I1, I2).

Similar failures to crosscheck and validate information can lead to other attacks, such as indicating whether there is pending voicemail for the user[51] (1, I1, I2), or where attackers may spoof incoming calls by directly connecting to a VoIP phone[52] (1, I1, I2).

Undocumented, on-by-default features are another source of vulnerabilities. These are often remnants from testing and debugging during development that were not disabled when a product shipped.[53] As a result, they often offer privileged access to services and data on a device that would not otherwise be available[54] (1, C1, I2). One particularly interesting vulnerability allowed an attacker to place outgoing calls through the web management interface[55] (4, I1, C2). A significant class of vulnerabilities in VoIP devices revolves around default configurations, and in particular default usernames and passwords[56] (2, C1 + I1, C2). Lists of default accounts are easy to find on the Internet via a search engine. Users often do not change these settings; this seems to be particularly so for administrative accounts, which are rarely (if ever) used in the home/Small Office Home Office (SOHO) environment. Other default settings involve Network Time Protocol (NTP) servers[57] and DNS servers[58] (2, C1 + I1, C2). Since the boot and VoIP stacks are not necessarily tightly integrated, interaction with one protocol can have adverse effects (e.g., changing the perceived location of the phone) in the other protocol[59] [2, C1, I2]). Other instances of such vulnerabilities involve improper/insufficient credential checking by the registrar or proxy[60] or by the SNMP server,[61] which can lead to traffic interception (2, C1, I2) and user impersonation (1, I1, I2). The integration of several capabilities in VoIP products, e.g., a web server used for the management interface, can lead to vulnerabilities being imported to the VoIP environment that would not otherwise apply. In the specific example of an integrated web server, directory traversal bugs[62] or similar problems (such as lack of proper authentication in the web interface)[63] can allow adversaries to read arbitrary files or other information from the device (1, C1, I2). SIP (or, more generally, VoIP) components integrated with firewalls may also interact in undesirable ways. For example, improper handling of registration requests may allow attackers to receive messages intended for other users[64] (2, C1, I2). Other such examples include failure to authenticate server certificates in wireless environments, enabling man-in-the-middle and eavesdropping attacks[65] (2, C1, I2).

Predictability and lack of proper use (or sources) of randomness is another vulnerability seen in VoIP products. For example, predictable values in SIP header messages[66] allows malicious users to avoid registering, but continue using the service (4, I1, I2). Protocol responses to carefully crafted messages can reveal information about the system or its users to an attacker. Although this has been long understood in limited-domain protocols (e.g., remote login), with measures taken to normalize responses such that no information is leaked, the complexity of VoIP (and other) protocols make this infeasible. As a result, information disclosure vulnerabilities abound[67] (1, C1, I2).

Some of the most serious nonimplementation type of vulnerabilities are those where the specification permits behavior that is exploitable. For example, certain vendors permit the actual Uniform Resource Indentifier (URI) in a SIP INVITE call and the URI used as part of the Digest Authentication to differ, which (while arguably permitted by the specification) allows credential reuse and toll fraud[68] (4, I1, P2). While rare, protocol-level vulnerabilities also exist. These represent either outright bugs in the specification, or unseen interaction between different protocols or protocol components. For large, complicated protocols such as SIP and H.323, where components (code, messages, etc.) are semantically overloaded and reused, it is perhaps not surprising that such emergent properties exist. One good example is the relay attack that is possible with the SIP Digest Authentication,[69] whereby an adversary can reuse another party's credentials to obtain unauthorized access to SIP or PSTN services (such as calling a premium or international phone line) (4, I1, P2). This attack is possible because in an authentication attack, both depicted in Figure 10.5, an authentication may be requested in response to an INVITE message that is not usable in, for example, placing fraudulent calls.

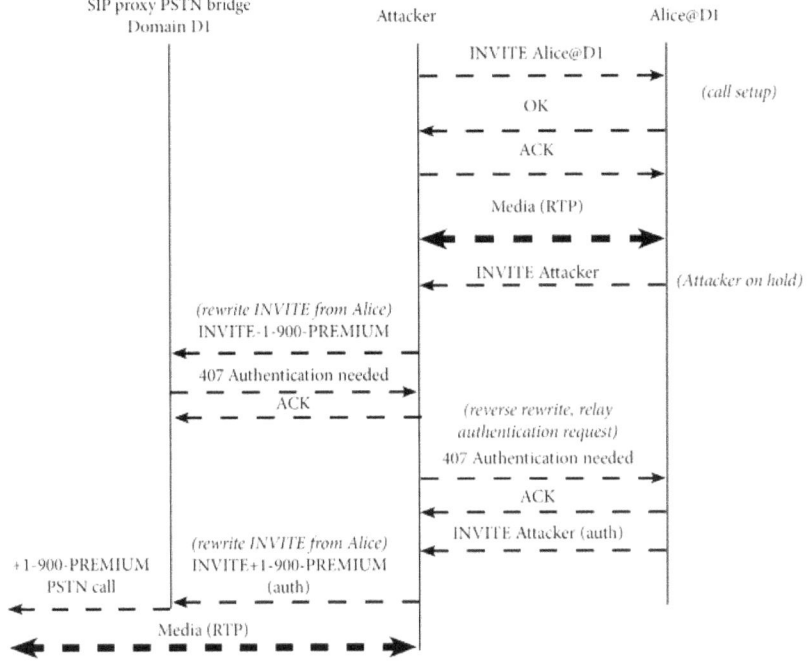

Figure 10.5. SIP Relay Attack.

DISCUSSION

Looking at the vulnerabilities we have considered, a few patterns emerge. First, as we can see in our informal classification of vulnerability effects shown in Figure 10.6, half of the problems lead to a denial of service in either an end-device (phone or soft phone) or a server (proxy, registrar, etc.). This is not altogether surprising, since denial of service (especially a crash) is something that is easily diagnosed. In many cases, the problem was discovered by automated testing, such as protocol or software fuzzing; software failures are relatively easy to determine in such settings. Some of these vulnerabilities could in

247

fact turn out to be more serious, e.g., a memory corruption leading to a crash could be exploitable to mount a code injection attack. The second largest class of vulnerabilities allows an adversary to control the device, whether by code injection, default passwords and services, or authentication failures. Note that we counted a few of the vulnerabilities (approximately 10 percent) more than once in this classification. The same pattern with respect to the predominance of denial of service vulnerabilities holds when we look at the breakdown according to the VOIPSA taxonomy, shown in Figure 10.7. It should not be surprising that, given the nature of the vulnerabilities disclosed in Common Vulnerabilities and Exposures (CVE), we have no data on physical access and (accidental) interruption of services vulnerabilities. Furthermore, while "Access to Services" was a non-negligible component in the previous breakdown, it represents only 4 percent here. The reason for this apparent discrepancy is in the different definitions of service: the specific element in the VOIPSA taxonomy refers to VoIP-specific abuse, whereas our informal definition covers lower-level system components which may not be usable in, for example, placing fraudulent calls. One state (data) resident on the system falls into the "access to data" category. The other observation here, is that while the VOIPSA taxonomy covers a broad spectrum of concerns or VoIP system designers and operators, its categories are perhaps too broad (and, in some cases, imprecise) to help with characterizing the types of bugs we have examined.

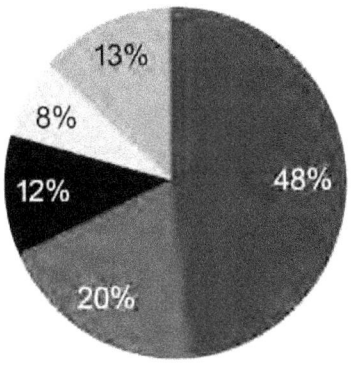

Denial of service
Attack the user
Access to services

Remote control of device
Access to data

Figure 10.6. Vulnerability Breakdown Based on Effect.

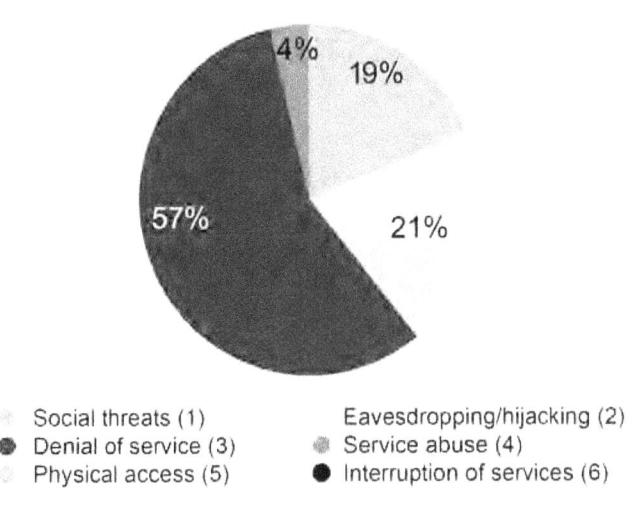

Social threats (1)
Denial of service (3)
Physical access (5)

Eavesdropping/hijacking (2)
Service abuse (4)
Interruption of services (6)

Figure 10.7. Vulnerability Breakdown Based on VOIPSA Taxonomy.

Most categories are self explanatory; "attack the user" refers to vulnerabilities that permit attackers to affect the user/administrator of a device without necessarily compromising the system or getting access to its data or services. XSS attacks and traffic eavesdropping attacks fall in this category, whereas attacks that compromise state (data) resident on the system fall in the "access to data" category.

The vulnerability breakdown according to the traditional CIA security concerns again reflects the predominance of denial of service threats against VoIP systems, as seen in Figure 10.8. However, we can see that integrity violations (e.g., system compromise) are a sizable component of the threat space, while confidentiality violations are seen in only 15 percent of disclosed vulnerabilities. This represents an inversion of the perceived threats by users and administrators, who (anecdotal evidence suggests) typically worry about such issues as call interception and eavesdropping. Finally, Figure 10.9 shows the breakdown based on source of vulnerability. The overwhelming majority of reported problems arise from implementation issues, which should not be surprising given the nature of bug disclosure. Problems arising from configuration represented 7 percent of the total space, including such items as privileged services left turned on and default username/passwords. However, note that the true picture (i.e., what actually happens with deployed systems) is probably different in that configuration problems are most likely undercounted: such problems are often site-specific and are not reported to bug-disclosure databases when discovered. On the other hand, implementation and protocol problems are prime candidates for disclosure. What is surprising is the presence of protocol vulnerabilities; one would expect that such problems were discovered and issued during protocol development, specification, and standardization. Their mere existence potentially indicates high protocol complexity. The vulnerability analysis contained in this chapter is, by its nature, static: we have presented a snapshot of known problems with VoIP systems, with no correlation with (and knowledge of) actual attacks exploiting these, or other vulnerabilities. A complete analysis of the threat space would also contain a dynamic component, whereby attacker behavior patterns and trends would be analyzed vis-à-vis actual, deployed VoIP systems or, lacking access to such, simulacra thereof.[70]

Figure 10.8. Vulnerability Breakdown Based on Source (I2, C2, P2).

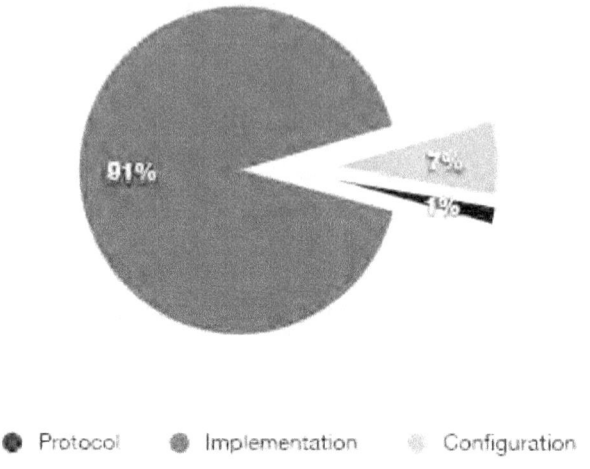

Protocol   Implementation   Configuration

**Figure 10.9. Vulnerability Breakdown Based
on Source (I2, C2, P2).**

CONCLUSIONS

We can draw some preliminary conclusions with
respect to threats and potential areas for future research based on the data examined so far. These can
be summarized as follows:

1. The large majority of disclosed threats focused
on denial of services attacks are based on implementation issues. While fault-tolerance techniques can be
applied in the case of servers (replication, hot standby,
Byzantine fault tolerance, etc.), it is less clear how to
provide similar levels of protection at acceptable cost
and usability to end user devices. Unfortunately, the
ease with which mass DoS attacks can be launched
over the network against client devices means that
they represent an attractive venue for attackers to
achieve the same impact.

2. Code injection attacks in their various forms (buffer overflow, cross-site scripting, SQL injection, etc.) remain a problem. While a number of techniques have been developed, we need to do a better job at deploying and using them where possible, and devising new techniques suitable for the constrained environments that some vulnerable VoIP devices represent.

3. Weak default configurations remain a problem, as they do across a large class of consumer and enterprise products and software. The situation is likely to be much worse in the real world, considering the complexity of securely configuring a system with as many components as VoIP. Vendors must make an effort to provide secure-by-default configurations, and to educate users on how to best protect their systems. Administrators are in need of tools to analyze their existing configurations for vulnerabilities. While there are some tools that dynamically test network components (e.g., firewalls), we need tools that work higher in the protocol and application stack (i.e., interacting at the user level). Furthermore, we need ways of validating configurations across multiple components and protocols.

4. Finally, there is simply no excuse for protocol-level vulnerabilities. While techniques exist for analyzing and verifying security protocols, they do not seem to cope well with complexity. Aside from using such tools and continuing their development, protocol designers and standardization committees must consider the impact of their decisions on system implementers, i.e., whether it is likely that a feature or aspect of the protocol is likely to be misunderstood and/or misimplemented. Simpler protocols are also desirable, but seem incompatible with the trends we have observed in standardization bodies. Our plans for future work include expanding the data set we used for

our analysis to include findings from academic work, adding and presenting more views (classifications) to the data, and developing dynamic views to VoIP-related misbehavior.

ENDNOTES - CHAPTER 10

1. R. Droms, "Dynamic Host Configuration Protocol," RFC 2131 (Draft Standard), March 1997, Updated by RFCs 3396, 4361, 5494.

2. P. V. Mockapetris, "Domain Names—Concepts and Facilities," RFC 1034 (Standard), November 1987, Updated by RFCs 1101, 1183, 1348, 1876, 1982, 2065, 2181, 2308, 2535, 4033, 4034, 4035, 4343, 4035, 4592; P. V. Mockapetris, "Domain Names—Implementation and Specification," RFC 1035 (Standard), November 1987, Updated by RFCs 1101, 1183, 1348, 1876, 1982, 1995, 1996, 2065, 2136, 2181, 2137, 2308, 2535, 2845, 3425, 3658, 4033, 4034, 4035, 4343.

3. K. Sollins, "The TFTP Protocol (Revision 2)," RFC 1350 (Standard), July 1992, Updated by RFCs 1782, 1783, 1784, 1785, 2347, 2348, 2349; R. Finlayson, "Bootstrap loading using TFTP," RFC 906, June 1984.

4. P. Srisuresh and K. Egevang, "Traditional IP Network Address Translator (Traditional NAT)," RFC 3022 (Informational), January 2001.

5. J. Rosenberg, R. Mahy, P. Matthews, and D. Wing, "Session Traversal Utilities for NAT (STUN)," RFC 5389 (Proposed Standard), October 2008.

6. D. Mills, "Network Time Protocol (Version 3) Specification, Implementation and Analysis," RFC 1305 (Draft Standard), March 1992.

7. D. Harrington, R. Presuhn, and B. Wijnen, "An Architecture for Describing Simple Network Management Protocol (SNMP) Management Frameworks," RFC 3411 (Standard), December 2002, Updated by RFC 5343.

8. T. Berners-Lee, R. Fielding, and H. Frystyk, "Hypertext Transfer Protocol – HTTP/1.0," RFC 1945 (Informational), May 1996; R. Fielding, J. Gettys, J. Mogul, H. Frystyk, L. Masinter, P. Leach, and T. Berners-Lee, "Hypertext Transfer Protocol – HTTP/1.1," RFC 2616 (Draft Standard), June 1999, Updated by RFC 2817.

9. T. Dierks and E. Rescorla, "The Transport Layer Security (TLS) Protocol Version 1.2," RFC 5246 (Proposed Standard), August 2008.

10. H. Schulzrinne, S. Casner, R. Frederick, and V. Jacobson, "RTP: A Transport Protocol for Real-Time Applications," RFC 3550 (Standard), July 2003, Updated by RFC 5506.

11. I. Johansson and M. Westerlund, "Support for Reduced-Size Real-Time Transport Control Protocol (RTCP): Opportunities and Consequences," RFC 5506 (Proposed Standard), April 2009.

12. J. Rosenberg, H. Schulzrinne, G. Camarillo, A. Johnston, J. Peterson, R. Sparks, M. Handley, and E. Schooler, "SIP: Session Initiation Protocol," RFC 3261 (Proposed Standard), June 2002, Updated by RFCs 3265, 3853, 4320, 4916, 5393.

13. 3GPP, "Generic Access Network," available from *www.3gpp.org/ftp/Specs/html-info/43318.htm, 2009.*

14. J. Franks, P. Hallam-Baker, J. Hostetler, S. Lawrence, P. Leach, A. Luotonen, and L. Stewart, "HTTP Authentication: Basic and Digest Access Authentication," RFC 2617 (Draft Standard), June 1999.

15. Rosenberg, Schulzrinne, Camarillo, Johnston, Peterson, Sparks, Handley, and Schooler, "SIP: Session Initiation Protocol."

16. J. Postel, "Transmission Control Protocol," RFC 793 (Standard), September 1981, Updated by RFCs 1122, 3168.

17. J. Postel, "User Datagram Protocol," RFC 768 (Standard), August 1980.

18. L. Ong and J. Yoakum, "An Introduction to the Stream Control Transmission Protocol (SCTP)," RFC 3286 (Informational), May 2002.

19. E. Rescorla and N. Modadugu, "Datagram Transport Layer Security," RFC 4347 (Proposed Standard), April 2006.

20. M. Handley, E. Rescorla, and IAB, "Internet Denial-of-Service Considerations," RFC 4732 (Informational), December 2006.

21. M. Handley, V. Jacobson, and C. Perkins, "SDP: Session Description Protocol," RFC 4566 (Proposed Standard), July 2006.

22. B. Ramsdell, "Secure/Multipurpose Internet Mail Extensions (S/MIME) Version 3.1 Message Specification," RFC 3851 (Proposed Standard), July 2004.

23. S. Kent and K. Seo, "Security Architecture for the Internet Protocol," RFC 4301 (Proposed Standard), December 2005.

24. S. Kent, "IP Encapsulating Security Payload (ESP)," RFC 4303 (Proposed Standard), December 2005.

25.C. Kaufman, "Internet Key Exchange (IKEv2) Protocol," RFC 4306 (Proposed Standard), December 2005, Updated by RFC 5282.

26. H. Haverinen and J. Salowey, "Extensible Authentication Protocol Method for Global System for Mobile Communications (GSM) Subscriber Identity Modules (EAP-SIM)," RFC 4186 (Informational), January 2006.

27. J. Arkko and H. Haverinen, "Extensible Authentication Protocol Method for 3rd Generation Authentication and Key Agreement (EAP-AKA)," RFC 4187 (Informational), January 2006.

28. J. Arkko, E. Carrara, F. Lindholm, M. Naslund, and K. Norrman, "MIKEY: Multimedia Internet KEYing," RFC 3830 (Proposed Standard), August 2004, Updated by RFC 4738.

29. Tom Berson, "Skype Security Evaluation," *Tech. Rep.*, October 2005; S. A. Baset and H. Schulzrinne, "An Analysis of

the Skype Peer-to-Peer Telephony Protocol," in *Proceedings of INFO-COM*, April 2006.

30. P. Biondi and F. Desclaux, "Silver Needle in the Skype," in BlackHat Europe Conference, March 2006, available from *www. blackhat.com/presentations/bh-europe-06/bh-eu-06-biondi/bh-eu-06-biondi-up.pdf*.

31. VoIP Security Alliance, "VoIP Security and Privacy Threat Taxonomy, version 1.0," October 2005, available from *www.voipsa. org/Activities/taxonomy.php*.

32. "Two charged with VoIP fraud," The Register, June 2006, available from *www.theregister.co.uk/2006/06/08/voip fraudsters nabbed/*; "Fugitive VOIP hacker cuffed in Mexico," The Register, February 2009, available from *www.theregister.co.uk/2009/02/11/ fugitive voip hacker arrested/*.

33. Examples of Common Vulnerabilities and Exposures are available from: *cve.mitre.org/cve/index.html*; CVE-2007-4753; CVE-2007-0431; CVE-2007-4553; CVE-2003-1114; CVE-2006-1973; CVE-2007-0648; CVE-2007-2270; CVE-2007-4291, 4292; CVE-2008-3799, 3800, 3801, and 3802; CVE-2009-1158; CVE-2004-0054; CVE-2001-0546; CVE-2002-2266; CVE-2004-0498; CVE-2004-2344; CVE-2004-2629; CVE-2004-2758; CVE-2007-4429; CVE-2006-5084; CVE-2005-3267; CVE-2004-1777; CVE-2003-1108-1113; CVE-2003-1115; CVE-2004-0504; CVE-2005-4466; CVE-2006-5445; CVE-2006-2924; CVE-2006-0739, 0738, and 0737; CVE-2007-6371; CVE-2007-5583; CVE-2007-5537; CVE-2007-4924; CVE-2007-4459; CVE-2007-4455; CVE-2007-4382; CVE-2007-4366; CVE-2007-3441-3445; CVE-2007-3436 and 3437; CVE-2007-3369, 3368; CVE-2007-3361-3363; CVE-2007-3348-3351; CVE-2007-3322 and 3321; CVE-2007-3318 and 3317; CVE-2007-2297; CVE-2007-1693; CVE-2007-1650; CVE-2007-1594; CVE-2007-1590; CVE-2007-1561; CVE-2007-1542; CVE-2007-1306; CVE-2007-0961; CVE-2008-0095; CVE-2008-0263; CVE-2008-1249; CVE-2008-1741; CVE-2008-1745; CVE-2008-1747 and 1748; CVE-2008-1959; CVE-2008-2119; CVE-2008-2732; CVE-2008-2733; CVE-2008-2734 and 2735; CVE-2008-3157; CVE-2008-3210; CVE-2008-3778; CVE-2008-4444; CVE-2008-5180; CVE-2008-6140; CVE-2008-6574 and 6575; CVE-2009-0871; CVE-2009-0636; CVE-2009-0630; CVE-2009-0631; CVE-2007-5591; CVE-2007-5556; CVE-2007-5369; CVE-2007-2886; CVE-2006-7121; CVE-2006-6411;

CVE-2006-5233; CVE-2006-5231; CVE-2005-3989; CVE-2004-1977; CVE-2002-0882; CVE-2002-0880; CVE-2002-0835;

34. "CVE-2007-4291," 2007, available from *cve.mitre.org/ cgi-bin/cvename.cgi?name=CVE-2007-4291.*

35. "CVE-2005-4464," 2005, available from *cve.mitre.org/ cgi-bin/cvename.cgi?name=CVE-2005-4464.*

36. "CVE-2007-5488," 2007 available from *cve.mitre.org/cgi-bin/ cvename.cgi?name=CVE-2007-5488.* CVE-2007-5411, CVE-2008-0582, CVE-2008-0583, CVE-2008-0454, CVE-2006-2925, CVE-2007-2191.

37. "CVE-2008-6509," 2008, available from *cve.mitre.org/cgi-bin/ cvename.cgi?name=CVE-2008-6509.* "CVE-2008-6573," 2008, available from *cve.mitre.org/cgi-bin/cvename.cgi?name=CVE-2008-6573.*

38. "CVE-1999-0938," 1999, available from *cve.mitre.org/cgi-bin/ cvename.cgi?name=CVE-1999-0938.*

39. "CVE-2008-1250," 2008, available from *cve.mitre.org/cgi-bin/ cvename.cgi?name=CVE-2008-1250.*

40. "CVE-2008-6708," 2008, available from *cve.mitre.org/cgi-bin/ cvename.cgi?name=CVE-2008-6708.*

41. "CVE-2007-4498," 2007, available from *cve.mitre.org/cgi-bin/ cvename.cgi?name=CVE-2007-4498.*

42. "CVE-2007-3319," 2007, available from *cve.mitre.org/cgi-bin/ cvename.cgi?name=CVE-2007-3319.*

43. "CVE-2007-3177," 2007, available from *cve.mitre.org/cgi-bin/ cvename.cgi?name=CVE-2007-3177,* 2007. "CVE-2007-0334," available from *cve.mitre.org/cgi-bin/cvename.cgi?name=CVE-2007-0334.*

44. Examples of Common Vulnerabilities and Exposures are available from: *cve.mitre.org/cve/index.html;* CVE-2003-1114, CVE-2003-1110, CVE-2003-1111, CVE-2005-4050, CVE-2007-4294, CVE-2007-4295, CVE-2004-0056, CVE-2004-0117, CVE-2005-3265, CVE-2004-1114, CVE-2003-0761, CVE-2006-4029, CVE-2006-3594,

CVE-2006-3524, CVE-2006-0359, CVE-2006-0189, CVE-2007-5788, CVE-2007-3438, CVE-2007-2293, CVE-2007-0746, CVE-2008-0528, CVE-2008-0530, CVE-2008-0531, CVE-2008-2085, CVE-2007-4489, CVE-2005-2081.

45. "CVE-2003-0819," 2003, available from *cve.mitre.org/cgi-bin/ cvename.cgi?name=CVE-2003-0819.*

46. "CVE-2005-1461," 2005, available from *cve.mitre.org/cgi-bin/ cvename.cgi?name=CVE-2005-1461.*

47. Examples of Common Vulnerabilities and Exposures are available from: *cve.mitre.org/cve/index.html*; CVE-2006-5084, CVE-2008-2545, CVE-2008-1805, CVE-2007-5989, CVE-2007-3896, CVE-2008-6709.

48. "CVE-2008-1334," 2008, available from *cve.mitre.org/cgi-bin/ cvename.cgi?name=CVE-2008-1334.*

49. "CVE-2006-2312," 2006, available from *cve.mitre.org/cgi-bin/ cvename.cgi?name=CVE-2006-2312.*

50. "CVE-2005-2181," 2005, available from *cve.mitre.org/cgi-bin/ cvename.cgi?name=CVE-2005-2181.*

51. "CVE-2005-2182," 2005, available from *cve.mitre.org/cgi-bin/ cvename.cgi?name=CVE-2005-2182.*

52. Examples of Common Vulnerabilities and Exposures are available from: *cve.mitre.org/cve/index.html*; CVE-2007-5791, CVE-2007-3347, CVE-2007-3320.

53. Examples of Common Vulnerabilities and Exposures are available from: *cve.mitre.org/cve/index.html*; CVE-2006-0305, CVE-2006-0302, CVE-2005-3804, CVE-2005-3724, CVE-2005-3715.

54. Examples of Common Vulnerabilities and Exposures are available from: *cve.mitre.org/cve/index.html*; CVE-2006-0360, CVE-2007-3439, CVE-2006-0374, CVE-2005-3723, CVE-2005-3721, CVE-2005-3718.

55. Examples of Common Vulnerabilities and Exposures are available from: *cve.mitre.org/cve/index.html*; CVE-2007-3440, CVE-2008-1248.

56. Examples of Common Vulnerabilities and Exposures are available from: *cve.mitre.org/cve/index.html*; CVE-2005-3718, CVE-2006-5038, CVE-2008-4874, CVE-2007-3047, CVE-2008-1334, CVE-2006-0834, CVE-2005-3803, CVE-2005-3719, CVE-2005-3717, CVE-2005-3716, CVE-2005-0745, CVE-2002-0881.

57. "CVE-2006-0375," 2006, available from *cve.mitre.org/cgi-bin/cvename.cgi?name=CVE-2006-0375*.

58. "CVE-2005-3725," 2005, available from *cve.mitre.org/cgi-bin/cvename.cgi?name=CVE-2005-3725*.

59. "CVE-2007-5361," 2007, available from *cve.mitre.org/cgi-bin/cvename.cgi?name=CVE-2007-5361*.

60. "CVE-2008-5871," 2008, available from *cve.mitre.org/cgi-bin/cvename.cgi?name=CVE-2008-5871*.

61. "CVE-2005-3722," 2005, available from *cve.mitre.org/cgi-bin/cvename.cgi?name=CVE-2005-3722*.

62. "CVE-2008-4875," 2008, available from *cve.mitre.org/cgi-bin/cvename.cgi?name=CVE-2008-4875*.

63. "CVE-2008-6706," 2008, available from *cve.mitre.org/cgi-bin/cvename.cgi?name=CVE-2008-6706*, 2008. "CVE-2008-6707," available from *cve.mitre.org/cgi-bin/cvename.cgi?name=CVE-2008-6707*.

64. "CVE-2007-6095," 2007, available from *cve.mitre.org/cgi-bin/cvename.cgi?name=CVE-2007-6095*.

65. "CVE-2008-1114," 2008, available from *cve.mitre.org/cgi-bin/cvename.cgi?name=CVE-2008-1114*, 2008. "CVE-2008-1113," available from *cve.mitre.org/cgi-bin/cvename.cgi?name=CVE-2008-1113*.

66. "CVE-2002-1935," 2002, available from *cve.mitre.org/cgi-bin/cvename.cgi?name=CVE-2002-1935*.

67. "CVE-2006-4032," available from *cve.mitre.org/cgi-bin/cvename. cgi?name=CVE-2006-4032*, 2006. "CVE-2008-3903," 2008, available from *cve.mitre.org/cgi-bin/cvename.cgi?name=CVE-2008-3903*.

68. "CVE-2007-5469," available from *cve.mitre.org/cgi-bin/ cvename.cgi?name=CVE-2007-5469*, 2007. "CVE-2007-5468," 2007, available from *cve.mitre.org/cgi-bin/cvename.cgi?name=CVE-2007 -5468*.

69. R. State, O. Festor, H. Abdelanur, V. Pascual, J. Kuthan, R. Coeffic, J. Janak, and J. Loroiu, "SIP Digest Authentication Relay Attack," March 2009, available from *tools.ietf.org/html/draft-state-sip-relay-attack-00*.

70. M. Nassar, R. State, and O. Festor, "VoIP Honeypot Architecture," in Proceedings of the 10th IFIP/IEEE International Symposium on Integrated Network Management, May 2007, pp. 109–118.

CHAPTER 11

TOWARD FOOLPROOF IP NETWORK CONFIGURATION ASSESSMENTS*

Rajesh Talpade

INTRODUCTION

Internet protocol (IP) networks have come of age. They are increasingly replacing leased-line data infra-structure and traditional phone service, and are expected to offer Public Switched Telephone Network (PSTN) - quality service at a much lower cost. As a result, there is an urgent interest in ensuring IP network security, reliability, and quality of service (QoS). In fact, regulators are now requiring compliance with IP-related mandates. This chapter discusses the complex nature of IP networks and how that complexity makes them particularly vulnerable to faults and intrusions. It describes regulatory efforts to mandate assessment, explains why many current approaches to IP assessment fall short, and describes the requirements for an effective solution to satisfy business, government, and regulatory requirements.

IP networks throughout the public and private sectors are now mainstream. Everyday, IP networks are responsible for transporting real-time and critical voice, video, and data traffic. As a result, it is no longer acceptable for IP networks to deliver "best-effort" service. They are expected to perform at carrier-grade level. However, it is enormously challenging to deploy

---

* This work was supported in part by the U.S. Department of Homeland Security Science & Technology Directorate under Contract No. NBCHC050092.

IP networks and assure consistent, and high quality service delivery, given that they are such complex and dynamic environments.

IP networks are comprised of devices such as routers, switches, and firewalls that are interconnected by network links. These devices are not "plug-and-play," rather, they must be provided with specific instructions, also known as scripts or configurations, which indicate exactly how they are to interact with each other to provide the correct end-to-end IP network service. This is why we refer to IP device configurations as the DNA of the network—they literally control the network's behavior.

Unfortunately, there is nothing simple or standard about these configurations. Each one must be manually programmed into the network devices, and every vendor uses a different configuration language for its devices. Furthermore, device configurations change virtually everyday in response to new application deployments, organizational or policy changes, new device or technology deployments, device failures, or any number of other reasons. Device configurations have an average of 500 lines of code per device. A Fortune 500 enterprise that relies on an IP can easily have over 50 million lines of configuration code in its network. But numbers of devices and lines of code are only part of the problem. Configurations can contain parameters for about 20 different IP protocols and technologies that need to work together. Those protocols and technologies must satisfy various, constantly changing service requirements, some of which are inherently contradictory, such as security and connectivity with the Internet. So configuration errors can easily occur due to entry mistakes, feature interaction, poor process, or lack of a network-wide perspective.

The labor-intensive and constantly changing nature of IP network operations is analogous to software development. The key difference, as illustrated in Figure 11.1, is that software development has matured to the point where errors are significantly reduced by having different people responsible for requirements, code writing, and testing. More importantly, testing in software development is a well-established process, while there is no similarly rigorous process in IP network deployment and operation. The impacts of configuration errors are well documented. The National Security Agency (NSA) found that 80 percent of the vulnerabilities in the Air Force were due to configuration errors, according to a recent report from Center for Strategic and International Studies (CSIS).[1] British Telecom (BT)/Gartner has estimated that 65 percent of cyber attacks exploit systems with vulnerabilities introduced by configuration errors.[2] The Yankee Group has noted that configuration errors cause 62 percent of network downtime.[3] A 2006 Computer Security Institute/FBI computer crime survey conservatively estimates average annual losses from cyber attacks at $167,000 per organization.[4]

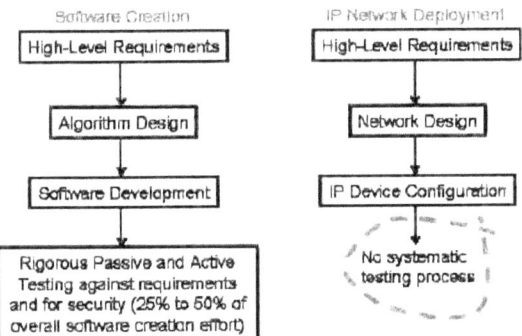

Figure 11.1. Inadequate Testing in IP Network Deployment Compared to Software Development.

CONFIGURATION ERRORS FOUND IN OPERATIONAL IP NETWORKS

IP network configuration errors are hard to detect since they can require validation of multiple protocols and device configurations simultaneously. These errors typically remain latent until they are exploited by cyber attackers, discovered by auditors, or result in network failures. Below are specific examples of configuration errors, and their potential impact on the organization. Many of these errors have been discovered in operational networks while performing configuration assessments.

Reliability.

Organizations that depend on the IP network to provide a very reliable service have to ensure that there are no single points of failure in the network. It is not sufficient to just provide redundant network devices and links at the physical level. It is also critical to ensure that the configurations of the network devices make use of the available redundant physical resources, and that the redundancy is ensured across multiple layers. Examples of misconfigurations that result in single points of failure include:
- Mismatched device interface parameters. This mismatch prevents devices from establishing logical connectivity even though physical connectivity exists.
- Hot Standby Routing Protocol (HSRP) inconsistently configured across two routers that are expected to mirror each other. The standby router will not take over when the main router fails.

266

- Access Control Lists (ACLs) or firewall rules stop specific application traffic on a path. Even if the path provides redundancy in general, the ACLs/rules still are a cause for a single point of failure to exist for the specific application traffic.
- Use of a single Open Shortest Path First (OSPF) Area Border Router (ABR). The OSPF areas that are connected by the ABR will become isolated if the ABR fails.
- Multiple VPN connections sharing a single physical link or device. The redundancy expected from the multiple VPN connections is not provided due to their dependence on a single physical resource.

In addition to the errors that introduce single points of failures as described above, other errors in configuration of IP routing protocols, such as Open Shortest Path First (OSPF), Border Gateway Protocol (BGP), Multi-Protocol Label Switching (MPLS), and Intermediate System to Intermediate System (IS-IS), can also impact network reliability. Examples of such errors include:

- Inconsistent routing parameters such as OSPF Hello and Dead interval across multiple routers. OSPF will not function efficiently if such parameters are inconsistent, resulting in ephemeral traffic loops and poor network performance.
- Best practices that are proposed by vendors and experts for routing protocols, such as the use of a full-mesh to connect all internal BGP (iBGP) routers, and that OSPF route summarizations should include IP addresses of all interfaces ex-

cept the loopback interface of a router, are not followed. Not adhering to best practices generally results in an unstable network that will have intermittent connectivity issues that are difficult to debug.

- Use of inappropriate IP addresses, such as addresses assigned to other organizations, or private addresses in parts of the network directly exposed to the Internet. Such networks will start advertising routes for IP addresses they do not own, resulting in Internet routing issues.

Security.

The most obvious configuration errors in this category can be found in firewalls, in the form of "holes" that are inadvertently left in firewall configurations. These holes are actually rules that permit specific application traffic to pass temporarily through the firewall, and then these rules are not removed after they are no longer needed. Cyber attackers scanning enterprise networks discover these holes and craft their attacks on the enterprise infrastructure through them. Apart from the obvious firewall holes, there are several other examples of errors that impact security, such as:

- Static route on device does not direct application traffic into IPSec tunnel. This results in sensitive traffic remaining unprotected as it transits the network instead of flowing through the secure IPSec tunnel.
- Best practices for Virtual LAN (VLAN) security, such as disabling dynamic-desire and using root-guard and Bridge Protocol Data Unit (BPDU)-guard on switch access ports, are not

followed. Leaving the dynamic-desire VLAN feature enabled in a switch allows an attacker that connects to the switch to monitor all traffic passing through the switch.

- Link left active between devices. If the devices belong to network segments that are not meant to have a direct connection, then a backdoor has been introduced that can be exploited by attackers.
- Mismatched IPSec end-points. This results in sensitive traffic remaining unprotected as it transits the network instead of flowing through the secure IPSec tunnel.
- Adequate authentication is not used between devices for exchanging routing protocol information. An attacker can connect to a network device and extract or inject spurious routing information.

Quality of Service.

IP traffic with demanding network latency and packet-loss rate requirements, such as Voice over IP (VoIP) and financial services applications, requires appropriate Differentiated Services and other QoS configurations in the network devices. In a large network, it is easy to make errors in the QoS configurations. Examples of such errors include:

- Incorrect bandwidth or queue allocation on device interfaces for higher priority traffic. During high-load periods, higher priority traffic will not receive its due bandwidth or queue, resulting in higher latency or packet-loss.
- Inconsistent QoS policy definitions and usage across multiple devices. The same QoS policy

may be implemented differently across multiple devices, resulting in application traffic receiving different treatment at the different devices, which can impact latency and packet-loss during periods of high-load.

REGULATORS EXPECT COMPLIANCE

The world's growing reliance on IP and the highly networked nature of government computing environments have also motivated a wave of regulations to improve security, reliability, and QoS.

In the United States, the Federal Information Security Management Act (FISMA) of 2002 requires federal agencies to develop, document, and implement security programs.[5] Office of Management and Budget (OMB) Circular A-130 (an implementation guideline for FISMA), establishes, among other things, a minimum set of controls to be included in automated, inter-connected information resources.[6] The National Institute of Standards and Technology (NIST) has promulgated security requirements, for protecting the confidentiality, integrity, and availability of federal information systems and the information handled and transmitted by those systems.[7] NIST's "Guideline on Network Security Testing"[8] recommends that security testing be a routine part of system and network administration. It also directs organizations to verify that systems have been configured based on appropriate security mechanisms and policy. In addition, laws such as the Sarbanes-Oxley Act and Health Insurance Portability and Accountability Act, among others, are fueling the push for network protection.

Outside the United States, organizations such as the British Standards Institute (BSI), International Organization for Standardization (ISO), and Information Technology Infrastructure Library (ITIL) recognize the complexity of IP networks and the importance of security. In 2006, BSI published "Delivering and Managing Real World Network Security," which explains that networks must be protected against malicious and inadvertent attacks and "meet the business requirements for confidentiality, integrity, availability, non-repudiation, accountability, authenticity and reliability of information and services.[9]

MANY ASSESSMENT APPROACHES PROVE DEFICIENT

Many of the solutions for IP network configuration assessment have proven woefully inadequate. They fall generally into three categories: manual assessment, invasive systems, and noninvasive systems.

Manual Assessments.

In many organizations IP device configurations are large, complex software systems that depend on a hands-on, highly skilled administrator base for creation, update, and troubleshooting. Given the size of many networks and the cost of labor, the manual approach has obvious limitations. One large U.S. federal agency, for example, has 10 five-person teams handling manual analysis of device configurations for its 120 locations.

Invasive Systems.

Invasive scanning solutions, such as ping, traceroute, and their commercial variants, send traffic to devices in the network and use the responses to assess compliance. Such approaches work for simple usage, such as demonstrating IP connectivity between network nodes and identifying the software version on the devices. However, when it comes to rigorous assessment, they have serious shortcomings, including:

- No root-cause analysis. They can detect problems, but offer little, if any, help in diagnosing the configuration errors that caused them.
- Nonscalable. They cannot deliver "all" or "none" results, which generally require a huge number of tests. For example, to confirm that "There is connectivity between all pairs of internal subnets," connectivity tests are required for the number of subnets squared.
- No testing requirements on contingencies. Contingencies may be security breaches, component or link failures, changes in traffic conditions, or changes in requirements themselves. It is impractical to simulate contingencies on a network that supports real-time and critical services. For example, to detect the existence of a single point of failure, one would have to fail each device and check whether the end-to-end requirement still holds.
- Potential to disrupt network operations. Invasive scanning can introduce malware into a network, or inadvertently exploit a vulnerability that brings down a device.

Noninvasive Systems.

Noninvasive solutions include network simulation tools and Network Change and Configuration Management (NCCM) systems, which are analogous to software version control systems like Concurrent

Versioning System (CVS) and Source Code Control System (SCCS). Such systems tend to treat configurations as "blobs," and support IP device configuration backups, upgrades, controlled rollbacks, and maintainability of device configurations. While these capabilities are important, they are not sufficient for detecting issues that must be proactively resolved to ensure that the network continuously satisfies service requirements.

Noninvasive assessment is preferable to manual and invasive assessment because it does not impact ongoing network operations, but many of the existing systems have limitations, including:

- Individual-device assessments. Configuration management tools assess individual devices in isolation using a template-based approach, even though structural vulnerabilities are often created by interactions between protocols across multiple devices. Even nonsecurity protocols can interact improperly to create structural vulnerabilities. For example, if redundant tunnels traverse the same physical router and that router fails, all tunnels fail.

- Nonscalable. Certain types of requirements, such as reachability, can be assessed by network simulation tools; however they can take hours to compute reachability for networks with more than 50 devices, because they simulate each and every transition of the state machine of each protocol, whether it is for routing, security, reliability, or performance.

TOWARD A SOLUTION THAT WORKS

Building on our long history of involvement in assuring all types of communications networks, Telcordia has spent years researching the issues of IP network reliability and security. Part of this work was funded by the Department of Homeland Security's HSARPA office. That work has yielded important insight into the features and functions that an effective IP network configuration assessment solution must have, and all are capabilities that are achievable today.

Desirable Features of a Solution.

A scalable and effective solution for performing IP network assessments to detect configuration errors needs to possess the following features:

- Automatic and proactive network-wide, multi-device, and multivendor assessments against a comprehensive and updatable knowledge base that considers the network in its entirety and not just at a per-device level. The knowledge base should include rules for best current practices, regulatory compliance, and customer-specific requirements.
- Findings should visualize noncompliant rules and devices down to the "root" cause, eliminating speculation about cause.
- Nonintrusive, detailed, multilevel visualizations for physical connectivity, IP subnets, routing, VLAN, VPN, and MPLS. These visualizations, and the service reachability analysis mentioned below, can be computed using graph theory algorithms on data from the configurations.

- Service reachability analysis that visualizes path and single points of failure between network devices without generating traffic on the network.
- Network change impact analysis using the rules knowledge base, so new or changed configurations can be analyzed to detect errors before deployment to devices.
- Automated reconciliation of configuration and inventory information to identify and eliminate inconsistencies and errors.

Configuration Extraction.

Network and security administrators are generally reluctant to share IP network device configurations because they include sensitive information such as passwords and IP addresses. IP address anonymization and password obfuscation tools are of limited benefit since their usage tends to result in critical information being removed and lost from the configurations. The loss of this information makes the configuration assessments less effective. So for any configuration assessment solution to obtain complete configurations from administrators, it needs to provide assurances that their configurations will be adequately protected.

The most effective approach for acquiring configurations is for the configuration assessment solution to have direct read-only access to the IP network devices for extracting the configurations using device vendor-supported technologies such as secure FTP or remote copy. This direct approach ensures that the most current configuration information is securely retrieved without modification by administrators, and any other device-specific data relevant for validation can also be retrieved. Another approach is to rely on backups of device configurations from a file-system. Most organizations maintain versions of their IP network device configurations on a file system as backups, to be used to recover a device after its failure or for rolling-back configurations after an unsuccessful configuration change. The configuration assessment solution can acquire these backed-up configurations automatically, either periodically or every time new configurations appear in the backup file-system.

Configuration Adaptors.

Supporting the desirable features identified above requires detailed information from the device configurations. Since every IP network device vendor has their individual configuration language, software adaptors are needed that can extract the detailed information from vendor-specific format (e.g. Cisco IOS, Checkpoint, etc.), and convert the information into a vendor-neutral representation. Based on our experience, the adaptors need to extract as many as 750 attributes from a single configuration to support the desired features, as compared to less than 100 that are extracted by NCCM systems.

Telcordia IP Assure.

Telcordia's IP Assure solution (www.telcordia.com/products/ip-assure) satisfies many of the requirements discussed previously for IP network configuration validation. Figure 11.2 illustrates the high-level information flow that is supported in IP Assure. Solution details can be obtained by contacting the author.

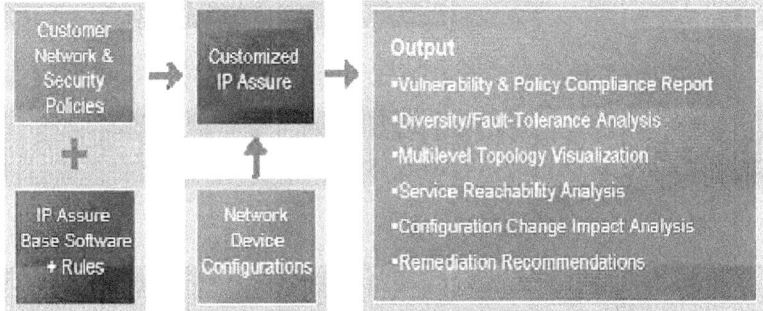

Figure 11.2. Telcordia IP Assure Information Flow.

SUMMARY

IP networks are no longer optional throughout the business and government sectors. This fact, along with the emergence of international regulations on security, reliability, and QoS, means that IP network assessment is a necessity. Many existing solutions on the market, including troubleshooting by skilled administrators, traffic-based vulnerability and penetration testing, NCCM software, and network simulation tools, do not (and cannot) fulfill the world's increasingly rigorous objectives. However, the technology exists today for a nonintrusive and comprehensive IP network assessment solution. Such a solution can provide auditable validation of regulations, eliminate IP network downtime caused by configuration errors, and stop the cyber attacks that exploit those errors. Telcordia IP Assure is an example of such a solution that is available today.

ENDNOTES - CHAPTER 11

1. "Securing Cyber Space for the 44th Presidency," Washington, DC: The Center for Strategic and International Studies (CSIS), December 2008, available from *www.csis.org/media/csis/pubs/081208_securingcyberspace_44.pdf*.

2. British Telecom/Gartner Study, "Security and business continuity solutions from BT," available from *www.btnet.cz/business/global/en/products/docs/28154_219475secur_bro_single.pdf*.

3. *Ibid.*

4. L. Gordon *et al.*, CSI/FBI Computer Crime and Security Survey, 2006, available from *www.cse.msu.edu/~cse429/readings06/FBI2006.pdf*.

5. Federal Information Security Management Act (FISMA) of 2002, available from *csrc.nist.gov/policies/FISMA-final.pdf*.

6. "Security of Federal Automated Information Resources," OMB Circular A-130, Appendix III, available from *www.whitehouse.gov/omb/circulars/a130/a130appendix_iii.html*.

7. "Minimum Security Requirements for Federal Information and Information Systems," FIPS-200, published by NIST, available from *csrc.nist.gov/publications/fips/fips200/FIPS-200-final-march.pdf*.

8. "Guideline on Network Security Testing," SP800-42, published by NIST, available from *csrc.nist.gov/publications/nistpubs/800-42/NIST-SP800-42.pdf*.

9. "Delivering and Managing Real World Network Security," British Standards Institute, 2006, available from *www.bsi-global.com/en/Standards-and-Publications/Industry-Sectors/ICT/ICT-standards/BIP-0068/*.

CHAPTER 12

ON THE NEW BREED OF DENIAL OF SERVICE (DOS) ATTACKS IN THE INTERNET

Nirwan Ansari
Amey Shevtekar

INTRODUCTION

Denial of Service (DoS) attacks impose serious threats to the integrity of the Internet. These days, attackers are professionals who are involved in such activities because of financial incentives. They bring higher sophistication to the attack techniques that can evade detection. A shrew attack is an example of such a new threat to the Internet; it was first reported in 2003, and several of these types of attacks have emerged since. These attacks are lethal because they can evade traditional attack detection systems. They possess several traits, such as low average rate and the use of TCP as attack traffic, which empowers them to evade detection. Little progress has been made in mitigating these attacks. This chapter presents an overview of this new breed of DoS attacks along with proposed detection systems for mitigating them. The analysis will hopefully lead to a better understanding of these attacks, and help to stimulate further development of effective algorithms to detect such attacks and to identify new vulnerabilities which may still be dormant.

The Internet has become an integral part of various commercial activities like online banking, online shopping, etc. However, the Internet has been plagued by a variety of security threats over the past several years.

The Distributed Denial of Service (DDoS) attacks received much attention after 2000 when yahoo.com was attacked. After that event, DDoS attacks have been rampaging throughout the Internet. DDoS News,[1] has since been keeping track of DDoS related news. A tremendous amount of work has been done in the industry and academia to mitigate DDoS attacks, but none have been able to successfully eradicate them. The motivations for launching attacks have shifted significantly. Initially, they were for publicity, but now they are for economic or political incentives. Thus, DDoS attacks are a prevalent and complex problem.

Figure 12.1 depicts the trend of DDoS attacks in the Internet. The x-axis indicates the efficiency of the attack, indicating how much damage it can cause to the good traffic. The y-axis indicates the detectability of the attack, indicating the exposure of the attack to defense systems. The early brute force attacks relied on sending high rate attack traffic continuously to a website. They are now easily detected because many defense systems can distinguish such anomalous attack traffic.[2] The shrew and Reduction of Quality of Service (RoQ) attacks are emerging low rate DoS attacks that are difficult to detect as compared to the brute force attack, but they primarily affect only long-lived TCP traffic. One major contribution of this chapter is to forewarn and model the emerging sophisticated attacks, because attacks have a higher impact on good traffic and yet they are very evasive.

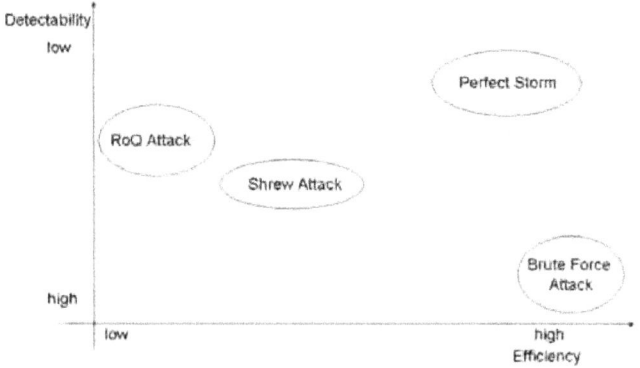

Figure 12.1. The Trend of DDoS Attacks in the Internet.

TRADITIONAL BRUTE FORCE ATTACKS

A Denial of Service (DoS) attack is defined as an attack that prevents a network or a computer from providing service to the legitimate users.[3] It typically targets the bandwidth of the victim. A DDoS attack is defined as an attack that uses multiple unwilling computers to send the attack traffic to the victim. A DDoS attack is more lethal since it exerts a large capacity of attack traffic as compared to a DoS attack. These attacks are also referred to as brute force attacks, since they send attack traffic at high rates and lack characteristics required to be stealthy. There are several types of brute force DDoS attacks that have been reported in the literature, a few of the commonly used attacks are described below. DDoS attacks can be characterized as shown in Figure 12.2.[4] DDoS attacks can be classified by the degree of automation, i.e., the level of sophistication of the attack mechanism.

Figure 12.2. Classification of DDoS Attacks.

Early attacks were manual, and were improved gradually. In a manual attack,[5] the victims are scanned for a particular vulnerability which is exploited by the attacker to gain access into the victim's system. An attacker then use commands to control the victim during the attack. In a semi-automatic attack, some steps of the attack procedure, which were originally manually performed become automated; for example, some of the victims are compromised to act as attack agents who coordinate the attack by issuing commands to conceal the identity of the real attacker even if the attack is detected.[6] The attack agents are preprogrammed with the necessary required commands. All of the recent attacks have been highly automatic requiring minimal communication between the attacker and the compromised machines once the attack was launched. All the attack steps are preprogrammed and delivered as a payload to infect clients, also referred to as zombies or bots. Some new attack payloads, which fail to detect a specific vulnerability in a victim machine, will automatically scan for another vulnerability in the same machine. Recent botnet attacks on Estonia's websites employed fully automated mechanisms.[7] Botnet is a network of bots or zombies controlled by a botmaster.[8]

Classification of DDoS attacks based on an exploited vulnerability takes into account the property of the network or the protocol used in the attack. The category to which the flood attack belongs is the simplest of all categories and is one in which an attacker relies on denying the network bandwidth to the legitimate users. The common example of this category is the UDP flood attack.[9] In a UDP flood, an attacker sends UDP packets at a high rate to the victim so that the network bandwidth is exhausted. UDP is a connectionless protocol, and therefore it is easy to send UDP packets at any rate in the network. Another attack in this category is the ICMP echo flood; it involves sending many ICMP echo request packets to a host. The host replies with an ICMP echo reply to each of the two ICMP echo request packets, and many such requests and reply packets fill up the network bandwidth.

In the category of amplification attack, an attacker exploits a protocol property such that few packets will lead to amplified attack traffic. The DDoS "SMURF" attack, which exploits the ICMP protocol,[10] falls in this category. It involves replacing a source IP address of the ICMP echo request packet with the address of the victim. The destination address of the ICMP echo request is the broadcast address of the LAN or so-called directed broadcast addresses. On receiving such a packet, each active host on a LAN responds with an ICMP echo reply packet to the victim. Typically, a LAN has many active hosts, and so a tremendous amount of attack traffic is generated to cripple the victim. To avoid such an attack, most system administrators are advised to disable the directed broadcast addresses.

In the category of protocol exploit, a property of the protocol is exploited. The SYN attack[11] exploits the TCP protocol's three-way handshake mechanism. Web servers use port 80 to accept incoming HTTP traffic that runs on top of the TCP protocol. When a user wants to access a webpage, it sends a SYN packet to the web server's open port 80. The web server does not know the user's IP address before the arrival of the SYN packet. The server, upon receipt of a SYN packet, sends a SYN/ACK packet, and thus puts the connection in the LISTEN state. A legitimate user's machine replies to the web server's SYN/ACK packet with an ACK packet and establishes the connection. However, if the SYN packet has been sent from an attack machine which does not respond to the server with an ACK packet, the web server never gets an ACK packet and the connection remains incomplete. Every web server has a finite amount of memory resources to handle such incomplete connections. The main goal of the SYN attack is to exhaust the finite amount of memory resources of a web server by sending a large number of SYN packets. Such an attack causes the web server to crash. Another similar protocol exploit attack is the PUSH + ACK attack,[12] which also falls in this category.

In the category of malformed packet attack, the packet header fields are modified to instigate a crash of the operating system of the receiver. An IP packet having the same source and destination IP address is a malformed packet.[13] In another kind of malformed packet attack, the IP options fields of the IP header are randomized, and the type of service bit is set to one. A ping of death attack involves sending a ping packet larger than the maximum IP packet size of 65535 bytes.[14] Historically, a ping packet has a size of 56 bytes, and most of the systems cannot handle ping packets of a larger size. Operating systems take more time to process such unusual packets, and a large quantity of such packets can crash the systems.

DDoS attacks can also be classified by their attack rates, namely: continuous vs. variable. Likewise, they can also be classified by their impacts: disruptive vs. degrading. Disruptive attacks aim for denial of service while degrading attacks aim for reduction of quality.

NEW BREED OF STEALTHY DoS ATTACKS

Internet security is increasingly more challenging as more professionals are getting into this lucrative business. An article in the *New York Times*,[15] describes one such business of selling the software exploits. Attacks are also getting more sophisticated, as the attackers are not merely interested in achieving publicity. The shrew attack is one such intelligent attack, which was first reported in Low-Rate TCP-Targeted Denial of Service Attacks in "The Shrew vs. the Mice and Elephants,"[16] followed by a series of variants.[17] This study considers these attacks as low rate DoS attacks. It is typically illustrated by a periodic waveform shown in Figure 12.3, where T is the time period, t is the burst period, and R is the burst rate.

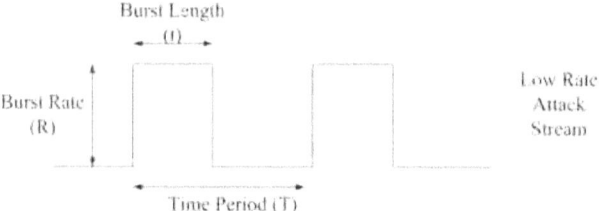

Figure 12.3. An Example of a Generic Low Rate
DoS Attack Pattern.

A shrew attack exploits widely implemented minimum RTO,[18] property of the TCP protocol. The following characterize the low rate TCP DoS attack:
- It sends periodic bursts of packets at one-sec-
  ond intervals.
- The burst rate is equal to or greater than the
  bottleneck capacity.
- The burst period is tuned to be equal to the
  round-trip times of the TCP connections; this
  parameter determines whether the attack will
  cause DoS to the TCP connections with small or
  long round-trip times.
- The exponential back off algorithm of the
  TCP's retransmission mechanism is eventually
  exploited.

In a Reduction of Quality of Service (RoQ) attack,[19]
the attacker sends high rate short bursts of the attack
traffic at random time periods, thereby forcing the
adaptive TCP traffic to back off due to the temporary
congestion caused by the attack bursts. In particular,
the periodicity is not well defined in a RoQ attack,
thus allowing the attacker to keep the average rate
of the attack traffic low in order to evade the regulation of adaptive queue management like RED and

RED-PD.[20] By sending the attack traffic, the RoQ attack introduces transients and restricts the router queue from reaching the steady state. The awareness of these stealthy attacks demands early fixes. For simplicity, the term "low rate DoS attack" refers to both the shrew and the RoQ attack, unless otherwise stated as shown in Figure 12.3. The attacker can also use different types of IP address spoofing to evade several other detection systems. Owing to the open nature of the Internet, IP address spoofing can still evade ingress and egress filtering techniques at many sites.[21] A low rate DoS attack can use IP address spoofing in a variety of ways like random IP address spoofing and continuous IP address spoofing.[22] The use of IP address spoofing most importantly divides the high rate of a single flow during the burst period of the attack among multiple flows with spoofed identities. This way, an attacker can evade detection systems that concentrate on finding anomalous traffic rate. The detection systems that rely on identifying periodicity of the low rate DoS attack in the frequency domain can detect the periodicity, but they fail to filter the attack traffic because it is difficult to know the IP addresses that an attacker will use in the future.

This problem is further exacerbated by the use of botnets; a botnet is a network of compromised real hosts across the Internet controlled by a master.[23] Since an attacker using botnets has control over thousands of hosts, it can easily use these hosts to launch a low rate DoS attack; this is analogous to a low rate DoS attack that uses random or continuous IP address spoofing. Now, with the use of botnets, the IP addresses of bots are not spoofed and so these packets cannot be filtered by spoofing-prevention techniques. In fact, these attack packets are similar to the HTTP flows. This random and continuous IP address spoofing problem described above is unique to the low rate DoS attacks, and is different from other types of DDoS attacks. These attacks[24] can be launched from any routers in the Internet; the edge routers can be easy targets as their capacities are small, and hence attackers can easily incite denial of service to the VoIP users traversing those routers. Low rate DoS attacks fall in the DDoS attack category of variable attack rate and degrading impact.

The perfect attack[25] is the latest attack model which is extremely lethal as compared to the attack models discussed before. The perfect attack has the ability to disguise itself as a normal traffic, thereby making detection difficult. It relies on using readily available botnets to send the attack traffic. Botnets are formed at an alarming rate today because of increasing vulnerabilities in various software applications. The users of these applications are often average users who are not security conscious, thus leaving their systems exposed to exploitations. Social engineering attacks are also used to increase the bot population. Thus, all these conditions create a breeding ground for rogues to develop new attacks. The perfect attack model consists of two parts: an initial, short, deterministic high-rate pulse, and a feedback-driven sustained attack period with a network-adaptive attack rate, as depicted in Figure 12.4.

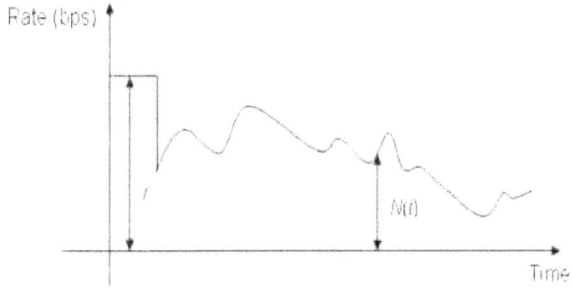

Figure 12.4. Attack Traffic for a Perfect DDoS Attack.

To accomplish the objectives identified above, a perfect attack is envisioned to be executed as follows. The attack traffic is injected from a botnet toward a target with a bottleneck queue as described in Figure 12.4. Initially, a high-rate pulse is sent at a rate of r for a duration of τ that overflows the buffer such that all packets are dropped. This pulse is similar to a shrew pulse, with the main difference that it only occurs at the beginning, once or twice, to drop all the packets in the queue. Thus, after this pulse, it is assumed that all long-lived TCP flows are in a timeout state, and thus do not send traffic. The only legitimate traffic that arrives immediately after the pulse is flow that is being established.

Thus, in the phase after the pulse, the attacker must fill the bottleneck queue with its own traffic as fast as possible and to sustain this level. Ideally, this filling ensures that only a small fraction of legitimate packets ever passes the bottleneck. Such a high drop rate per flow implies that: (1) a large number of SYN packets are dropped; (2) TCP flows experience packet loss already in slow start; and (3) other non-TCP traffic incurs significant packet loss. Thus, in this second phase, the attack traffic is sent according to the following pattern. Denote $B(t)$ as the available bandwidth at the bottleneck and C as the link capacity of the attack target link. Then, the sustained attack traffic $N(t)$ Equation (1) is: $N(t) = C + B(t)$

Under the assumption that all or the vast majority of the bottleneck bandwidth is consumed by the attack traffic, Equation (1) aims at maintaining a steady consumption. This attack traffic is the TCP traffic at a rate equivalent to the link capacity C. To fill the bottleneck and to compensate for drops in the TCP attack rate, UDP traffic at a rate of $B(t)$ is injected into the network. Note here that the UDP traffic is a function of the available bandwidth rather than the capacity as in a shrew attack or an RoQ attack. $N(t)$ is periodically updated and adjusted with the time period T. The update contains a rate adaptation but also the chance to exchange the zombies in the attack to create a diverse traffic pattern from different traffic sources. Thus, at the bottleneck, $N(t)$ creates a traffic pattern consisting of a superposition of many TCP flows, with a small fraction of UDP traffic, whose sources vary over time. After each period T, a new set of TCP flows are directed at the bottleneck link. These TCP flows begin in the slow start phase of TCP and end in the slow start phase as well. It is important to keep the attack TCP flows in slow start because they have been shown to affect long-lived TCP flows on shorter timescales, and also introducing a new TCP connection allows the congestion window to grow rapidly, otherwise attack TCP flows will enter congestion avoidance phase and will try to share the bandwidth with the legitimate TCP flows. The period T can be random so as to evade detection particularly for systems that try to find the deterministic attack pattern. Note that this interplay between TCP and UDP further complicates the detection. In contrast to the shrew attack where the repetitive pulses can be relatively detected, the perfect attack does not create such a repetitive pattern. Instead, the dynamics lead to an ever changing traffic pattern that cannot be observed and captured by the defense.

DEFENSE SYSTEMS

Mitigating DDoS attacks is a widely studied problem, and some of the popular approaches are described below. Defense systems can be broadly classified based on their functions. There are four main categories of defense systems: intrusion prevention, intrusion detection, intrusion response, and intrusion mitigation.[26]

Intrusion prevention systems prevent an attack from occurring. Ingress and egress filtering control IP address spoofing that is used in the attack. Ingress filtering only allows packets destined for the source network to enter the network, thereby filtering all other packets. It is implemented at the edge routers of the network, and it limits the attack traffic from entering the network. Egress filtering is an outbound filter that allows only packets with source IP addresses originated from the source network to exit the source network. Use of egress filtering controls attack traffic going to destination networks.[27] Disabling IP broadcasts prevents smurf attacks. Honeypots are network decoys,[28] that study attack behavior before the onset of an attack. Honeypots act as early warning systems. Honeypots mimic all aspects of a real network like a web server and a mail server to lure attackers. The primary goal of the honeypots is to determine/derive the exploit mechanism of the attack in order to build defense signatures against the exploit. Intrusion prevention systems cannot completely prevent an attack, but they contain the damage of the attack. They allow building better defense systems by analyzing the attack.

Intrusion detection systems detect an attack based on attack signatures or anomalous behaviors. Snort is a popular signature based network intrusion detection system.[29] It performs protocol analysis and content matching to passively detect a variety of attacks like buffer overflows, port scans, and web application attacks. Snort uses Berkeley's libpcap library to sniff packets. It uses a chain structure to maintain rules. The header of each chain is a tuple of source IP address, destination IP address, source port, and destination port. Various rules are then attached to the header so that packet information is matched to a header and the corresponding rules to detect an intrusion.

Anomaly detection systems rely on detecting shift in the normal traffic patterns of the network. The Reference A network management system is widely deployed in the Internet and is effectively used for intrusion detection. Consider the ping flood attack in which many ICMP echo request packets are sent to the target. The SNMP ICMP MIB group has a variable icmpInEchos, which shows the sudden increase in its count during the ping flood attack. During the UDP flood attack, SNMP UDP MIB group's udpInDatagrams shows a similar increase in its count. To detect localized variations in important MIB variables, a time series is segmented in small sub-time series which are compared to the normal profiles. In a DDoS attack, variations are so intense that averaging the time series on properly chosen time intervals enables anomaly detection.

The examples discussed above are network based intrusion detection systems, but intrusion detection can also be performed at a host. A data mining based approach is one such method.[30] Datasets consisting of normal and abnormal data points are gathered and fed to a classification algorithm to obtain classifiers. Once trained on these classifiers the training datasets are then used to find abnormal data points. D-WARD[31] is an intrusion detection system to be installed at the network edges to detect attack sources. It monitors network traffic rates to determine asymmetry in the traffic rate. Typically in a DDoS attack like the SYN attack, there are more SYN packets leaving the network as compared to ACK packets entering the network. D-WARD attempts to stop the attacks close to the sources so that network congestion is reduced. Attack traffic even affects traffic not intended for the victim, and thus D-WARD also minimizes the collateral damage from the attack. Figure 12.5 shows the conceptual diagram of the PPM scheme where each router marks packets probabilistically so that the victim can reconstruct the entire path from the source router.[32]

Intrusion response systems are required to find the source of the attack in order to stop the attack. Blocking the attack traffic is sometimes done manually by contacting network administrators who change the filtering policies to drop the attack traffic at routers. If an attacker is using source IP address spoofing, manual filtering is not useful and schemes like IP traceback are required. IP traceback traces the IP packets back to their sources and helps reveal attack sources.[33] In probabilistic packet marking (PPM)[34] shown in Figure 12.5, routers mark their addresses on packets that traverse through them. Packets are selected randomly with some fixed probability of marking. Upon receiving many packets a victim can construct the route back to the sources by reading router marks. Router vendors need to enable the marking mechanism, so ISP participation is required. This scheme does not require additional overhead bandwidth, which is an important advantage of this scheme. In contrast, a scheme referred to as deterministic packet marking (DPM),[35] shown in Figure 12.6, only marks packets passing through edge routers of the network. At the victim, a table is maintained for mapping between source addresses and router interface addresses. This facilitates the reconstruction and identification of the source of the packets. Some countermeasures to mitigate the low rate DoS attacks in the Internet have been reported although none of them has made a comprehensive attempt to address such attacks with IP address spoofing.

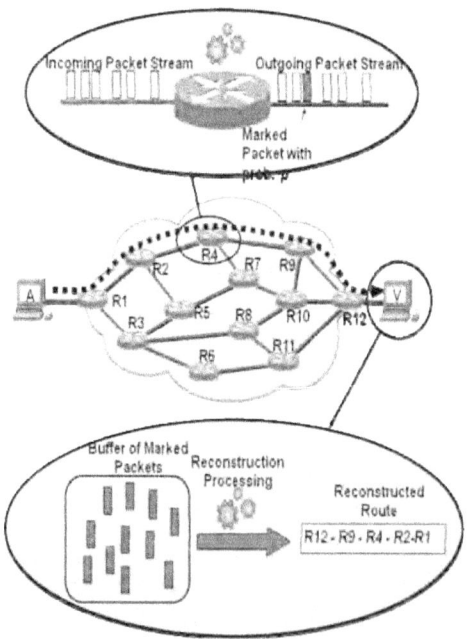

Figure 12.5. Conceptual Diagram of the PPM Scheme.

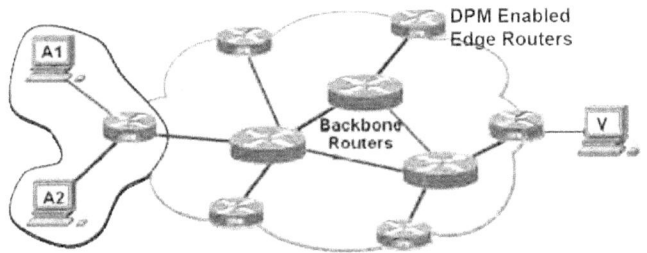

Figure 12.6. Conceptual Diagram of the DPM Scheme.

Pushback, also known as aggregate congestion control scheme (ACC),[36] drops DDoS attack traffic by detecting the attack and sends signals to drop the attack traffic closer to the source as shown in Figure 12.7. The rationale behind the pushback scheme is that the attack traffic has a unique signature in an attack, where the signature consists of identifiers such as port numbers, IP addresses, and IP prefixes. By detecting a signature in the aggregate attack traffic, upstream routers can be instructed to rate-limit flows that match the signature. A router in a pushback scheme has two components: a local ACC mechanism and a pushback mechanism.

The local ACC mechanism is invoked if the packet loss percentage exceeds a threshold of 10 percent. It then tries to determine the aggregate congestion signature and correspondingly tries to rate limit the aggregate traffic. If the rate limiting does not reduce the arrival rate of the attack traffic below a predefined target rate, ACC invokes the pushback mechanism which sends pushback messages to the upstream routers to filter the attack traffic. By repeating this scheme upstream, pushback aims at rate-limiting the attack traffic at the source network. Throttling is another approach to defend web servers from a DDoS

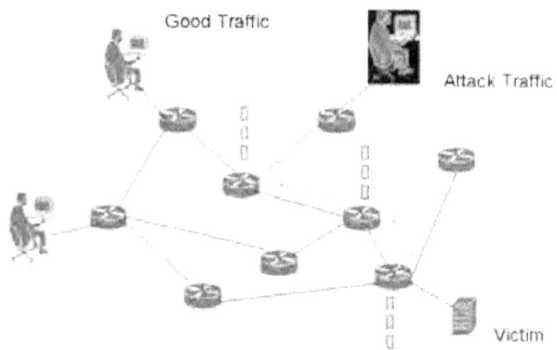

Good Traffic

Attack Traffic

Victim

: Pushback messages to upstream routers to drop attack traffic near the source

: Attack Packets are dropped by the pushback routers

Figure 12.7. Conceptual Diagram of the Pushback Scheme.

attack. It uses max-min fairness algorithm to compute the rate to drop excess traffic. Upstream routers also participate in the scheme so as to drop the attack traffic near the source. There have been several ways to mitigate specific DDoS attacks like SYN attacks. A technique, referred to as a SYN cookie, avoids giving server resources to the SYN packet until a SYN/ACK is received.[37]

The autocorrelation and dynamic time warping algorithm[38] relies on the periodic property of the attack traffic to detect the low rate DoS attacks. It proposes a deficit round-robin algorithm to filter the attack flows; however, it fails to drop attack packets when the attacker uses the continuous cycle and randomized IP address spoofing since each attack flow is a combination of multiple flows and each will be treated as a new flow. Thus, the attacker can easily evade the filtering mechanism. The randomization of RTO proposed to mitigate the low rate TCP DoS attack cannot defend against the RoQ attack, which targets the network element rather than the end host. The main idea reported in "Collaborative Detection and Filtering of Shrew DDoS Attacks using Spectral Analysis," *Journal of Parallel and Distributed Computing*,[39] is to randomize the minimum RTO instead of setting it to be one second. However, it ignores the advantages of having the minimum RTO of one second, which was chosen as a balance between an aggressive value and a conservative value.

The Collaborative Detection and Filtering scheme proposed in, "Collaborative Detection and Filtering of Shrew DDoS Attacks using Spectral Analysis,"[40] involves cooperation among routers to throttle and push the attack traffic toward the source. They rely on the autocorrelation property to distinguish the periodic behavior of attack traffic from legitimate traffic. Thus, it needs extra DSP hardware for implementation and extra memory to store the flow information of the attack packets to be dropped. The scheme maintains a malicious flow table and a suspicious flow table, which can be overwhelmed under the presence of the IP address spoofing. The novel part is the cumulative traffic spectrum that can distinguish traffic with and without the attack. In the traffic spectrum with the attack, the energy is found more localized at lower frequencies. The attacker can randomize the attack parameters in the RoQ attack. This work does not provide clear guidelines to activate the filtering of attack packets.

The wavelet based approach identifies the abnormal change in the incoming traffic rate and the outgoing acknowledgments to detect the presence of low rate TCP DoS attacks.[41] This approach cannot regulate the buffer size so that the attack flows can be detected as high rate flows by the RED-PD filter, and therefore the approach was subsequently dropped.[42] This work does not consider the RoQ attack in their analysis; it is difficult for this approach to detect the RoQ attack because the average rate of an RoQ attack is very low. The buffer sizing scheme fails if an attacker uses IP address spoofing because the high rate attack flow is a combination of multiple low rate individual flows. A modified AQM scheme referred to as HAWK[43] works by identifying bursty flows on short timescales, but lacks good filtering mechanisms to block the attack flows that can use the IP address spoofing. This approach can penalize the legitimate short bursty flows, thereby reducing their throughput. A filtering scheme similar to HAWK is proposed to estimate the bursty flows on shorter and longer time scales.[44] The main idea is to use per-TCP flow rate as the normal rate, and anything above that rate is considered abnormal. The identification of flow rates is done online. On a shorter time scale, it is very easy to penalize a normal flow as a bursty flow. The proposal did not consider the random IP address spoofing, where every packet may have a new flow ID. It uses a very complex filtering technique. With the use of the IP address spoofing, it is difficult to come up with the notion of a flow, because the number of packets per flow can be randomized in any fashion during every ON period.

An edge router based detection system is proposed to detect low rate DoS attacks based on time domain technique.[45] Each edge router acts as an entry and exit point for traffic originating from that local area network; essentially all incoming and outgoing traffic will pass through this point. The proposed detection system can be deployed at the edge routers of a local area network in which the server is present. For illustrative purposes, it is assumed that all clients are outside the local area network in which the server is present, so that the detection system can monitor all flows connecting to the server.

Figure 12.8 shows the basic layout of the system. It has three basic blocks, namely, flow classifier, object module, and filter. Each block functions as follows. The flow classifier module classifies packets based on the flow ID by means of a combination of the IP source address, IP source port, IP destination address, and IP destination port. Flow information is obtained from these packets, and packets are forwarded as usual by the routing mechanism resulting in no additional delay apart from the lookup delay. The object module consists of various objects for each flow that is monitored. A flow is monitored until it is considered normal. The filter is used to block flows that are identified as malicious by the object module. Consider a DoS attack which tries to exploit protocol shortcomings. The object module maintains per flow information by creating objects per flow called flow objects. A thin data structure layer is designed to keep track of these flow objects. It maintains only those parameters which are exploited in the attack. This thin structure keeps track of information about flows classified as malicious. This information is then relayed to the filter module.

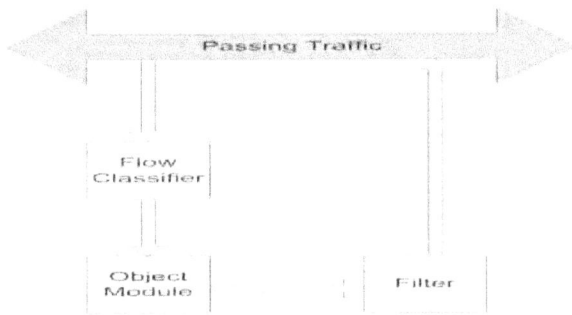

Figure 12.8. The Detection System Architecture.

The flow objects maintain the arrival times of packets at the edge router in the pseudo transport layer. The malicious flow detection submodule of the object module computes the time difference of consecutive packets of each flow. The submodule computes the average high and low of the time difference values. The average high value of the time difference repeats periodically for the attack flow; other flows do not exhibit this property. The malicious flow detection submodule then estimates the burst length of a flow based on the packet arrival times. A flow exhibiting periodicity in the time difference graph is marked malicious, since no legitimate flows will show such periodicity. The time difference technique uses a per-flow approach to store the arrival times of the packets belonging to each flow, and computes the interarrival times between the consecutive packets to detect periodicity. The attacker using IP address spoofing can easily deceive this simple per-flow approach as the time difference approach will not be able to detect periodicity in the attack flow, which is no longer a single flow.

FUTURE RESEARCH DIRECTIONS

Mitigating perfect attack and low rate DoS attacks is extremely critical. Router based solutions that can identify and drop malicious attack traffic can be a possible defense approach. Currently, both perfect and low rate DoS attacks are facilitated by botnets. Mitigation of botnets can be another important step to prevent stealthy DoS attacks. Botnet detection and mitigation is a serious challenge, because attackers find new vulnerabilities at a rapid pace. Secure software development that would be void of vulnerabilities is desirable. These research goals are known and emerging everyday. On the other hand, isolating bots from accessing the network by using better CAPTCHAs can be another approach to defend against botnets until such a time that we can completely eliminate bots.

CONCLUSION

In this chapter, we have presented a survey of several traditional brute force DoS attacks and examples of more recent stealthy DoS attacks. We have also introduced defense systems discussed in the literature, and identified some of their shortcomings. The focus of this chapter was to present some of the latest advances in the area of DoS attacks to stimulate research for better defense systems and to reveal vulnerabilities that may exist.

ENDNOTES - CHAPTER 12

1. DDoS News, available from *staff.washington.edu/dittrich/ misc/ddos/*.

2. C. Douligeris and A. Mitrokotsa, "DDoS Attacks and Defense Mechanisms: Classification and State-of-the-Art," *Computer Networks*, Vol. 44, No. 5, 2004, pp. 643-666.

3. *Ibid.*

4. *Ibid.*

5. *Ibid.*

6. *Ibid.*

7. DDoS News.

8. D. Dagon, Z. Zhou, W. Lee, "Modeling Botnet Propagation Using Time Zones," Network and Distributed System Security (NDSS) Symposium, 2006.

9. "UDP Port Denial-of-Service Attack," available from *www. cert.org/advisories/CA-1996-01.html.*

10. "Smurf Attack," available from *www.nordu.net/articles/ smurf.html.*

11. W. Eddy, "TCP SYN Flooding Attacks and Common Mitigations," IETF RFC 4987, 2007.

12. "Push + Ack Attack," available from *www.csie.ncu.edu. tw/~cs102085/DDoS/protocolexploit/push%2Back/description.htm.*

13. Douligeris and Mitrokotsa.

14. "Ping of Death Attack," available from *insecure.org/sploits/ ping-o-death.html.*

15. "A Lively Market, Legal and Not, for Software Bugs," available from *www.nytimes.com/2007/01/30/technology/30bugs.ht ml?ex=1327813200&en=99b346611df0a278&ei=5088&partner=rssny t&emc=rss.*

16. A. Kuzmanovic and E. Knightly, "Low-Rate TCP-Targeted Denial of Service Attacks (The Shrew vs. the Mice and Elephants)," ACM SIGCOMM, 2003, pp. 75-86.

17. M. Guirguis, A. Bestavros, and I. Matta, "Exploiting the Transients of Adaptation for RoQ Attacks on Internet Resources," IEEE ICNP, 2004, pp. 184-195; S. Ebrahimi-Taghizadeh, A. Helmy, and S. Gupta, "TCP vs. TCP: a Systematic Study of Adverse Impact of Short-lived TCP Flows on Long-lived TCP Flows," IEEE INFOCOM, 2005, pp. 926-937; X. Luo and R. K. C. Chang, "On a New Class of Pulsing Denial-of-Service Attacks and the Defense," NDSS, 2005; A. Shevtekar and N. Ansari, "Do Low Rate DoS Attacks Affect QoS Sensitive VoIP Traffic?" IEEE ICC, 2006, pp. 2153-2158; R. Chertov, S. Fahmy, and N. Shroff, "Emulation versus Simulation: A Case Study of TCP-Targeted Denial of Service Attacks," Tridentcom, 2006, pp. 316-325.

18. V. Paxon and M. Allman, "Computing TCP's Retransmission Timer," IETF RFC 2988, 2000.

19. Guirguis, Bestavros, and Matta.

20. R. Mahajan, S. Floyd, and D. Wetherall, "Controlling High-Bandwidth Flows at the Congested Router," IEEE ICNP, 2001, pp. 192-201; Y. Xu and R. Guerin, "On the Robustness of Router-based Denial-of-Service (DoS) Defense Systems," *ACM Computer Communications Review*, Vol. 2, 2005, pp. 47-60; S. Floyd and V. Jacobson, "Random Early Detection Gateways for Congestion Avoidance," IEEE/ACM, *Transactions on Networking*, Vol. 1, No. 4, 1993, pp. 397-413.

21. R. Beverly and S. Bauer, "The Spoofer Project: Inferring the Extent of Source Address Filtering on the Internet," USENIX SRUTI, 2005, pp. 53-59.

22. Xu and Guerin.

23. Dagon, Zhou, and Lee.

24. Guirguis, Bestavros, and Matta.

25. A. Shevtekar, N. Ansari, and R. Karrer , "Towards the Perfect DDoS Attack: The Perfect Storm," IEEE Sarnoff Symposium, 2009, pp. 1-5.

26. Douligeris and Mitrokotsa.

27. P. Ferguson and D. Senie, "Network Ingress Filtering: Defeating Denial of Service Attacks which Employ IP Address Spoofing," IETF RFC 2827, 2001.

28. W. R. Cheswick, "An Evening with Berferd, in Which A Cracker Is Lured, Endured, And Studied," USENIX Winter Conference, 1992, pp. 163-174.

29. Snort IDS, available from *www.snort.org*.

30. W. Lee and S. Stolfo, "Data Mining Approaches for Intrusion Detection," USENIX Security Symposium, 1998, pp. 79-93.

31. J. Mirkovic, G. Prier, and P. Reiher, "Attacking DDoS at Source," IEEE ICNP, 2002, pp. 312-321.

32. A. Belenky and N. Ansari, "On IP Traceback," *IEEE Communications Magazine,* Vol. 41, No. 7, 2003, pp. 142-153.

33. *Ibid.*; Z. Gao, and N. Ansari, "Tracing Cyber Attacks from Practical Perspective," *IEEE Communications Magazine*, Vol. 43, No. 5, 2005, pp. 123-131.

34. S. Savage, D. Wetherall, A. Karlin, and T. Anderson, "Network Support for IP Traceback," IEEE/ACM, *Transactions on Networking*, Vol. 9, No. 3, 2001, pp. 226-237.

35. A. Belenky and N. Ansari, "IP Traceback with Deterministic Packet Marking," *IEEE Communication Letters*, Vol. 7, No. 4, 2003, pp. 162-164.

36. R. Mahajan, S. Bellovin, S. Floyd, J. Ionnadis, V. Paxson, and S. Shenker, "Controlling High-bandwidth Aggregates in the Network," ACM SIGCOMM CCR, Vol. 32, No. 3, 2002, pp. 62-73.

37. SYN cookies, available from *cr.yp.to/syncookies.html.*

38. H. Sun, J. C. S. Lui, and D. K. Y. Yau, "Defending Against Low-rate TCP Attack: Dynamic Detection and Protection," IEEE ICNP, 2004, pp. 196-205.

39. Y. Chen, K. Hwang, and Y. Kwok, "Collaborative Detection and Filtering of Shrew DDoS Attacks using Spectral Analysis," *Journal of Parallel and Distributed Computing*, 2006, available from *gridsec.usc.edu/files/publications/JPDC-Chen-2006.pdf.*

40. *Ibid*.

41. X. Luo and R. K. C. Chang, "On a New Class of Pulsing Denial-of-Service Attacks and the Defense," NDSS, 2005.

42. S. Sarat and A. Terzis, "On the Effect of Router Buffer Sizes on Low-Rate Denial of Service Attacks," IEEE ICCCN, 2005, pp. 281-286.

ABOUT THE CONTRIBUTORS

NIRWAN ANSARI joined The New Jersey Institute of Technology (NJIT) Department of Electrical and Computer Engineering as an Assistant Professor in 1988 and has been a full professor since 1997. Dr. Ansari is a senior technical editor of the *IEEE COMMUNICATIONS MAGAZINE*, and also serves on the Advisory Board and Editorial Board of five other journals. He has been serving the IEEE in various capacities such as: Chair of IEEE North Jersey COMSOC Chapter; Chair of IEEE North Jersey Section, Member of IEEE Region 1 Board of Governors; Chair of IEEE COMSOC Networking TC Cluster; Chair of IEEE COMSOC Technical Committee on Ad Hoc and Sensor Networks; and Chair/TPC Chair of several conferences/symposia. His current research focuses on various aspects of broadband networks and multimedia communications. He has contributed around 30 patent applications, three have been issued and others are pending. Dr. Ansari authored *Computational Intelligence for Optimization* (New York: Springer, 1997, translated into Chinese in 2000) with E.S.H. Hou; and edited *Neural Networks in Telecommunications* (New York: Springer, 1994) with B. Yuhas. He also contributed over 300 technical papers, over one third of which were published in many noted journals/magazines. Dr. Ansari holds a B.S.E.E. (summa cum laude, gpa=4.0) degree from NJIT, Newark, NJ; an M.S.E.E. degree from University of Michigan, Ann Arbor, MI; and a Ph.D. degree from Purdue University,West Lafayette, IN.

MIKE CHUMER teaches and conducts research within the Information Systems Department of the New Jersey Institute of Technology. His research focuses on command and control as used by the military and its application to emergency response during multi-agency collaboration such as experienced in Katrina and the recent Tsunami disasters. Dr. Chumer has written about command and control and is incorporating that knowledge into command center operations that benefit the public and private sectors during Homeland Security enabled emergency management. As a Marine Corps Officer, he started the first Systems Analysis and Design function at the United States Marine Corps (USMC) Automated Services Center on Okinawa, Japan, and consulted with the Chinese Marines on Taiwan for the development of large mainframe and communication systems. He also worked with the C4 (command, control, communication, computers) organization at Headquarters Marine Corps, assisting in the design of satellite based battlefield information systems. He is co-editor of "Managing Knowledge: Critical Investigations of Work and Learning," a book that investigates issues surrounding the present formulation of IT based Knowledge Management. Dr. Chumer holds a Ph.D. from Rutgers University in communication and information science.

ADEL ELMAGHRABY is Professor and Chair of the Computer Engineering and Computer Science Department at the University of Louisville. He has also held appointments at the SEI-CMU, and the University of Wisconsin-Madison. He is a Senior Member of the IEEE and is active on editorial boards and conference organizations. Professor Elmaghraby's research focus is in Network Performance and Security Analysis, Intelligent Multimedia Systems, Neural Networks, PDCS, Visualization, and Simulation with applications to biomedical computing, automation, and military wargames.

ANUP GHOSH is a research professor at George Mason University and Chief Scientist in the Center for Secure Information Systems. He is also Founder and Chief Executive of Secure Command, Inc., a venture-backed security software start-up organization developing next generation Internet security products. He was previously Senior Scientist and Program Manager in the Advanced Technology Office of the Defense Advanced Research Projects Agency (DARPA) where he managed an extensive portfolio of information assurance and information operations programs. He is currently a member of the Committee on Information Assurance for Network-Centric Naval Forces for the Naval Studies Board, National Research Council. Dr. Ghosh is also author of three books on computer network defense.

THOMAS J. HOLT is an assistant professor in the School of Criminal Justice at Michigan State University specializing in computer crime, cybercrime, and technology. His research focuses on computer hacking, malware, and the role that technology and the Internet play in facilitating all manner of crime and deviance. He is also the project lead for the Spartan Devils Chapter of the International Honeynet Project and a member of the editorial board of the International Journal of Cyber Criminology. Dr. Holt has published in academic journals, including *Deviant Behavior* and the *Journal of Criminal Justice*.

LOUIS H. JORDAN, JR., is the Deputy Director of the Strategic Studies Institute, U.S. Army War College, Carlisle, Pennsylvania. He recently returned from a deployment to Afghanistan where he served as Senior Military Advisor to the Afghan Deputy Minister of Interior for Counter Narcotics. He is a graduate of Fordham University in the Bronx, NY, where he received a bachelor of arts degree in sociology. Colonel Jordan's formal education includes a master's degree in strategic studies from the U.S. Army War College and certification in strategic planning from the American Management Association. Colonel Jordan has served in aviation assignments from company through brigade and the national level including service at the National Guard Bureau as an operations officer, branch chief, and as the Deputy Division Chief of the Aviation and Safety Division. Colonel Jordan has commanded at the battalion, brigade, and joint task force level to include command of Joint Task Force Raven, the aviation task force for Operation JUMP START along the Southwest Border in Arizona.

DEBORAH WILSON KEELING is currently Chairperson of the Department of Justice Administration University of Louisville, KY, and is responsible for academic programs as well as the Southern Police Institute and National Crime Prevention Institute. Dr. Keeling has conducted numerous applied research projects for local, state, and federal criminal justice agencies. She has organized police training programs in the People's Republic of China, Hungary, Romania, and the Republic of Slovakia. Dr. Keeling holds a Ph.D. in sociology from Purdue University.

ANGELOS KEROMYTIS is an associate professor in the Computer Science Department at Columbia University, New York. He is also the director of the Network Security Lab. His main research interests are in computer security, cryptography, and networking. He is an active participant in the Internet Engineering Task Force and, in particular, the IPsec and IPSP working groups. He occasionally contributes to the OpenBSD operating system. He has been working on the KeyNote trust-management system and the STRONGMAN access control management system. Other projects he is/was involved in include AEGIS and SwitchWare.

YEHIA H. KHALIL worked from 1995-2005 as a researcher at the Informatics Technology Institute, Egypt, which provides IT consulting and training services. He has several publications and is a student member of IEEE. Mr. Khalil's research is focused on methods to identify and augment cyber infrastructure resiliency. He holds a B.S. in computer science and statistics from Alexandria University, Egypt, a master's degree in operations research and computer science from the Arab Academy of Science and Technology, Egypt, and is currently a Ph.D. candidate in computer science and engineering at the University of Louisville, KY.

MICHAEL LOSAVIO is an attorney working on issues of law, society, and information security in the Department of Justice Administration and the Department of Computer Engineering and Computer Science at the University of Louisville; he is also teaching and training in these areas. He holds a J.D and a B.S. in mathematics from Louisiana State University.

TAREK N. SAADAWI is Professor and Director of the Center for Information Networking and Telecommunications (CINT), City College, The City University of New York. His current research interests are telecommunications networks, high-speed networks, multimedia networks, AD-HOC mobile wireless networks and secure communications. Dr. Saadawi has been on the Consortium Management Committee (CMC) for ARL Consortium on Telecommunications (known as Collaborative Technology Alliances on Communications and Networks, CTA-C&N), 2001-2009. He has published extensively in the areas of telecommunications and information networks. Dr. Saadawi is a co-author of the book, *Fundamentals of Telecommunication Networks* (New York: John Wiley & Sons, 1994) which has been translated into Chinese. He was the lead author of the *Egypt Telecommunications Infrastructure Master Plan* covering the fiber network, IP/ATM, DSL, and the wireless local loop under a project funded by the U.S. Agency for Independent Development. He joined the U.S. Department of Commerce delegation to the Government of Algeria addressing rural communications. Dr. Saadawi is a Former Chairman of IEEE Computer Society of New York City (1986-87). He holds a B.S. and M.S. from Cairo University, Egypt, and a Ph.D. from the University of Maryland, College Park.

DOUGLAS SALANE has held positions with Exxon Corp., Sandia National Laboratories, and Argonne National Laboratories. He has been a faculty member at John Jay College of Criminal Justice, The City University of New York, since 1988. For 12 years, he served as coordinator of the College's Computer

Information Systems Major and is currently a member of the graduate faculty in Forensic Computing. He teaches graduate courses in network forensics and data communication security. In 2006, Dr. Salane became the director of the Center for Cybercrime Studies at John Jay. The Center brings together expertise in law, computing, and the social sciences in an effort to understand and deter computer related criminal activity. Dr. Salane is a member of the Association for Computing Machinery (ACM), Institute of Electrical and Electronics Engineers (IEEE), and the Society for Industrial and Applied Mathematics (SIAM). Dr. Salane holds a Ph.D. in applied mathematics with a specialization in numerical analysis.

AMEY SHEVTEKAR completed an internship at Deutsche Telekom Laboratories, Berlin, Germany, in 2007. He has contributed several technical papers and has filed two U.S. patents. He is currently working for Lumeta Corporation. His research focuses on network security. Dr. Shevtekar holds a B.S. in electronics and telecommunications engineering from University of Mumbai, India, an M.S. degree in telecommunications from the New Jersey Institute of Technology (NJIT), and a Ph.D. in computer engineering from NJIT.

J. EAGLE SHUTT is a former prosecutor and public defender and currently is an assistant professor at the Department of Justice Administration, University of Louisville, KY. He also serves as a JAG officer with the South Carolina National Guard. His research interests include biosocial criminology, culture, public policy, and law. Dr. Shutt holds a J.D., an M.C.J., and a Ph.D.

STUART STARR is a Distinguished Research Fellow at the Center for Technology and National Security Policy, National Defense University, Fort McNair, Washington, DC. Concurrently, he serves as President, Barcroft Research Institute (BRI), where he consults on Command and Control (C2) issues, serves on senior advisory boards to defense industry (e.g., Northrop Grumman, Titan), lectures to audiences worldwide on C2 issues, and participates on Blue Ribbon panels (e.g., member of the Army Science Board [ASB]; member of the National Research Council Task Force on Modeling and Simulation [M&S] to support the Transformation of DoD). He was a Fellow at MIT's Seminar XXI during 1989-90. Dr. Starr holds a B.S. in electrical engineering from Columbia University, and an M.S. and a Ph.D. in electrical engineering from the University of Illinois.

RAJESH TALPADE is Chief Scientist and Director of the Information Assurance Group at Telcordia Applied Technology Solutions, with over 15 years experience in Internet, telecom, wireless, and security areas. He currently has responsibility for a new Telcordia software product in IP network management, and has led all product stages from concept to market. He has been the principal investigator for several Government-funded R&D projects, such as cyber attack traceback, IP device configuration error detection, and Distributed Denial of Service attack detection. Dr. Talpade holds and has several patents pending, has been guest editor of multiple journals, has given multiple invited talks, and has published numerous refereed papers and IETF RFC 2149. Dr. Talpade holds an M.B.A. from Columbia University and a Ph.D. in Computer science from the Georgia Institute of Technology.

EDWARD WAGNER has worked as an information technology professional for clients within the Department of Defense. He has worked at the executive level within the Office of Secretary of Defense, and supported Joint and Service level programs. Mr. Wagner is currently a Project and Department Manager for Northrop Grumman. In addition to his professional career, he is a Reserve Lieutenant Colonel and the commander of the North East Information Operations Center. He is an adjunct professor for Strayer University.

LARRY WENTZ is a Senior Research Fellow at the Center for Technology and National Security Policy, National Defense University, Fort McNair, Washington, DC, and consults on Command and Control (C2) issues. He is an experienced manager, strategic planner, and C4ISR systems engineer with extensive experience in the areas of Nuclear C2, continuity of government C2, multinational military C2 and C3I systems interoperability, civil-military operations and information operations support to peace operations and numerous other military C4ISR activities. He also has extensive experience in business process reengineering, strategic planning, and commercial telecommunications and information systems and their use in support of military C2. Mr. Wentz is a writer, author, and lecturer on multinational C4ISR systems interoperability, information operations, and civil-military operations. He was a contributing author to the AFCEA International Press book, *The First Information War and CYBERWAR 2.0* and Canadian Peacekeeping Press book, *The Cornwallis Group Series*.

www.ingramcontent.com/pod-product-compliance
Lightning Source LLC
Chambersburg PA
CBHW051441170526
45166CB00001B/72